Japan Copes with Calamity

JAPAN COPES WITH CALAMITY

Edited by Tom Gill, Brigitte Steger
and David H. Slater

Peter Lang Oxford

Peter Lang Ltd
International Academic Publishers
52 St Giles, Oxford
Oxfordshire OX1 3LU
United Kingdom

www.peterlang.com

Contents

vi

Preface to the Second Edition

We are very happy to see this new edition of *Japan Copes with Calamity* published. The first edition has already been reprinted, as has the Japanese edition, which was also published in 2013. The demand for the book reflects the continuing lack of closely observed ethnographic studies of the 3.11 disasters but the enduring interest in the human aspect of the disasters. The book has received a warm response from informants in the disaster zone and many of them have told us they are glad that their voices have been heard.

We would like to take this opportunity to offer a brief update on post-disaster Japan as seen from a standpoint eighteen months on from the original publication.

'Is everything back to normal now?' This is what we are asked frequently, when we return from our visits to Tohoku. Coming from people living well away from the disaster zone, it is an understandable question. Three or four years after the earthquake, tsunami and nuclear disasters, life outside the zone has moved on. The flood of news items about the disaster has slowed to a trickle. The government of prime minister Abe Shinzo has engineered a temporary economic recovery under the name of 'Abenomics', a fashionable word that really means using the time-honoured pump-priming methods of the Liberal Democratic Party: injecting trillions of yen[1] of borrowed money into the economy, much of it spent on public works.

Occasionally, people are reminded of the Fukushima accident when they hear of another anti-nuclear demonstration and when they hear that the leaks of contaminated water were actually much bigger and more damaging than they had been told, but generally they prefer to believe in the reassurance of the government that the Fukushima plant, the post-disaster recovery process, the economy and things in general are under control.

---

[1]   At the time of the disaster, in March 2011, the US dollar was trading at about 80 yen. As this book went to press, the US dollar was worth about 115 yen.

Along the Sanriku coast of Tohoku, the situation is quite different. Clearing flat areas on mountains and securing land to provide safe building space has only just started in some areas. Giant cranes and Caterpillar tractors are everywhere. The huge piles of wreckage have been sorted and moved away for recycling and a few former beaches have been prepared for holiday makers. However, locals still feel uncomfortable to relax in the bay, where they know that tons of rubbish was washed away and many people were drowned, many of them never discovered.

In Iwate, Miyagi and Fukushima, the three Tohoku prefectures directly impacted by the disasters, prices for building plots, materials and construction work have soared. For the last three years, districts located on high ground in the tsunami zone have occupied the top five places in the whole of Japan in rankings of land-price increases. Shirasagidai, a district of Ishinomaki, has been number one for three years in a row, with a cumulative increase of 129 per cent.[2] These days the reconstruction drive is in competition with demand from Tokyo to prepare infrastructure for the 2020 Olympic Games. One result of this has been a serious labour shortage – another factor holding up reconstruction.

The most significant series of events for most communities surrounds the creation of a 'recovery plan' (*fukkō-an*), a rebuilding plan for each community, required by the state and approved by each prefecture. But with many coastal zones declared too dangerous for habitation, these plans have faced the intractable challenge of finding land that is both large enough to allow the relocation of whole communities, and close enough to the original site to preserve social and economic systems.

The recovery plans were supposed to give communities a say in relocation decisions, but there was internal division among residents and pressure from different business interests that conflicted with community desires. Eventually local residents often had plans foisted upon them that were so complicated and vague that even civil engineers had trouble understanding them. What was supposed to be community building has as often as not been a source of strife and conflict. Even if there were available housing,

---

2 See *Fudōsan Onrain*, <http://fudousan.zuuonline.com/archives/2323> accessed 1 November 2014.

the money that residents could patch together from compensation payments, insurance and savings was often not enough to allow them to buy back into their own community. The net result has usually been smaller, poorly constructed and more expensive housing and the break-up of neighbourhoods and communities.

The challenge of agreeing on and executing recovery plans has seriously held up the disbursement of government reconstruction funding. As of November 2014, only 2,700 housing units had been completed in the tsunami zone, less than 10 per cent of the 29,000 units planned. The government had already transferred 5.5 trillion yen in reconstruction funds to local authorities in Iwate, Miyagi and Fukushima prefectures, but some 60 per cent of that money remains unspent in local bank deposits.[3]

A few families have already been able to move into newly built accommodation, some into houses, but many more into apartment blocks, a cheaper option for rapid construction. Sadly, however, many of these units remain empty, reflecting poor planning in cases where housing was built without first obtaining solid commitments from households to move in. Families used to living in large rural homesteads are reluctant to move into small apartments, while many single or elderly people prefer to stay on in the temporary housing complexes. Though rudimentary, the temporary housing units are rent-free, and a kind of alternative community life has developed in the complexes. That community life will be destroyed when people move to the widely scattered 'recovery housing' units. Moreover, most of the newly constructed apartment blocks are quite far away from where people have lived before and often lack infrastructure, such as accessible shops and bus services.

Thus, the net result of the rehousing programme includes a tragic irony – that people who were driven from their *furusato*, or home town, and have improvised a new community in the temporary housing complexes, may find themselves expelled from home, or a place that feels like home, for a second time when the housing complexes are finally closed down. At

3   See for example Reuters Special Report, 'Tsunami evacuees caught in $30 billion Japan Money Trap', 31 October 2014. <http://www.reuters.com/article/2014/10/31/us-japan-reconstruction-specialreport-idUSKBN0IK00220141031> accessed 1 November 2014.

present, however, most of the complexes are being kept open, their period of use extended from the initially planned two years to three, then four years.

The fishing industry of the Sanriku coast shows a mixed picture. The disasters have accelerated some trends. For instance, a large number of fishermen have retired early, given that it would have been impossible for them to pay back a huge loan to buy a new boat to replace one destroyed in the tsunami. However, fishing activities in Iwate and Miyagi prefectures have recovered to a large extent, and 7 per cent of the fishers operating there are newcomers (a phenomenon that could also be observed after the great tsunami of 1896 and 1933).[4] After three years of cultivating, farmed oysters and clams can now be harvested again. The biggest challenge is to keep one's clients, as they naturally switched to other producers during the years when aqua farmers had to invest but could not harvest.

As a result of high levels of radiation, there is no fishing being done in the area around the Fukushima nuclear power plant except for experimental purposes, but even further up the coast, fishers are very aware of the problem. To avoid *fūhyō higai*, or 'damaging rumours' that depress sales, they subject their harvest to strict radiation testing to demonstrate that they are safe to eat. Not everyone is convinced. In September 2013 Korea prohibited the import of *hoya* (sea squirt, used in the production of *kimchi*) from the Sanriku coast. For *hoya* farmers this means that they have lost the majority of their clients, and they are now trying to promote *hoya* as a regional specialty. Other strategies have included direct sales, branding of products to associate them with the locality rather than with the disaster zone, and the seeking out of supporters who will become shareholders in cooperative sales ventures.

A highly controversial issue in communities along the Sanriku coastline is the construction and repair of seawalls. Some 400 km of seawalls are planned, at tremendous expense to the taxpayer. Often these big-ticket construction projects are decided at the prefectural level and local communities have often opposed them, for many reasons: they impede fishing operations, disrupt the local ecology, create new dangers by reducing the

---

4   Shūichi Kawashima (2012). *Tsunami no machi ni ikite* [My life in the town of tsunamis]. Tokyo: Fūzambō International, 54.

visibility of the sea and spoil the view, thereby discouraging tourists. They also prevent water from running back to the sea after a tsunami, instead pooling it behind the walls and thereby worsening damage and hindering post-tsunami clean-up. Furthermore, the future expense of maintaining the walls will be prohibitive for coastal communities faced with a dwindling and ageing population.

Critics also question the effectiveness of seawalls as safety barriers, since some communities with high walls suffered high mortality rates in the 2011 tsunami after being lulled into a false sense of security. Strong community ties leading to well-organized evacuations appear to have been more effective at reducing tsunami damage. Many of the worst affected communities have been forced to relocate to higher ground anyway, meaning that there will be little or no housing for the seawall to protect.

In October 2014, the prefectural government of Miyagi gave in to sustained opposition and agreed to cancel plans for new seawalls in three communities in Ishinomaki that had been vehemently opposed to them: Yoriiso, Fukkiura and the island of Aji. The local movements against seawall construction have been less noticeable to outsiders than the nationwide movement against nuclear power plants, but their occasional successes in delaying or cancelling seawall construction show that grassroots movements can sometimes influence the major centers of political power.

The health and welfare of people living in remote rural districts affected by the disasters is another serious problem. There are few incentives for doctors to live in remote areas and the disasters have further depressed the appeal of work in Tohoku. In Brigitte Steger's research site of Yamada (Iwate prefecture), for instance, there is no gynaecologist or paediatrician in a town of about 17,000 inhabitants. One private clinic re-opened in the town centre in the summer of 2014, but the prefectural hospital in Yamada was destroyed by the tsunami and replaced by a prefabricated 'temporary day clinic'. By the summer of 2014 there was only one physician employed their full time: Hiraizumi Sen. Hiraizumi trained as a surgeon and studied at Harvard, but he now works as a general practitioner, especially in geriatric and palliative care.

He sees patients at the clinic all morning. In the afternoon, he and two nurses make home visits to take temperatures, give drip-feed infusions, prescribe medicine and change diapers of elderly bed-ridden people. On weekends, the clinic is closed, and Hiraizumi goes on home visits alone. With his self-sacrificing commitment to home visiting, he ensures that bed-ridden patients can stay with their families in a familiar environment and at low cost. He also saves lives, especially in emergencies. Yet there are not many physicians like him, and home care in general is not well developed. For many families, driving their elderly relatives to a far-away hospital is the only way to get care.

Volunteers continue to go to the disaster zone, though the numbers have dwindled as the immediate physical needs of the people there have diminished with time. They still help farmers and fishers with tasks such as preparing the ground, transplanting crops, cleaning tools, seeding seaweed, etc. In the Shobutahama neighbourhood of Shichigahama, which was 80 per cent destroyed by the tsunami (see Johannes Wilhelm and Alyne Delaney in this volume), volunteers carry the *mikoshi* (portable shrine) in a local festival; even by the summer of 2014, there were not enough young local men able to perform this task. Nationally, there is a continued rhetoric of service and many universities are setting up programmes of 'service learning' to institutionalize this sentiment and experience.

However, much of the assistance now required – such as for legal advice on making claims for compensation or psychological help in the form of '*kokoro no kea*' (care of the heart) – requires longer term commitments and more training than even locally based volunteers groups can provide. Much of the work now shifts back to the state.

The Fukushima nuclear disaster continues to cast a long shadow over Japanese society. As of November 2014, all fifty of Japan's nuclear reactors were shut down. Two reactors, at the Ōi nuclear power plant in Fukui prefecture, were restarted in July 2012, despite formal objections from both the city and prefecture of Osaka, the biggest consumer of electricity from Ōi. In September 2013 the two reactors were shut down for regular inspections and since then there has been no nuclear power generated in Japan. Many of Japan's nuclear reactors are located on or close to geological fault lines, and there is intense argument as to whether those fault lines are active or not. Moreover, all of the reactors are located close to the sea and therefore exposed to some degree of risk from future tsunamis. The Abe government has attempted to keep nuclear power as part of Japan's energy mix by setting new safety standards that it claims are the toughest in the world to be enforced by a specially created body called the Nuclear Regulation Authority.

By the summer of 2014, the NRA had received applications to restart eighteen reactors at eleven power plants, and in September 2014 it issued its first ever approval – for two reactors at the Sendai plant in Satsumasendai, Kagoshima prefecture, southern Kyushu. At the time of writing it seems possible that the two reactors at Sendai could be reactivated early in 2015, ending a period of well over a year in which Japan generated no electricity from nuclear reactors.

In Fukushima the economy continues to struggle with the challenge of persuading consumers that agricultural produce from the prefecture is safe. According to the latest survey conducted by the Consumer Affairs Agency, Government of Japan, in August 2014, 19.6 per cent of respondents said they were hesitant to purchase produce from Fukushima, with a further 28.4 per cent naming wider areas of Tohoku from which they were hesitant to buy. In the same survey, 25.9 per cent of people did not know that food was being tested for radioactivity to ensure safety.[5]

Meanwhile, anti-nuclear demonstrations have continued. Though the scale and frequency of demonstrations has declined, there have been interesting developments in the range of people involved and the ways in which the anti-nuclear movement works. In the three decades before 3.11, most political activity had been organized by labour unions in which participation was mainly by men employed in regular jobs from urban locations. This has changed in a number of ways. First, young people who took the initiative in the early days of the disaster (see Tuukka Toivonen in this volume) have often been leaders in organizing and networking of anti-nuclear protests. Organizations like the Metropolitan Coalition Against Nukes and the Twitter-based TwitNoNukes have mobilized a new generation of socially disaffected, previously politically unengaged, and technologically sophisticated young people. The events they stage are as likely to reference European precarity events as post-war labour demonstrations.

---

5   Consumer Affairs Agency (2014). 'Regarding the 4th Survey on Consumer Consciousness about Fuhyo'. <http://www.caa.go.jp/safety/pdf/141001kouhyou_1.pdf> accessed 12 November 2014.

Second, patterns of geography and gender have been upset. While many of the most visual protests are in Tokyo, the rate of participation is probably higher among people from Tohoku, and especially Fukushima. People confronted with the most immediate threats to health have found support and information that has led to local activism. Sometimes organized through NPOs, agricultural producers or consumer groups, at other times through less formal, even neighborhood groups, their alliances cut across age and occupation in ways that make new spaces for residents to question governmental prioritization of economic recovery over concerns for safe food, land and water.

These groups are often led by women: young mothers and older environmental activists, as Morioka Rika observes in this volume.[6] While younger generations tend to recoil from the stigma of fist-raging radical activism, some have formed a style of 'gentle' protest, aspiring to a lifestyle different from those of their postwar generation parents devoted to Japan Inc. For them, nuclear power plants symbolize the wrongness of economy-centered policies. The disaster in 2011 provided common ground to unite generations of protesters. Sometimes the geographical gaps between Tokyo and Tohoku are bridged, too, as in the case of Fukushima Women Against Nukes, a group that has garnered international media attention through their presence at Tokyo demonstrations, while keeping local ties with Fukushima communities and families.

In Fukushima, about 130,000 people remain displaced by the nuclear disaster, and for many of them there is no prospect of returning to their communities for decades to come, if ever. The prolonged operations of stabilizing the crippled reactors at the Fukushima No.1 plant, staunching the emission of radiation into the local environment and decontaminating the surrounding area proceed at a snail's pace. An interim waste storage site has now been agreed at a site straddling the two townships of Futaba and Ōkuma, where the No.1 nuclear power plant itself is located. These townships will not be inhabitable for decades, so there is a certain

---

6   See also Rika Morioka (2014). 'Gender difference in the health risk perception of
     radiation from Fukushima in Japan: The role of hegemonic masculinity', *Social Science
     & Medicine*, 107, 105–112.

inevitability about the decision to create the contaminated waste storage site there. Compensation payments to the two townships will total some 300 billion yen.

The deal over the interim dump site included a legal guarantee that the waste materials contained at the facility would be moved outside the prefecture within thirty years. Still, the deal offers a temporary answer to the question of where to put some 20 million cubic metres of radioactive waste, currently stored in piles of bags at some 54,000 locations around Fukushima prefecture.[7]

The issue of compensation for the victims of the nuclear disaster is also ongoing. For people in the worst affected areas, total compensation to date for the psychological damage of forced relocation has reached about 15 million yen per person, or 75 million yen for a household of five. Many households now have enough money to buy a house elsewhere, and a growing number of them have done just that. For example, by autumn 2014, roughly 300 out of the 1,800 households in Iitate village had bought houses, including 30 of the 71 households in Nagadoro hamlet (see Tom Gill in this volume). With every house bought, the number of villagers likely to return after decontamination is reduced; as a result, at this point there seems to be no chance that village life will return to anything like what it was before the disaster. What is true of Iitate is even truer for the communities closer to the nuclear power plant, such as Namie, Tomioka and, of course, Futaba and Ōkuma. These communities have almost certainly been dispersed permanently.

So the answer to the question 'is everything back to normal now?' is that pre-disaster normality is gone forever. We can but hope that in the years to come, a new kind of normality can slowly be established by the victims of the terrible disaster that was 3.11. Japan will still be coping with calamity for many years to come.

—THE EDITORS, November 2014

7 <http://ajw.asahi.com/article/0311disaster/fukushima/AJ201409020061> accessed 12 November 2014.

Preface and Acknowledgements to the First Edition

This collection of ethnographic studies explores how people experienced the aftermath of the tsunami and nuclear disasters that afflicted Japan on 11 March 2011. By focusing on the period between the initial chaos caused by large-scale and sudden destruction and the formation of a recognizable trajectory of rebuilding, it aims to enhance our understanding of 3.11 and more generally of the human consequences of disaster. This was the period when outsiders, be they from nearby Sendai, from Tokyo or Osaka, or from abroad, ventured into the areas of north-eastern Japan where the tsunami had hit to provide aid and relief. New sets of relationships were being forged or negotiated in evacuation shelters and temporary housing. People were frantically trying to assess the effects of becquerels and millisieverts on human health while the search for bodies under the debris was still going on. Communities were hatching relocation plans and imagining possible futures, even as rituals for the dead were being performed. It was a period when people struggled to find narratives that could explain what had happened, but nevertheless had to sort out how to move ahead.

It is impossible to make overarching scholarly or even systematic generalizations about this important, complex and chaotic phase. The contributors to this volume have thus looked at specific issues in specific locations to explore the uneven fits and starts of relief and recovery, the tentative, incomplete, sometimes misguided attempts to recover community and lost social relations, and the efforts to build something new out of the wreckage. This book was conceived as an urgent ethnographic response to the disasters. All of its authors shared a desire to get the voices of disaster victims heard as rapidly and as clearly as possible amid the welter of reportage, polemic and rumour that the disaster generated. We hope this collection will form a bridge between the studies rushed out in the immediate aftermath, and the more authoritative analyses of the disaster and aftermath that will doubtless appear in the years to come.

We have been helped along the way by many friends. We held a symposium in Yokohama on 19 August 2011, where we received advice and constructive criticism from Yamashita Shinji, Kariya Takehiko, Michael Shackleton, Ramona Bajema, Alex Vesey and others. At a workshop on 13 November 2011, also in Yokohama, we were advised by James Roberson, Earl Kinmonth, Michael Watson and Susanne Klein. In the long process of turning those symposium papers into the present volume, we benefited from the insights of Mark Selden, John Traphagan, Jerry Eades, Harumi Befu and the anonymous reviewer of Peter Lang. Individual papers were helped by many other people, who are acknowledged in those papers. Mary Anketell proofread several of the chapters for us, supported by a Cambridge Humanities Research Grant. Carla Takaki Richardson provided timely and professional indexing. We thank all of these, named or otherwise, who helped us create this book.

Our publisher, Peter Lang, has been consistently helpful, patient and understanding. We wish to thank all those who worked on the book and especially Laurel Plapp, who has been in overall charge of publication.

We wish to express our deep gratitude to the Japan Foundation for making the whole project viable by supporting us with a grant. This financed the two events in Yokohama, offset costs of the present volume, and enabled us to translate and produce a Japanese volume, *Higashi-Nihon daishinsai no jinruigaku: Tsunami, genpatsu jiko to hisaishatachi no 'sono go'* (Anthropology of the Great Eastern Japan Disaster: The tsunami, the nuclear accident and what happened next to the victims), published by Jinbun Shoin of Kyoto in March 2013. The three maps in this book were originally drafted by Jinbun Shoin, and we thank them for allowing us to reproduce translated versions of them. The English and Japanese volumes contain the same collection of ten papers, but during the process of editing, the two volumes diverged considerably.

Publication in Japanese has enabled us to communicate with readers in Japan, including some of the people this book is about – the victims of 3.11. It is of course to them that we owe our biggest debt of gratitude. They found the time and kindness to talk to strangers like us at times of extreme personal stress. We can never thank them enough.

— THE EDITORS, July 2013

Technical Note: Japanese names are written with the family name first. Macrons are used to indicate long vowels, principally ō and ū.

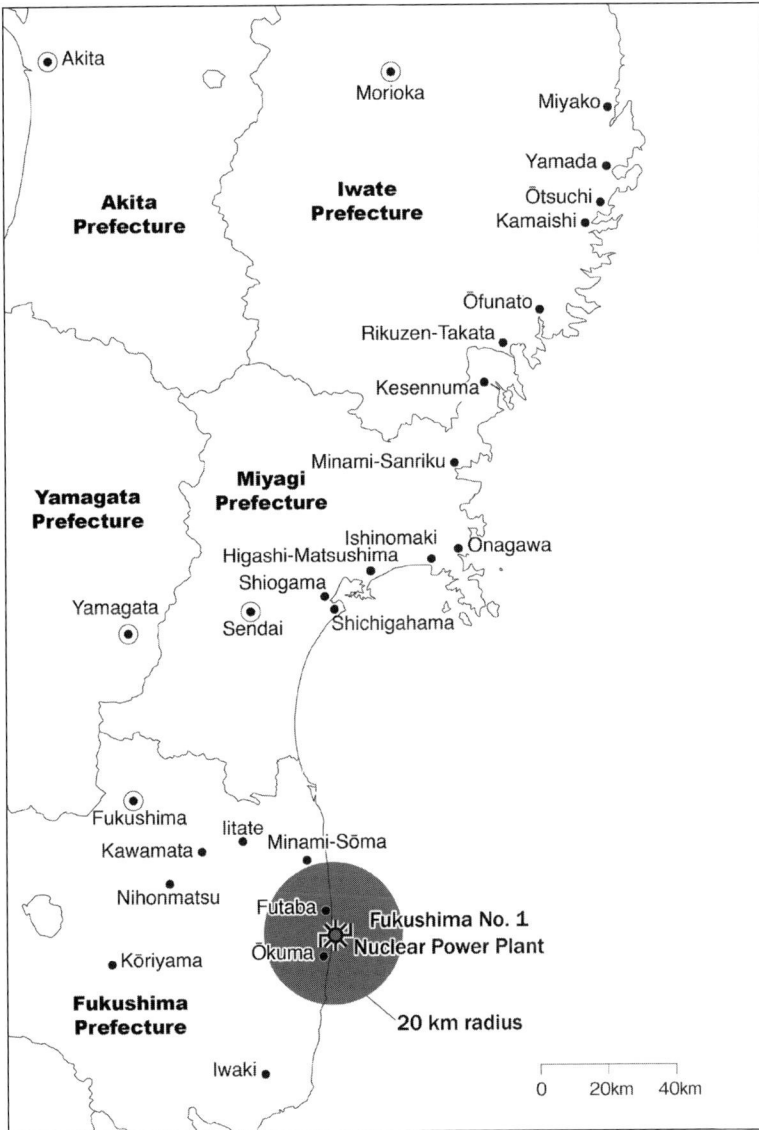

Map of Tohoku (North-eastern Japan), displaying places mentioned in the text. Reprinted and translated from Gill et al., *Higashi Nihon daishinsai no jinruigaku* (Jinbun Shoin, 2013), p. 4.

INTRODUCTION

TOM GILL, BRIGITTE STEGER AND DAVID H. SLATER

The 3.11 Disasters

The earthquake

On Friday, 11 March 2011, at 2.46pm, an earthquake of magnitude 9 occurred 70 kilometres off Japan's north-eastern coast. It was the strongest ever recorded in Japan.[1] All over eastern Japan buildings shuddered violently, clearing bookshelves, knocking over tables and counters, and ripping out built-in furniture. Those who fled found the pavements buckling and crumbling beneath their feet, the asphalt undulating strongly enough to knock them to the ground. The earthquake knocked out electricity, gas and water supplies, and severely disrupted telecommunications. Even in Tokyo, several hundred kilometres away from the epicentre, high-rise buildings swayed and public transportation was paralyzed, forcing millions of people to walk home in the small hours. At a major landfill project in Urayasu, just east of Tokyo, the earth was liquidized, leaving hundreds of houses tilting alarmingly. In nearby Ichihara an oil refinery caught fire and blazed for days.

Remarkably, the earthquake itself caused relatively few fatalities. A precise count of how many houses were destroyed by the earthquake and how many by the tsunami is impossible, but one estimate[2] suggests that 268 people were killed by the shaking, mostly crushed in collapsed buildings, and another 165 died in fires and landslides. Though bad enough, these death tolls are very low for such a major earthquake. With a long history

---

[1]   The 1923 Great Kanto earthquake had a magnitude of 8.3; the 1995 Kobe earthquake registered 7.2.

[2]   <http://earthquake-report.com/2012/03/10/japan-366-days-after-the-quake-19000-lives-lost-1–2-million-buildings-damaged-574-billion/> accessed 23 June 2013.

of earthquakes and sophisticated technology and infrastructure to resist them, Japan was well prepared. Most buildings remained standing; all the bullet trains had built-in earthquake alarms and came to a safe halt. And yet, any sense of relief would last for no more than forty minutes.

The tsunami

People living along Japan's north-eastern coast know from long experience that earthquakes can trigger a major tsunami. The one caused by the Meiji Sanriku earthquake in 1896 killed about 22,000 people, mostly in Iwate prefecture. The Showa Sanriku earthquake (1933) and the Chile tsunami (1960), although less disastrous, were still in older people's memories (Hagami 2012: 10–12) and had been well documented (Ōfunato Shiritsu Hakubutsu-kan 1990). Many attended annual tsunami evacuation training or other disaster prevention exercises (Yamori 2007: 111–113). Much of the coast was lined by an ugly protective wall, six to seven metres high, with metal gates for access to the sea, which had been built over several decades. Along the Pacific coast, tsunami alarms went off three minutes after the quake. Unfortunately, technical and systemic failings prompted the Meteorological Agency (JMA) to understate the seriousness of the situation by forecasting the height of the tsunami at '3 metres or more', that being the highest category of warning in the system, thereby worsening the confusion.[3] Still, as soon as the worst of the shaking had stopped, local residents took evasive action. Shopkeepers hurriedly moved their stock upstairs; garage mechanics drove their clients' cars to higher ground; fire-fighters rushed to close the gates in the tsunami protection walls; nurses

3   On 8 August 2011, the JMA formally admitted that it had underestimated the height of the tsunami and announced an overhaul of its procedures. The biggest change was that it would no longer try to estimate the height of a tsunami, and would instead use expressions such as 'huge' (see Cyranoski 2011).

and doctors led their patients onto the roofs of their hospitals. Fishermen had to decide whether to sail into the open sea to try and save their boats[4] or abandon the boats and try to take care of their families. Groups and individuals drove or ran to designated evacuation areas on higher ground. Mothers and fathers rushed to pick up their children from school. Others thought it safer to shelter at home or were not mobile enough to run. 'When the tsunami comes, leave everything behind and flee!' This was always the standard advice, and most people followed it. Even so, the size and speed of the tsunami were underestimated by most – partly because of misleading warnings, but also because people cannot easily imagine their own houses destroyed and their own loved ones killed by a disaster, even when they are aware of a threat. Abe and Kazama (1985) describe this kind of psychological denial in their account of the fire that destroyed some 1,700 houses at Sakata, Yamagata prefecture, in 1976.

When the waves reached the coast some forty minutes after the earthquake, they dwarfed everyone's worst fears. The tsunami towered up to 12 metres high, and reached points up to 40 metres above sea level,[5] sweeping inland as far as 10 kilometres. It pulverized buildings, swept away major roads and displaced landmasses. Supposedly safe evacuation zones were deluged in a flash. Entire coastal communities were wiped off the map.

Many people in the afflicted areas never saw the tsunami. They sat it out at school grounds, temples and other safe havens well inland. They were the lucky ones. Others, who had fled on first instinct, returned home to fetch valuables or necessities. Many died that way. Others were caught in their cars, on their way to pick up children from school or driving home along the coastal road, parallel to the coast, when they should have been

---

4   A tsunami wave is much smaller while still out in the deep sea than when it hits land; thus fishermen generally know that they should head towards the open sea rather than towards the shore.

5   The highest wave recognized by the JMA was 11.8 metres at Ofunato, Iwate prefecture: <http://www.jma.go.jp/jma/kishou/books/saigaiji/saigaiji_201101/saigaiji_201101_01.pdf> accessed 23 June 2013. The highest run-ups were around 40 metres, in narrow inlets around Miyako and Yamada, Iwate prefecture (see e.g. Okayasu et al. 2012).

driving inland. Most of the deaths occurred in just a few minutes – people smashed by the ferocious impact of the waves, drowned in the rising waters, or dragged out to sea by the undertow as the waters receded, leaving many others trapped under collapsed buildings and in overturned cars. The wave of water turned black with dirt and debris, toxic with oil and chemicals. Fires broke out and destroyed many houses that had survived the onslaught, colouring the night-sky red.

The first line of defence was the local community. The rescue teams had to struggle through impassable streets in darkness and chaos. Until they arrived, family and neighbours were left to help each other. It is documented that some 66,000 people were rescued by the Self-Defence Forces (SDF, *Jieitai*) in the first three days after the earthquake.[6] But it is probable that many more were saved by undocumented local solidarity. The local fire brigades also pulled many thousands from the rubble.

In round numbers,[7] 3.11 killed about 18,600 people, of whom 94 per cent were killed by the tsunami and 6 per cent by the earthquake and related fires, landslides, heart-attacks, cold, exposure, hunger, etc. That figure includes some 2,700 whose bodies were never found. About 130,000 buildings were totally destroyed (*zenkai*), 104,000 by the tsunami and 26,000 by the earthquake. About 250,000 buildings were 'half-destroyed' (*hankai*), 140,000 by the tsunami and 110,000 by the earthquake. Another 710,000 buildings were less severely damaged, and here the tsunami accounted for 67,000 and the earthquake for 633,000. The damage was highly concentrated in three prefectures: Miyagi, Iwate and Fukushima. Miyagi suffered roughly 10,800 deaths, Iwate 5,800 and Fukushima 1,800, with only about seventy people killed anywhere else in Japan. Damage to property was also concentrated in these three prefectures. As Johannes Wilhelm and Alyne Delaney show in this volume, the tsunami devastated the local fishing industry, where for example it destroyed 90 per cent of all the fishing boats in Miyagi prefecture.

---

6   <http://factsanddetails.com/japan.php?itemid=1677> accessed 5 June 2013.
7   All data in this paragraph comes from the National Police Agency of Japan. <http://www.npa.go.jp/archive/keibi/biki/higaijokyo_e.pdf> accessed 5 June 2013.

The pattern is clear enough from the statistics. The earthquake caused widespread damage; the tsunami was much more localized but accounted for the vast majority of the serious destruction and most of the deaths.

Survival and shelter

Because the earthquake hit in the middle of the afternoon, families were often spread out across the villages and towns, at home, at work and at school, with no way to communicate their whereabouts due to the disrupted phone service. Town officials were still at work when the disasters occurred. While this facilitated fast response and co-ordination of rescue efforts in some towns, elsewhere the town halls were destroyed by the tsunami and many officials who stayed at their posts were killed, depriving the immediate relief effort of leadership and increasing the chaos. As the evening set in, people began to gather at designated evacuation shelters such as school gymnasiums and community halls. Blankets and cushions were handed out, and a little water and food distributed. Medical teams were formed in urban centres and provided emergency care. However, most towns and villages in Tohoku are scattered, so people in the smaller and more remote hamlets had to rely on themselves and their neighbours. They stayed wherever they could find protection from the cold: private houses, temples, department store aisles or any other fairly dry place. Others slept in their cars. During the first night, the earth continued to shake. Survivors had to endure twenty-three aftershocks of magnitude 6 to 7.9 in the first twenty-four hours after the main quake, with many more in the following days and weeks.[8]

---

8   See: Japanquakemap.com (accessed 5 June 2013). As a comparison, the earthquake that destroyed large areas of Haiti on 12 January 2010 with an estimated 220,000 dead reached magnitude 7. The earthquake at Christchurch on 4 September 2010 and the one near Van in Turkey on 23 October 2011 both had a magnitude of 7.1.

In the morning, there was debris and rubble everywhere, with houses crushed and ships marooned on rooftops. Some small factories and houses were burning, others had been washed away. Houses that survived the tsunami often had their ground floor saturated, forcing residents to retreat upstairs in search of shelter or to rescue their belongings. In other cases, the upstairs part of the house had been ripped from the foundation, picked up and deposited elsewhere. Streets near the coast were not passable, indeed not even recognizable. People tried to find their way to the community centres over small mountain roads, hoping to find their relatives there, praying that they were safe. Lists of those missing were posted on the walls of evacuation shelters, pored over and updated. The local newspapers made it one of their major jobs to compile the diverse and incomplete lists and put them online (Matsuo 2012). Many searched desperately for their loved ones under the debris. In some areas, large fires had broken out. The tsunami had knocked out the hydrants, leaving the fire brigade helpless, and the Self-Defence Forces struggled to extinguish fires from the air. Short winter days and the need to look out for possible survivors under the debris further hampered clean-up activities. Meanwhile, official and unofficial shelters (*hinanjo*) rapidly filled up. Most of the sick and elderly were soon evacuated to places further inland, but limited capacity meant many could not find a place. Others refused to leave their homes, determined to wait for relatives to come back and look for them, or to protect their homes from looting.

In the first weeks, the shelters were almost always overcrowded. Lack of running water, electricity, toilets and other basic facilities posed formidable challenges. Deliveries of food, blankets, clothes and medicine were irregular with many streets impassable, railway lines crippled and petrol hard to come by. The shelters were very diverse, ranging from gymnasiums to hot spring hotels. Many found it increasingly stressful to share their living space with strangers and left as soon as they could. Others, especially elderly people who had hitherto lived alone on a small income, appreciated the company of others after their horrific experience, and desperately needed the regular medical care and meals that the evacuation shelters provided. 'It's downright paradise!' (*Marude tengoku desu*), a colleague of ours was told by an elderly lady, while volunteering at a shelter. After routines had been restored, donations of food and daily necessaries were plentiful. But for the vast majority, the ordeal of sleeping on cold, hardwood floors, with little privacy and personal space, was immensely stressful. There was a sense of community, but as the weeks and months passed by, the virtue of endurance (*gaman*), for which people in Tohoku are well known, was severely tested.

Temporary housing

After two to three months, temporary housing gradually became available. Places were allocated by lottery, but priority was given to families with sick or elderly members or small children, so these were usually the first to move out of the evacuation shelters. In some locations, this broke up families and created new problems.

The quality of the temporary housing was diverse, but they were all prefabricated units with little or no insulation, which could get very cold and damp in the long Tohoku winter. Curtis (2011) reports that the government had to spend up to US $30,000 per unit to make the accommodation inhabitable in winter, and the Japan Red Cross was among many other bodies working to 'winterize' the temporary housing (American Red Cross 2012). Initially people were told that this housing was for a maximum of two or three years, but that period has passed now, and people in many parts of the coast are well aware that they will have to wait several more years before the towns and villages can be rebuilt. Where it is clear that return will never be possible, as in the case of coastal communities whose former site has been declared uninhabitable, the challenge for local authorities is to construct 'reconstruction housing' (*fukkō jūtaku*) for permanent residence, of decent quality and at an affordable price with low-interest loans to help victims buy them. How far from the original community they should be sited, and whether they should be houses or apartments – these are hotly debated issues.

A typical temporary housing unit is a single story terraced house with a kitchen/dining-room just inside the front door, usually of about ten square metres, and one or two smaller rooms in the back. By now, many houses have an additional little porch, added on some time later to help keep the wind out and to provide some additional space for shoes and coats. They have a toilet and a tiny bathroom. The units have gas, water and electricity and are generally air-conditioned. There is a futon for each resident and a standard set of six household electrical items: a fridge/freezer, a rice cooker, a washing machine, a vacuum cleaner, a microwave oven and a television. Such housing units are designed for up to four people, but sometimes more are accommodated in order to keep the family intact. It is better than the floor of a gymnasium, but there is almost no storage space and again little privacy among family members.

Arguably, a bigger problem than the design of the temporary housing is its location. With few empty public spaces available close to the affected area but safe from potential new tsunamis, some of the housing sites are in quite remote inland areas. Initially, food could only be bought from a truck that came once a day at most, and one had to go miles to get other daily necessities. Few residents had cars,[9] and bus services, limited at the best of times, took considerable time to be restored.

Understandably, many tried to avoid the temporary housing. Some moved into relatives' or even neighbours' homes, but this put stress on personal relationships. Some left the area entirely. Others found a place to rent on the open market, in which case they generally received the same six items of equipment and a guarantee that their rent would be reimbursed, initially for two years and typically up to a maximum of 90,000 yen a month. With the post-disaster phase in its third year at the time of writing, there is some anxiety as to how long these subsidies will last.

Another primary problem was employment. The fishing industry was decimated. Not just the fishermen's boats, but the repair shops, the

9   Thousands of cars were destroyed but, unlike the case with housing, the government did not provide compensation. Yet for many people in these rural areas, a car is a necessity of everyday life.

processing plants, the transportation companies, in effect, the whole fishing industry was brought to a grinding halt. As the government started pumping public money into recovery programmes, however, employment recovered. Many people were employed in reconstruction and relief work. During 2012, unemployment in the three devastated prefectures fell below the national average, and for the first quarter of 2013 it stood at 4.0 per cent in Miyagi, 3.5 per cent in Fukushima and 3.4 per cent in Iwate, against the national average of 4.3 per cent.[10] The major long-term concern is what will happen to employment in the disaster zone once the artificial construction boom and welfare jobs fuelled by special government spending come to an end.

The nuclear disaster

Initially unknown to outsiders, the earthquake and tsunami had caused serious damage to the six nuclear reactors at the Fukushima No.1 plant run by Tokyo Electric Power Company (TEPCO). Over the next three days the cooling systems failed and a series of horrifying hydrogen explosions blew the roofs off reactors No.1, No.2 and No.3.[11] At 9.23pm on 11 March,

---

10   <http://www.stat.go.jp/data/roudou/pref/index.htm> accessed 5 June 2013.

11   There were also explosions at the No.4 reactor, which was fuelled but not operational at the time. The No.5 and No.6 reactors were in cold shutdown, although there were serious difficulties with cooling spent fuel rods there. Four more reactors at the Fukushima No.2 plant a little further down the coastline survived the tsunami. But the disaster naturally led to questions about the policy of putting so many reactors close together in an area known to be prone to earthquakes and tsunami. By the end of September 2013, all fifty-three of Japan's nuclear reactors had been shut down. However, the landslide victory of the Liberal Democratic Party in the general election of December 2012 brought in a new government under Abe Shintarō with a much more favourable view of nuclear power. By 2014, it seemed likely that nuclear power generation would gradually be resumed at most of Japan's reactors, though not at those found to be situated on active fault-lines.

people living within a 3 kilometre radius were ordered to evacuate, followed by those within 10 kilometres at 5.44am on 12 March. The first of
the explosions occurred at 3.36pm that day and at 6.25pm the evacuation
radius was expanded to 20 kilometres. Then on 15 March Prime Minister
Kan Naoto paid a dramatic visit to the headquarters of TEPCO at 5.30am
to order the company not to withdraw its workers from the stricken plant,
which the company had spoken of doing to protect the workers' lives. That
would have left the crippled reactors unmanned, with fuel rods exposed
and cooling water evaporating – pushing Japan towards an unimaginably
bigger disaster. On the same day, the government ordered those in the 20
to 30 kilometre ring to stay indoors (*shitsunai taihi*). Meanwhile the US
government urged its citizens to get at least 80 kilometres away from the
plant and the French government even advised its nationals in Tokyo, 250
kilometres away, to evacuate. This made the Japanese government's evacuation plan look very inadequate to many Japanese when they learned of the
very different evacuation standards declared by other countries, although
of course applying the American or French standards to Japanese nationals
would have been a logistical nightmare, because of the incomparably larger
numbers of people involved and the fact that, unlike most foreigners, they
did not necessarily have anywhere else to go. Thus evaluation of risk was
never made in a vacuum but was always constrained by what was feasible.

    The official data from the Ministry of Education on evacuee numbers
in Fukushima prefecture[12] make interesting reading. Four days after 3.11,
102,648 people had been evacuated. The number of evacuees then *declined*
to 89,309 on 25 March and further to 84,021 by 22 April. Their numbers then
climbed steadily, passing 150,000 in mid-August 2011, and remained at that
level, registering 156,234 at the end of 2012.[13] The evacuees left behind some
35,000 buildings in the evacuation zone viewed as intact but, for varying

---

12   <http://www.mext.go.jp/b_menu/shingi/chousa/kaihatu/016/shiryo/__icsFiles/
      afieldfile/2011/11/25/1313502_3.pdf > accessed 5 June 2013.
13   <http://wwwcms.pref.fukushima.jp/download/1/kikaku_chosei_honbusiryo19–1-4.
      pdf> accessed 5 June 2013.

periods of years, judged to be uninhabitable due to radiation. Roughly 100,000 were forced to evacuate by the government; the other 50,000 did so voluntarily and largely at their own expense.

These figures testify to the mixed messages sent out by the government regarding the radiation risk. As we have seen, the evacuation zone defined by the government was small compared with the American and French response. Once the first week had passed, the government created the impression that things were calming down in the disaster zone and people started to return home – including many of the villagers observed by Tom Gill (this volume). Then the government started to lose confidence in its risk-analysis, and ordered fresh evacuations – including some areas where the most dangerous phase had already passed. Meanwhile many people lost faith in the government and made their own evacuation arrangements. Most of those who left have still not come back. The population of Fukushima prefecture fell by about 75,000, from 2.024 million to 1.950 million, over the two years following the disaster.[14]

Like the tsunami evacuees, victims of the nuclear disaster have been housed in a mixture of prefabricated temporary housing units and rental properties subsidized by the prefectural government. But plans for long-term housing are still unsettled and bitterly contested between local and national governments, and even between different groups within a single community. With fears that some of this land will be uninhabitable for the foreseeable future, the issue of decontamination versus permanent relocation is likely to end up in the courts (see Gill's chapter in this volume).

Meanwhile the victims of the nuclear disaster must deal with stigma and discrimination in addition to material harm. The Japanese language uses four different writing systems: Chinese pictograms or *kanji*, two syllabaries (*hiragana* and *katakana*) and the Roman alphabet. The place-name 'Fukushima' is now sometimes written in the *katakana* syllabary rather than

---

14   Fukushima prefecture home page <http://wwwcms.pref.fukushima.jp/> accessed 23 June 2013. As the figure of 150,000 evacuees suggests, roughly half the evacuees had left Fukushima prefecture, the others having evacuated to a location within Fukushima.

the usual Chinese *kanji* pictograms to distinguish the disaster from the prefecture and city of the same name. The same was done with the names of Hiroshima and Nagasaki, and with the common element of nuclear incident and radiation, Fukushima has become associated with those other victimized sites (see Ikeda Yoko's chapter in this volume). Aware of how problematical the way of writing 'Fukushima' can be, some activists prefer to write it in *hiragana*, the other syllabary in the complex Japanese script.[15] The Fukushima prefectural government also frequently writes 'Fukushima' in hiragana in official publications and on-line.[16] Just to remind ourselves, no deaths have so far been officially attributed to the Fukushima meltdowns, whereas at least 150,000 people were killed in the two atomic bombings, so it is perhaps understandable that the people of Fukushima feel uncomfortable about being bracketed with Hiroshima and Nagasaki, though this has become one of the political gambits in the antinuclear movement.[17] Even the pure chance of assonance between the two names 'Hiroshima' and 'Fukushima' has increased the tendency to draw parallels between two places that, in truth, suffered very different disasters.

Partly this may be because people in Japan today find it easier to blame the Tokyo Electric Power Company than to blame the gods – a theme that we will now discuss in some detail.

---

15   For example the NPO *Fukushima Shien: Hito to Bunka Nettowāku* (Fukushima Support: People and Culture Network) uses *hiragana*. Organizer Gunji Mayumi told us that using *hiragana* is a way of stating that 'Fukushima' the disaster is different from Fukushima the place, but not in the same way that 'Hiroshima' the disaster is different from Hiroshima the place. Such subtleties are impossible to convey in English.

16   See for example <http://www.new-fukushima.jp/>.

17   See for instance the work of the anonymous Tokyo street artist 281_Anti Nuke (Mitchell 2013). He refers to the Fukushima disaster as 'the third bomb'.

Tensai/jinsai: 'Natural' versus 'man-made' disaster narratives

> Disasters occur at the interface of society, technology, and environment
> and are fundamentally the outcomes of the interaction of these features.
> In very graphic ways, disasters signal the failure of a society to adapt
> successfully to certain features of its natural and socially constructed
> environment in a sustainable fashion.
>
> — OLIVER-SMITH 1996: 303

We would agree with this general analysis of disasters, but add that when people try to account for disasters, they tend to foreground some of these elements more than others. Such an immense and complex event as 3.11 is inevitably simplified as people and institutions try to think about it and respond. The result is a set of framing narratives that inform some of the most intimate levels of interaction here. They are not uniformly imposed dominant discourses so much as shared explanations of situations that are often too terrible and/or too complex to be easily grasped and rendered. Having some ways to collectively narrate these events can provide solace and restore some cognitive order. As Brigitte Steger's contribution to this volume reminds us, people often lose their memories of events in posttraumatic situations, and collective narrative helps people to fill the gaps and put some shape on the chaotic events they experienced. But these narratives can also distort reality and become a source of conflict.

Two primary framing narratives have emerged from the melee. The tsunami, and the damage it caused, is often referred to as a *tensai*, or natural disaster. The nuclear disaster, in contrast, is described as a *jinsai*, or man-made disaster, a label that also includes the stigma suffered by people, places and products because of fears of health-risks from radiation due to the meltdowns (*fuhyō higai*, or damage by rumour; see Ikeda in this volume). The earthquake, although the immediate cause of both events, features less prominently in the narratives as it caused fewer deaths and less direct damage.

Duus (2012: 176) names 'blaming' as the first phase in people's response to disaster, followed by coping, hoping, learning and forgetting. We cannot accept such a formulaic view of the order of events and would point out that the pattern was not even consistent between the two 3.11 disasters. In the case of the nuclear disaster, a lot of blaming went on, as we shall see below, but in the case of the tsunami, blaming was well down the list of responses. These two disasters have to be treated separately.

The concept of *tensai* (literally 'heavenly disaster', usually translated as 'natural disaster') is sharply different to that of *tenbatsu* (literally 'heavenly punishment', usually translated as 'divine punishment'). When Tokyo governor Ishihara Shintarō described the earthquake/tsunami as *tenbatsu* he was isolated and forced to retract the statement.[18] None of the contributors to this volume found evidence that Tohoku people seriously thought that they were being punished by the gods or by fate – though many were affiliated to Shinto and Buddhism, two religions that do have a concept of divine punishment. Rather, the term *tensai* brings with it a sense of resignation and even fatalism: the disaster was a force of nature, and so cannot be helped. One of David H. Slater's informants, an 85-year-old woman from an old fishing family of Ishinomaki, Miyagi prefecture, explained, 'We all knew this would come – it was only a matter of time. Of course, we were not waiting for it, we were not thinking of it at all. But I guess if you asked us, any of us would have been able to tell you that it could come at any time'.

What sort of responsibility this knowledge entails is not made clear. In Ishinomaki, as in most coastal areas, there has been a steady creeping of residential housing closer to the shore, despite the lessons of the disastrous Sanriku tsunamis of 1896 and 1933. Many local residents did not view this as irresponsible. Another informant, an older fisherman from Minami Sanriku who lost his boat, expressed something echoed by many: 'You cannot prepare for everything ... You cannot live your life waiting for a disaster. It comes when it comes.' For many coastal inhabitants, living by the

---

18   <http://www.guardian.co.uk/world/2011/mar/15/tokyo-governor-tsunami-punishment> accessed 6 June 2013.

sea was not so much an irresponsible ignoring of risk as a sober willingness to accept risk as part of the larger set of choices that their lifestyle entailed.

This fatalism in the face of natural disaster often spilled over into other related domains where human agency and responsibility were more obviously involved, such as the timely distribution of relevant and accurate information, the drafting and executing of evacuation and rehousing plans, and the allocation of budgets for rebuilding. The logic of a narrative, in this case the fatalistic acceptance of hardship, was analogically extended to other domains. There were many victims, but no-one was to blame. There was nothing for the local residents to reproach themselves for, and no consistent attribution of failure to local or national government. True, there has been some criticism of poorly designed flood defences, and both local and national government were criticized for their slow and bureaucratic response. There have also been some lawsuits, such as the one brought against the Hiyori kindergarten in Miyagi prefecture by parents who blamed the management for the deaths of their children. But, by and large, in this narrative neither the local residents nor the government were held responsible, and we have seen little political protest around these issues in the tsunami zone.

It was only later, when cases of fraud with money allocated for reconstruction and regeneration became known in public, that some people felt that they were now facing another man-made disaster. For example, two years into the recovery process, the NPO Daisetsu Ribaanetto ('Big Snow River Net') from Hokkaido found itself facing trial accused of misusing most of a 790 million yen budget to employ local people on various recovery projects. The money was largely unaccounted for or had been spent on luxury items, some of which were put up for auction in an attempt to retrieve some of the funds.[19] The issue was further complicated by the fact that some local tsunami victims who had been employed by the NPO also participated in the extravaganza by not questioning unusually high salaries and luxurious gifts.

19   See for example <http://mainichi.jp/select/news/20130404mog00m040014000c. html> accessed 29 June 2013.

This was just one of many scandals over the misuse of relief funds. In June 2013, the central government announced that it would demand the return from local authorities of 100 billion yen in unspent relief funds.[20] In summer of 2013 it emerged that even the nuclear power plant operators had come in for a small share of the disaster relief budget, to the anger of many.[21] However, all those recriminations would come later. In the immediate aftermath of the tsunami, people generally viewed it phlegmatically, as an unavoidable force of nature. It was the subsequent flood of money that raised issues of responsibility and blame.

The second narrative is quite different, focusing on different geographical areas, different aetiology and different patterns of responsibility. While the tsunami obviously necessitated the evacuation of coastal regions, some inland areas of Fukushima suffered little if any observable physical damage but had to be evacuated due to their proximity to the stricken nuclear power plant. Their forced evacuation was based on the invisible and poorly understood threat to health from radiation in air, water, soil and food. The narrative that foregrounds the sheer bad luck of a 'once-in-a-millennium tsunami'[22] has not been seen as sufficient excuse for TEPCO among local residents or the media, local or national. Instead, as David McNeill notes in this volume (p. 133), the nuclear disaster generated 'a smouldering resentment and urge to apportion blame'. Some of that blame has been directed at journalists and activists accused of overreacting to the

---

20   NHK, 22 June 2013. <http://www3.nhk.or.jp/news/html/20130622/k1001550386 1000.html>.

21   'Funds from disaster relief budget given to nuclear operators'. *Japan Today*, 29 June 2013. <http://www.japantoday.com/category/national/view/funds-from-disaster-relief-budget-given-to-nuclear-operators?utm_campaign=jt_newsletter&utm_medium=email&utm_source=jt_newsletter_2013-06-29_PN>.

22   This expression, often used by defenders of TEPCO, was based mainly on the questionable assumption that there had not been a tsunami that big since the Jōgan Earthquake of 869. Some critics have argued that the Keichō Earthquake of 1611 was in fact of comparable scale. In any case, past seismic activity is not a reliable guide to future seismic activity. Another group of critics has argued that the principle cause of the meltdowns may have been the earthquake rather than the tsunami, which would further complicate risk analysis.

disaster, or at the prime minister of the day, Kan Naoto, for his allegedly poor management (Duus 2012: 178; Samuels 2013: 37, etc.). However, the events themselves at reactor No.1 have been firmly blamed on corporate greed, poor planning and compromised governmental oversight in the years leading up to 11 March 2011. This view received official backing in July 2012, when a parliamentary inquiry chaired by University of Tokyo emeritus professor Kurokawa Kiyoshi famously concluded that what happened at Fukushima No.1 'cannot be regarded as a natural disaster. It was a profoundly man-made disaster – that could and should have been foreseen and prevented'.[23] After insisting for a year and a half that it had done everything it could to protect the power plant, TEPCO started to change its tone in the autumn of 2012, creating an advisory body to its board of directors called the Nuclear Reform Monitoring Committee, chaired by Dale Klein, former Chairman of the US Nuclear Regulatory Commission. On 29 March 2013, this committee issued a report, accepted by TEPCO, placing the bulk of responsibility for the disaster at the company's door: 'TEPCO admits that one of the causes of the Fukushima Daiichi Accident was from deficiencies in the facilities at the Fukushima Daiichi Nuclear Power Plant, and deeply regrets having betrayed local trust because of its inability to ensure nuclear safety'.[24] TEPCO president Shimokobe Kazuhiko was one of the five members of the committee. Self-justification had given way to self-flagellation.

In the media and blogosphere, TEPCO has been characterized as a wicked tempter, actively seeking out economically struggling villages for reactor locations, and then locking them into long-term contracts of dependence. Not surprisingly, there was a far more political response to the radiation issue, not only in Tohoku, but also in Tokyo and all over Japan, and public demonstrations were large, frequent and sustained. But the blame is not all placed on TEPCO. A secondary narrative takes a

---

23 The Kurokawa Report is available at <http://warp.da.ndl.go.jp/info:ndljp/ pid/3856371/naiic.go.jp/en/report/>. Kurokawa's comment is included in the 'message from the chairman'.

24 See <http://www.nrmc.jp/en/report/detail/1226308_5233.html> accessed 23 June 2013.

moralistic view of the local communities that accepted nuclear power plants, attracted by sweeteners such as large subsidies, new infrastructure, and jobs for local people in areas which generally had a very depressed local economy (Sumihara 2003: 12). This element of perceived complicity with the enemy has caused self-doubt within, and resentment between, communities (see Gill in this volume). Then again, the governmental narrative identifying nuclear energy as an important, even necessary part of national energy policy and autonomy cast the people of Okuma and Futaba, where the Fukushima No.1 plant was sited,[25] as sacrificial victims, bravely accepting risk for the benefit of the nation. Despite these moral complexities, the nuclear disaster was clearly framed as being 'man-made'.

The relatively slow pace of the unfolding of the nuclear disaster rendered events yet more malleable to narrative crafting. In contrast to the immediate and tragic loss of life and infrastructure that the tsunami brought, there have been no deaths as yet definitively attributable to radiation. The social chaos of relocating 150,000 people due to fears of radiation contamination mirrored that of the tsunami-affected communities, but the moral implications were complicated by the fact that the evacuations left behind perfectly intact houses that were declared uninhabitable by the same government that initially described many of them as safe. One of Gill's informants from the nuclear disaster zone confessed that he 'envied' the people in the tsunami zone. It may seem strange that someone from a community that suffered no deaths and minimal visible damage could use such a word about one that suffered many thousands of deaths, yet his feeling is understandable. What he meant was that in the tsunami zone, at least the worst is known; in the radiation zone, the worst may not be known for decades. A number of Slater's and Steger's informants from the tsunami zone also echoed this sentiment: they sympathized with the radiation victims, saying that not knowing if one's own land would ever be habitable again would be almost too much to bear.

---

25   Like many nuclear power plants, Fukushima No.1 was located on a site straddling two local authorities. Some critics see this as a deliberate device to weaken local opposition to its siting.

In the months after 3.11, information on radiation risks was only gradually and patchily released. Food contamination was reported in products all over Japan, although methods of measurement and the interpretation of this data were both scientifically and politically disputed. Two years on from the disaster, avoidance of foods from anywhere in eastern Japan had largely given way to a more narrowly defined avoidance of products from Fukushima prefecture, although as many farmers point out, even within the prefecture, levels of detected radiation vary widely. Fear and uncertainty among the population is focused not on an event in the horrific recent past (the tsunami), but more on one in the undisclosed future – a time to come when today's children may find themselves victims of disease, social stigma, or both.

One only has to think for a moment to see that this dualistic narrative is a gross over-simplification. It is obvious that some of the tsunami damage could be blamed on walls that should have been higher, warnings that should have been more accurate, evacuation procedures that should have been better implemented, and above all, on the building of settlements too close to a notoriously dangerous coastline. Likewise the nuclear disaster would never have happened if it had not been for an exceptionally powerful earthquake and tsunami – indeed, TEPCO's plaintive and much derided defence was that the disaster was 'outside established parameters' (*sōteigai*). Then too, there are some who suffered a double blow – people living in coastal communities close to the No.1 nuclear power plant. Those people deserve a book all to themselves. Nevertheless, we offer this distinction between natural and man-made disaster as a heuristic device to frame the ethnographies to follow. For the people we spoke to in the various towns and villages along the Sanriku coast, this distinction was clearly important in how they coped with the disasters by which they were confronted. Painting with very broad brushstrokes, we can say that initially at least, the sudden outrageous calamity of the tsunami tended to unite people in shared victimhood, while the slow and ambiguous unfolding of the nuclear disaster tended to divide people over issues of human responsibility.

References

Abe Kitao and Kazama Ryoichi (1985). 'A Physiological Analysis of the Evacuation Behavior at the Great Sakata Fire', *International Journal of Mass Emergencies and Disasters*, 3 (1), 133–146.

American Red Cross (2012). 'Japan Earthquake and Tsunami: One Year Update'. <http://www.redcross.org/images/MEDIA_CustomProductCatalog/m6340390_JapanEarthquakeTsunami_OneYear.pdf> accessed 5 July 2013.

Curtis, Gerald (2011). 'Tohoku Diary', *Columbia College Today*, Winter 2011–2012, 20–27.

Cyranoski, David (2011). 'Japan's Tsunami Warning System Retreats: Lessons from Tohoku Wave Lead to Drop in Early-warning Precision', *Nature*, online edition, 11 August. <http://www.nature.com/news/2011/110811/full/news.2011.477.html> accessed 23 June 2013.

Duus, Peter (2012). 'Dealing with Disaster'. In Jeff Kingston (ed.), *Natural Disaster and Nuclear Crisis in Japan: Response and Recovery after Japan's 3/11*, pp. 175–187. London: Routledge.

Hagami Tarō (2012). 'Rupo: Hitobito no 3.11: Tsunami no genjō kara: Iwate-ken Yamada-machi. Kioku to kiroku to taiken to' (Reportage: The people's 3.11: From tsunami ground zero: Yamada town, Iwate prefecture. Memories, records, experiences'). In Kurihara Akira et al. (eds), *3.11 ni towarete: Hitobito no keiken o meguru kōsatsu* (Challenged by 3.11: Thoughts on the experiences of people), pp. 1–21. Tokyo: Iwanami Shoten.

Matsuo Hisato (2012). 'Hankyō yonda hinansha meibo' (The lists of evacuees that had an impact). In *Iwate Nippōsha henshūbu* (ed.), *Fūka to tatakau kishatachi. Wasurenai Heisei Sanriku ōtsunami* (Journalists fighting against forgetting. We won't forget the great Heisei Sanriku tsunami), pp. 44–53. Tokyo: Waseda University Press.

Mitchell, Jon. '281_Anti Nuke: The Japanese Street Artist Taking on Tokyo, TEPCO and the Nation's Right-wing Extremists', *The Asia-Pacific Journal: Japan Focus,* <http://www.japanfocus.org/-Jon-Mitchell/3959> accessed 5 July 2013.

Okayasu Akio, Shimazono Takenori, Sato Shinji, Tajima Yoshimitsu, Liu Haijiang, Takagawa Tomohiro, and Hermann M. Fritz (2012). '2011 Tohoku Run-up and Devastating Damage around Yamada Bay, Iwate: Surveys and Numerical Simulation', *Coastal Engineering*, 33. <http://journals.tdl.org/icce/index.php/icce/article/view/6977> accessed 23 June 2013.

Oliver-Smith, Anthony (1996). 'Anthropological Research on Hazards and Disasters', *Annual Review of Anthropology*, 25, 303–328.

Samuels, Richard J. (2013). *3.11: Disaster and Change in Japan.* Ithaca, NY: Cornell University Press.

Sumihara Noriya (2003). 'Flamboyant Representation of Nuclear Powerstation Visitor Centers in Japan: Revealing or Concealing, or Concealing by Revealing?' *Agora: Journal of International Center for Regional Studies*, 1, 11–29.

Yamori Katsuya (1997). 'Disaster Risk Sense in Japan and Gaming Approach to Risk Communication', *International Journal of Mass Emergencies and Disasters*, 25(2), 101–131.

DAVID H. SLATER

Urgent Ethnography

The tsunami and nuclear disasters of 3.11 have triggered a huge and diverse literature on the 3.11 disasters and their aftermath. With the rise of fast output such as social media, blogs and websites, and online publishing by news outlets of stories that were often longer than conventional print would permit, there is probably no other disaster which has received as much documentation (see Slater, Nishimura and Kindstrand 2012). So, what is the specific contribution that this book is trying to make and how does it differ from other works? Let us first briefly look at the range of literature on 3.11.

The largest and most revealing body of literature on 3.11 is first-person accounts of how people experienced the disasters. Most of them are of course in Japanese. They range from haphazard tweets and texts, photos and videos to systematic reports of visits and relief work.[1] In contrast to many disasters around the world where documentation often comes from official or outside sources, insider or local accounts are some of the most detailed and sustained sources of information. This gives us a more immediate view, one from the inside, a view not normally available when we try to understand what has happened. Since communication channels were initially cut off, local communities and journalists also made an effort to get people's voices heard. After the crisis, one of the first things done by many communities (village or city offices, or later, temporary housing units) was to start a new website, blog, or Twitter account relating to 3.11 issues, or reorient an existing one. This was a way both to keep one's own

---

[1]   See for example the Harvard digital archive <http://www.jdarchive.org/ja/home> or the Tohoku University digital archive <http://irides.tohoku.ac.jp/eng/archive/shinrokuden.html>. Both sites accessed 17 August 2013.

community informed and to communicate with the outside world.[2] NPOs also kept blogs of their own work, the status of their communities, and wrote reports for their stakeholders.[3] Many of these digital accounts have been collected by journalists, community leaders or academics and turned into books, accompanied by an introduction. Some have become bestsellers (Kanebishi 2012; Kondo 2012; Saijō et al. 2012; Yamagata et al. 2012). Photo and video collections are also very popular (Yamada-machi 2013), particularly for the local community as residents seek to recover lost memories and images. Some journalists and volunteers recorded and transcribed people's accounts of what had happened (for example, Yamagata 2012). These publications are important for the disaster victims, not only because their voices are heard, but also because later, reading about what happened and how things were before, during and after the disaster, helps them to remember and to make sense of what has happened. Akasaka Norio, one of the most prominent folklorists of Tohoku, goes one step further, having survivors interviewing other survivors (Akasaka 2012a), an approach that is also taken with the collection of video material by Sendai Mediatheque.[4]

While the material posted and collected on these sites represents just a small fraction of the chaos and complexity of the events of 3.11, the raw immediacy of these accounts is still shocking today, so much so that some of our informants cannot bear to look at them. They often dwell upon the horrific first moments of the disaster, and include the larger historical or socioeconomic context only when they happen to crop up in these first-hand accounts (Blue Shoe 2011; Gakuranman 2011; Shibuya 246 2011). They are rarely annotated nor given much editorial context, but they represent the deepest collection of survivor (and aid-giver) voices today.

---

2   The home pages of Kesennuma <http://www.city.kesennuma.lg.jp/> and Minami-
     Sōma: <http://www.city.minamisoma.lg.jp/> are good examples. Both accessed 21
     June 2013.

3   See for example sites run by the NPOs On The Road <http://ontheroad.weblogs.
     jp/>, Urato Fukushikai <http://ameblo.jp/npo-urato/> and Peace Boat Disaster
     Volunteer Center < http://pbv.or.jp/blog.html>. All sites accessed 21 June 2013.

4   Their online collection of user-generated video about the events around 3.11, in both
     English and Japanese, can be seen at <http://recorder311.smt.jp/> accessed 17 August
     2013.

Other blogs are written from a more academic perspective (see for instance Blogos Henshūbu 2012 and Iryō Gabanansu Gakkai 2011). These are shorter and told at a certain remove by outsiders, intending to give both an update on the recovery and reconstruction efforts of different communities.

A second type of data consists of field reports by journalists, ethnographers or other fieldworkers. Most of the journalistic accounts contain only sound-bites from survivors, but we did see a substantial amount of feature reporting from Tohoku in the mass media. One of the reasons for the huge rise in social and self-generated media was the perceived failure of the mass media to provide accurate and reliable information about the situation in the affected communities. Nonetheless, all Japan's major news companies have collected a huge range and volume of stories, many archived at their websites (*Asahi Shinbun* 2011; *Mainichi Shinbun* 2011; *Nihon Keizai Shinbun* 2011; *Yomiuri Shinbun* 2011; *Kahoku Shinpōsha* 2011). These are significant archives.

Scholars of what is sometimes translated as regional or rural sociology (*chi'iki shakaigaku*), one of the most productive branches of Japanese sociology since the Showa period, have made valuable contributions to the post 3.11 scholarship. These include broad-based studies of the place of Tohoku within Japan, putting the 3.11 disasters in the context of long-term problems such as the dwindling and ageing population and the decline of agriculture and fisheries (Yamashita 2012).

Another group of studies focuses on place-making, which in this post-3.11 period takes on an immediacy that was previously not fully realized. While these are rarely 'ethnographic', in the sense of focusing on the voices of local residents as key data or employing local experience as the primary analytical frame, they provide an unusually systematic overview of the shifts since 3.11 in terms of social structure and the local economy. More specifically, these include the topics of regional revitalization (*chi'iki saisei*), or on a smaller scale, town rebuilding (*machizukuri*; see for example, Kinoshita 2007). The challenges faced by such extreme dislocation of the population and the wiping out of whole residential and commercial areas could not have been anticipated by this literature – as one informant noted, 'When we used to speak of "town rebuilding" we did not mean it to start from zero'. Still, the discipline rallied, and at the end of 2011 produced a powerful collection of papers looking at new approaches to farming and fishing, ecotourism, alternative ecological lifestyles, the role of citizens' movements, and how to pay for it all (Satō 2011). Hamada Jinzaburō, in that collection, addresses the specific challenge of how to create hamlet-style communities in the temporary housing projects where many evacuees are now living (Hamada 2011).

Other revealing analyses of life since 3.11 come from a group of ethnologists or folklorists in a field sometimes referred to as Tohoku Studies (*Tōhoku-gaku*). One of the most prominent critical scholars in this sub-field, Akasaka Norio, Professor of Folklore and head of the Yanagita Kunio Museum in Tono, Iwate prefecture, had been working on Tohoku for more than a decade prior to 3.11, experience that allowed him to contextualize the disasters unusually perceptively (Akasaka 2012b). The distinctive contribution of these works is to situate 3.11, and disasters more generally, as a recurring component of Tohoku history and culture. They take a critical look at the history of Tohoku, situating Tohoku as an internal colony exploited by Tokyo-centric capital, a relationship emphasized by the disaster at the nuclear power plant in Fukushima (Akasaka 2000, 2009; Sone 2010).

The foreign-language materials are of course far fewer and take a somewhat different shape. Alongside technical accounts focusing on the threat of tsunami damage or nuclear contamination, few works have tackled the human side of the disasters. One early exception was a trio of brief field reports published online at *Japan Focus* in 2012 (Thompson and Grimes-MacLellan 2012). These were valuable as early and widely available first-hand accounts of trips by scholars, often doing volunteer work, in some of the most affected areas. While they were not ethnographies as such, they are informed by an ethnographic sensibility, allowing us to glimpse many of the same topics we address in our volume: volunteer work, community cohesion, local leadership, and the ideas of future planning as they were still forming. Another type of literature, rather than being ethnographic portraits, take as their focus the voices and narratives of local residents. One example is Birmingham and McNeill (2012), which introduces personal accounts by six individuals. Others include Corbett (2011), Our Man in Abiko (2011) and JCEJ (2013).

Reflecting the small number of scholars with relevant expertise publishing in English, some of the first English-language academic contributions to evaluate the sociocultural effects of the disasters were multidisciplinary collections. Perhaps more than almost any other topic, the study of disasters requires a multi-disciplinary approach. While thematically various, the advantage of these volumes is that they bring together a variety of perspectives, thereby enhancing the value of each chapter by providing useful context and expertise that no single author could provide. Jeff Kingston (2012) brought together scholars from nine different fields to produce the first such scholarly efforts to very good reviews. More recently, Adelstein et al. (2013) distil the political 'lessons learned', with an emphasis on policy and possible economic effects. If the literature on 3.11 follows the same sort of path that other disasters have established, both inside and outside Japan, we can expect to see a trend towards discipline-specific analyses of systemic failures of policy, of institutional structure and practice, and of implementation aimed at reducing future risk. This flow of studies has started at the intersection of nuclear development, policy and regulation, including Hirose (2011), Suzuki and Kaneko (2013), and Samuels (2013) among others. While all of these studies make valuable contributions, local experience and voices usually figure in this literature only rarely, and then, primarily as illustrations of analysis, rather than as the focus of the analysis itself.

Collections of cultural analyses in English, mostly by anthropologists and sociologists, and fieldworkers in related disciplines, come closer to our own project. The special collection edited by Adachi et al. (2012) in the *International Journal of Japanese Sociology* points out that many of the questions posed by the 3.11 disasters were questions that could and should be applied to Japanese society more generally – about uneven development; industrialization and demographics; incoherent policy in Tokyo and inconsistent implementation in Tohoku; the failure of media as a crucial social tool; stalled social movements; and the uneven distribution of risk. Most authors in this collection use the 1995 Kobe Earthquake as a reference point to see what has changed, and what has not. This makes for an interesting contrast with the rural sociologists working in Japanese quoted above who more often use Tohoku society as their primary point of reference.

While the range of topics that this collection covers is similar to our own, the methods are quite different. For example, on topics such as the choice to leave or return to affected areas (Ueda and Torigoe 2012), or to trust in government and fellow residents (Hommerich 2012), the data collected were from questionnaire surveys, rather than from ethnography. The approaches are complementary. Quantitative data can tell us the aggregate outcomes of difficult choices, such as whether to leave a damaged community or stay on; we hope to show *how* such choices are made. Both Ikeda and Gill show cases of people from the same milieu, even from the same family, with totally different responses to radiation risk – ranging from staying put in government-designated danger-zones, to emigrating from Japan. Morioka shows how schools in Tohoku foisted decisions about whether or not to let children play outdoors onto parents, so that risk was defined differently for children in the same class. While survey data can find a metric to gauge levels of trust, we hope to show what 'trust' means to those in the affected areas as they are forced to negotiate difficult choices in the context of highly disrupted practices of daily life.

The journal *Asian Anthropology* published a collection that came out of one of the first meetings of anthropologists after the disaster, asking disciplinary questions about the role of 'public anthropology'. Yamashita Shinji, probably the leading cultural anthropologist to address the cluster of issues related to 3.11, posed this challenge: that 'anthropology and anthropologists should go beyond their narrow academic discipline to engage in the broader public sphere by contributing to the analyses of public issues, and offering solutions' (Yamashita 2013: 23) by taking part in what he calls the 'new public sphere' (*atarashii kōkyō*). By this he means a new kind of civil society, created by citizens themselves without guidance from the authorities.[5] The authors in Yamashita's collection represent a diverse mix of area and thematic specializations. Kimura and Hayashi are both disaster specialists working on Turkey and Oceania respectively; Yamashita primarily works on tourism in Southeast Asia; Numazaki is a gender specialist on

5   In this volume, Tuukka Toivonen addresses this issue with his analysis of spontaneously emerging NPOs such as Youth for 3.11, many with a social-entrepreneurial style rather new for Japan.

Taiwan, etc. The diversity of scholarly backgrounds points to an important feature of our understanding of disaster and the fullest sort of academic engagement with the public sphere. In times of disaster, scholars from a wide range of backgrounds put aside other things to see what sort of help and insight that they can share. In a sense, this is the epitome of a public intellectual – bringing their scholarly training to bear on most pressing needs of society, but not being limited by their disciplinary boundaries. Across literatures and languages, this is one of the most heartening features of how academics have responded to the disaster.

And the results of this collection are impressive. Kimura (2012) situates the study of disaster within the mainstreams of anthropological theory, and shows us the ways that this perspective sensitizes us to the differential patterns of disaster vulnerability as we think about the 'lessons' learned. Hayashi (2010) shows us the importance of aspects of local culture, be they folk performances or material cultural properties, as resources for both coming to grips with tragedy (what he calls 'mourning work') and also as ways to rethink the future. Okada compares 3.11 with the Kobe earthquake and interestingly argues that the former generated a multicultural discourse, as people from different walks of life came together to help out, while 3.11 has been framed by a more nationalistic discourse, partly because of the sheer scale of the disaster, and partly because the more remote, rural disaster site was so much less accessible to outsiders than Kobe (Okada 2012). In each case, we see a revealing invocation of theoretical framing and relevant comparative work that allows us to start thinking outside of the immediacy of the disaster itself.

And yet, caution is also called for. Yamashita reminds us that it is 'too early to say anything definitely, and the disaster and its aftermath is a long process' and warns anthropologists not to make an 'easy "grandstand play"' (2012: 24). Numazaki, in the same collection, goes further: he reminds us that anthropology is a 'slow science' and says that 'parachuting anthropologists doing a quick ethnography of disaster' would be 'quite unanthropological, to say the least, if not downright exploitative of the afflicted' (Numazaki 2012: 33). We fully appreciate their concerns. On the other hand, even a slow science has to start somewhere, and there is a risk that excessive fear that one might be exploitative of the ravaged communities could become an excuse for inaction. While many have suggested that the disaster may indeed be, to quote Numazaki's title, 'too big, too wide, too complicated to understand', this is perhaps a narrow academic concern, reflecting the discipline's ambition to achieve systematic explanation, a cautiousness stemming more from a desire to protect itself from critique. In fact, to wait until all things are neatly explained (whenever that might be and whatever that would look like) can work against the possibility Yamashita envisions of anthropology or related disciplines actually participating in the public sphere by contributing relevantly, if imperfectly, in a timely fashion. Moreover, as almost anyone who has spent enough time in the field to get to know people has seen, most survivors want their stories told; they want the word to get out. It is for this reason that so many survivors are glad to have their stories told by scholars willing to invest a serious amount of time and effort in the project.

None of the chapters in Yamashita's volume is ethnographic, in the sense of being a descriptive account of a society and its people based on data collected through extended participant observation. It may be characterized as a manifesto – it provides frames of reference, historical context and useful theoretical tools, and calls for anthropology to respond carefully and sensitively to the giant challenge of 3.11 in order to address it in ways that will help the understanding of the general public, rather than just an academic coterie. Although not all the authors here are anthropologists, our volume is one attempt to respond to that call. While acknowledging the risks of rushed fieldwork, we do believe that urgent ethnography is an important contribution to the understanding of disasters like 3.11, as we will now discuss.

Methodological situation of disaster fieldwork: Urgent ethnography

As Anthony Oliver-Smith and Susanna Hoffman (1999) point out, 'every disaster has a past, present and future'. Our volume is situated in the present, but of course any study of ethnographic or narrative methods, focusing on the immediate situation of disaster, requires fuller contextualization. In this sense, we might call it 'urgent ethnography', responding first to the immediate needs that local residents faced in this unfolding disaster. It is necessary to have a pre-history of disaster, some backward tracing of players and policy, of technology and adaptability, of geographies and capital, that are linked together in ways that will reveal the trajectory of disaster and the patterns of vulnerability. While quantitative and historical methods are better suited to capture the wider situation through aggregate sampling and to capture the diversity within that scope, only ethnography can capture the complexity of the moment. Without ethnographic research, these other methods provide context without a core. Yamashita correctly calls for long-term engagement. Yet, without urgent ethnography, without listening to the voices of the people as early as possible, without the detailed accounts of everyday life in the immediate aftermath, those long-term engagements may be seriously compromised. Memories fade quickly, particularly in post-traumatic situations; people get used to the situation and forget the details of events and thoughts of the first days, weeks and months. To understand the situation, it is necessary to have some direct accounting, however provisional and selective, fragmentary and partial, of life on the ground, as close as possible to the moment of the event. This is what we have attempted to provide.

Few studies of disaster are actually based on data gathered while events are unfolding (see Hoffman 1999 for an exception). The vast majority of disaster studies are undertaken years after the event, usually through surveys or formal interviews, and sometimes through archival sources, often generating very perceptive studies. Some excellent ethnographic works have also been written long after the event, including Oliver-Smith's 1986 study of a Peruvian town devastated by earthquake sixteen years previously; Shimizu's 2003 work on the Aeta communities that survived the 1991 eruption of Mount Pinatubo in the Philippines; and Bernd Rieken (2010) on the 1999 avalanche which buried the village of Galtür in Austria.

Even in those cases where the disaster occurs in urban centres with a higher concentration of ethnographers on the ground, who are presumably ready to enter 'the field' right away (Adams 2013 working on Hurricane Katrina), this postponement is not uncommon. While there are surely

many good reasons for this timing, there are also costs. These delayed
studies capture the outcomes of past actions, once those have become settled, apparent, sorted out. They document remembrances of disasters past,
capturing established narratives after chaos has become turned into stories
with clear beginnings, middles and especially endings, once the significance
of these events has been decided. It is certainly possible to see behind the
accepted narratives, and feminist criticism has pointed out the importance
of capturing 'counter-hegemonic' narratives (Anderson and Jack 2006).
In contrast, most of our work sits at the pre-hegemonic point, before narratives have been smoothed out by their retelling, before they have been
situated in a larger narrative of heroic recovery, before moments of bitter
resentment, fear, uncertainty and confusion were forgotten or re-narrated.
The fieldwork that generated our collection, mostly conducted during the
months just after 3.11, thus makes a contribution to our understanding of
how individuals and groups actually coped in Tohoku, also preserving for
future studies ethnographic data that could not have been gathered at any
other time.

   We focus on those factors that constitute (or undo) families, communities and identities, and that lead people to consolidate networks of
support and trust among trusted individuals. We also examine those factors
that lead others to reach out, often to strangers, in times of need. We ask
how people deal with sudden grievous loss; evacuation and becoming a
refugee in their own land; the disruption of routines and rituals; the scat-
tering of families and communities; and the dissolution of many features
of everyday life that were assumed to secure foundations for social life.
The effects of these disruptions are far-reaching, changing over time and
in different ways in different parts of society.

   One issue of both ethnographic and methodological significance is
memory, how people remember and what they forget, and how they patch
together the often fragmentary pieces of memory with commonly agreed
narratives. Some harrowing experiences will never be forgotten. However,
after a relatively brief period of accessibility, a time when they are still available to share with others, they may not be talked about for many years,
either because they are too traumatic and hence repressed, or because they
do not fit the dominant narratives that grow and become accepted within a

community. On the other hand, mundane facts of everyday life will often be forgotten. Steger in this volume finds that there were gaps and distortions developing in the memories of victims even in the first months. So another purpose of our work is to preserve memories of experiences, thoughts and feelings at least as they were during our time in the field. Given the situation of our research, rather than seeking to make some systematic evaluation or a complete portrait of the disaster, our researchers address very local concerns, following the words and actions of informants, while seeking to situate this ethnography within the wider context of disaster, relief and recovery in ways that we hope will be of some use to our readers and subsequent researchers. As ethnographers, we collectively seek to identify and analyse the various cultural forms and social dynamics that structure individual and collective understanding and generate 'reasonable' choices in times of confusion and often desperation. That is, we are able to see cultural persistence as well as cultural innovation, adaptation and compromise. Through an ethnographic approach, we are able to document many of the mundane facts of daily life in the context of disaster, those that have often escaped the sensationalist glare of mainstream media, things that might have been taken for granted by the blogs and tweets.

Some of the ethnographic detail recorded here is far from obvious. It may be surprising to learn that an elementary school, and even a local school board might ignore a request to allow a child to bring a bottle of water to school (Morioka); that some of the shrines in stricken areas would be deconsecrated at a time when spiritual reintegration of communities was so important (Peterson); that in certain areas, the elderly would outnumber the youthful among the volunteers going to Tohoku (Toivonen); that women living in shelters would rather throw away their underwear after one use than hang it out to dry in public (Steger); that an old people's home would be kept open in an area declared unfit for human habitation (Gill); and that many of the residents in Fukushima felt blamed by the rest of Japan for polluting the whole country (Ikeda). These details, no less than the statistics of destruction and reconstruction, tell the story of 3.11.

The contributors to this volume have all spent considerable time in Tohoku, albeit a relatively short time by the standards of classical anthropological fieldwork. They are researchers with a long-established association with Japan, most as publishing scholars, many being long-term residents. None of us were specialists on disaster or relief, and obviously none of us was prepared for such a project when the disaster hit, though some had a head start – Wilhelm and Delaney knew their field sites and informants well from long before the disaster, and Ikeda is a native of Fukushima prefecture, from where she experienced and observed the events unfolding. The rest were starting from scratch.

Nevertheless, we have gathered together a diverse group of ethnographers who were in the field just months, weeks and sometimes only days after the disaster. As noted above, this immediate ethnography provides an important perspective, often lacking, to a complex, rapidly unfolding situation. Most scholarly framing or citation from existing scholarship came long after the fieldwork began. For most of us, our first urgent necessity was to get into the field; our aim was to understand ground-level situations as we found them. As such, any theoretical insights that have been generated are very literally 'grounded theory' – grounded in the mud and rubble of a disaster zone. Nevertheless, the papers have gained insight from existing studies of disasters, and collectively will contribute to this literature. We review this connection below.

In much disaster-related literature, the social or cultural approach is divided into three subthemes or stages (Oliver-Smith and Hoffman 1999). The first covers immediate responses to desolation and hardship, evacuation and relocation; the second, cultural interpretations of risk and disasters, or the making sense of a much-changed social and physical landscape; and the third, the longer-term post-disaster study of social and cultural change. Our own volume concerns the first two of these three stages, but with aspirations to provide some useful material for future researchers to explore the third. Taken together, our chapters problematize the heuristic categorization of the three stages, in part, due to how quickly most of us were in the field.

According to Hoffman, a social anthropologist specializing in disasters, and herself a disaster survivor, during and just after a major disaster, there is usually a period when '[s]ocial form and fabric have dissolved, and survivors find themselves on their own'. Separated from family and community, often physically removed from familiar landmarks and shelter, sometimes without sufficient food and appropriate clothing, they are nevertheless surrounded by various groupings – of fellow survivors, aid-givers and governmental agents. Each individual, whether separately or in a group, 'both recounts and reinvents their culture system' (Hoffman 1999: 137). That may be so at the moment of impact. But our ethnographies reveal a persistent and even systematic invocation of familiar cultural and social schema in individuals' attempts to deal with often radically altered circumstances. In times of crisis and extreme dislocation, established cultural schemes, shared ethos and cultural orientations can be the only thing that keeps individual people directed and groups cohesive, and able to act in effective, co-ordinated ways. Steger shows how rules of hygiene were briefly suspended as tsunami victims crowded into a school gymnasium – but soon reinforced, to the point where evacuees were shocked to see indoor shoes being worn outdoors. Slater finds a determination to adhere to gift-exchange etiquette among people whose houses have been destroyed and who thus have virtually nothing to give. Sometimes, the adherence to older ways in the face of drastically changed circumstances can make things worse, as we follow established paths and expectations that have been rendered impossible by circumstances. The failure of some local bureaucracies to change their management style in the face of catastrophe would be a case in point. Where people do appear to take on new styles of behaviour, as in the housewives-turned-activists described by Morioka, their activism may turn out to be founded on an appeal to their traditional role as mothers who are expected to defend their children's health. Old schema and values are often adapted to radically different circumstances.

In almost all cases, surviving disaster requires compromise, navigating between diverse uncertainties and risks; there is no perfect solution. Often the result is some sort of mixed form of behaviour: pragmatic, tactical attempts to adjust to unfamiliar situations while still pursuing familiar goals. Often, the remixing of familiar routines and rituals under dramatically shifted circumstances can lead to novel and creative solutions; it is impossible not to be moved by the improvised grave markers and memorials observed by Peterson, for example, or the one-man attempt to reduce radiation readings in his hamlet described by Gill. We see this bricolage all over our ethnographies – a recombination of older forms in new ways, usually tactical rather than strategic, reacting piecemeal to a situation that is only partially understood and evolving too quickly for anyone to grasp. Wilhelm and Delaney describe how fishermen used to working in fierce rivalry with each other have joined co-operative groups, albeit grudgingly, required to do so under government compensation programmes. That is a case of change enforced from above, but it is also something that had to be negotiated at the very immediate level of personal (and capital) relations. The emergence of local politicians like Mayor Sakurai Katsunobu of Minami-Sōma as YouTube heroes, described by McNeill, is an example of spontaneous improvization at a time when the usual channels seemed to be failing. The fact that the mayor's staff had been turning away the very assistance he was calling for is striking evidence of the social-systemic barriers to creative innovation.

Theoretical shift from revealing deep structures to documenting practical logics

> The arrangements of society become all the more visible when challenged by crisis.
>
> — ERIC WOLF (1990)

The theoretical justification for the cultural study of disaster is often a variant of scholarly interest in any pattern of social change, as eloquently articulated by Eric Wolf here. The argument goes something like this: in times of change, the internal workings of society are shifted out of their systematic patterns and smooth relationships, thereby revealing what is at other times obscure. Disaster reveals all the more because the degree of change is greater. Inherent in this assumption is that in the recombination or reworking, even in the dysfunction that is often characteristic of social change, things that are taken for granted by both local residents and researchers 'become strange' in some sense because they do not proceed as usual. Kimura Shūhei (2013: 67) writes that disaster becomes a 'natural labo-ratory' – a specialized, and in some sense privileged case of Levi-Strauss's imperative to seek out moments that are 'good to think with'. In an oft-quoted passage, Hoffman and Oliver-Smith (2002: 10) write that disasters

> ... unmask the nature of society's social structure, including the ties and resiliencies of kinship and other alliances. [...] Disasters provide a unique view of society's capacities for resistance or resilience in the face of disruption. The basic social organizational forms and behavioural tenets of a society are exhibited and tested under conditions of stress. By exposing the capacities and ethos to cope with the immediate forms of duress due to impact and emergency and with the sustainability of these efforts over long-term periods of reconstruction, disasters facilitate the study of human sociability.

So far, so good. But what are we to make of what we find? How do we consider this 'data' and how to handle it in a theoretically disciplined way? One way to conceptualize it is as Oliver-Smith and Hoffman do when they write that disaster 'draws researchers as close to basic elements of culture and society as ever found. Disasters take people back to fundamentals. In their turmoil, disassembly and reorganization, they expose essential rules of actions, bare bones of behaviour, the roots of intuitions, and the basic frameworks of organizations' (Oliver-Smith and Hoffman 1999: 11).

Again, Hoffman and Oliver-Smith echo this theoretical framing when they note that 'deeply pervasive custom as opposed to mutable surface detail is made plain' (2002: 11). They also say that disasters 'undrape canons and law, custom and practices, the novel from the entrenched traditions. In this manner, disaster often reveals the deeper social grammar of a people that lies behind their day to day behaviour' (2002: 10).

This sort of model of depth ('entrenched traditions' and 'grammar') and surfaces ('mutable detail' of the 'novel') seems to be a structural-func-tionalist remnant from an older and now quite challenged approach. The theoretical task stated appears to be one of grammatical reconstruction, an almost philological task of finding deeply embedded coherence.

The problem with this approach is two-fold. First, it seems to assume a pre-disaster community that is organic and coherent, maybe even 'cold' (in the Levi-Straussian idiom). There might be a temptation, especially when the disaster is understood as an extrinsic event, an act of nature, that impinges upon a community from the outside, to idealize that community, not only as coherent but also as timeless, a temptation compounded when the community in question is rural. The communities we studied in Tohoku are often assumed by outsiders, be they from Tokyo or from outside of Japan, to represent some primordial Japanese way of life. In fact, while retaining some of their social structure (the small settlements known variously as *chiku*, *shūraku* or *buraku*) from earlier times, this district has gone through drastic changes in the postwar period: a rapidly dwindling and ageing population, a shift from full-time agriculture to a mix of wage labour and part-time farming, and a succession of bureaucratic interventions that have merged many towns and villages together (*gappei*) while others have simply disappeared. Peter Matanle and Anthony S. Rausch (2011) give a good overview of these issues. Kelly (2012) points out that because of these mergers 'every coastal village and town, directly destroyed by the tsunami is administratively embedded in a larger local political unit'. This greatly complicates the politics and economics of reconstruction, and also the identity of the people. Gill in this volume shows how the perceived interests of a village and its constituent hamlets can be sharply divergent.

The communities we studied confound culturalist assumptions in other ways too. Farming has diversified into horticulture and alternative crops (Andean tubers in Gill's hamlet), while fisheries have developed thoroughly modern fish-farming and seaweed cultivation techniques (Wilhelm and Delaney). The image of an ancient, unchanging way of life does the people of Tohoku a disservice, just as the image of Fukushima as an irradiated wasteland does a grave disservice to the people of that prefecture (Ikeda). There is a thin and fuzzy line between admiration – for maintaining a 'traditional' way of life – and contempt – for unsophisticated country bumpkins, or *imo* ('potatoes'). There is a similarly thin and fuzzy line between sympathy – for the victims of nuclear folly – and discrimination – wondering whether one would want to marry someone who you think might develop thyroid cancer or give birth to a deformed child.

While one may argue for a deeper structural 'grammar' below these massive changes, the social structure of the Tohoku countryside was already being patched together before 3.11, along with the invented traditions that were supposed to explain it. This ethno-historical context, along with the temporal proximity after disaster, may help to explain why our studies tend to reveal conflict rather than deeper patterns of coherence. Sometimes that conflict was generated by the disaster itself; at other times, it was already there, its disruptive potential kept in check in calmer times. We are talking here for instance of gender conflict (Morioka), of conflict between socio-economic classes (Ikeda), between local power centres and their margins such as the 'village' and the 'hamlet' (Gill), or between grassroots groups of fishermen and the bureaucratized co-operatives (Wilhelm and Delaney).

Another group of papers shows conflict arising from the interaction between insiders and outsiders: between urban volunteers and rural victims (Slater), and between journalists and the communities they covered, and also between foreign and domestic media (McNeill). Toivonen reveals conceptual conflict between the propaganda of voluntarism and the reality of risk avoidance at universities. Perhaps only Steger and Peterson have come up with accounts where solidarity seems to outweigh conflict. Why is this the case? Again unlike the widespread perception of a homogeneous Tohoku, or a homogeneous pattern of disaster effect on the different communities, there are as many ways to suffer, and survive, as there are communities and individual people. Sometimes communities rally together, bond, and create new forms of collectivity, even unity. At other times, this is not the case. Where we saw less conflict, it was usually in cases where outsiders were not involved, money was not involved, and, being at the other end of the disaster area from the Fukushima No.1 plant, radiation was not involved. While it is too early to try to generate a typology of conditions and patterns of effects – a longer-term project – this is the sort of question that we would hope our data could be used to address in the future.

Disaster tactics: Ethnography of bad options

This brings up our second problem with the assumption of disaster as revealing deep structure or essential rules. Actually, we imagine that one of the significant theoretical contributions of disaster ethnography might lie in the documentation of individual and collective efforts to tactically work around the obstacles they suddenly face; capturing a practical logic, a 'making-do' (de Certeau 1984) within the compromised situation of survival. This making-do can take many forms. Of course, there are times when the official version of events is challenged by experience, when established sources of authority become questioned – such as when your government tells you that your community is safe but the radiation counters suggest otherwise (Gill, Morioka). But often we find a number of equally legitimate principles in conflict, suggesting different framing of the situation, different principles for action, and different patterns of practice. For example, how do you justify taking badly needed aid from a stranger, when you cannot live up to the expectations to reciprocate (Slater)? When does one sacrifice the principle of equality (everyone getting their share), so necessary for some sort of community coherence, in order to meet the immediate needs of some? What does a mother do when her felt obligation to provide her children with safe food comes into conflict with the village's desire to suppress fear and prevent rumours of local radiation from jeopardizing the reputation of the village, its farmers and crops (Morioka)? How do we deal with this sort of dilemma? Which principle is deeper? Which is more fundamental? Which is 'deep grammar' and which is trivial surface ephemera?

Being ethnographers rather than moralists, we refrain from passing judgment on those questions, asking rather how people, when faced with an untenable situation and no good choice, make do. What are the principles of practice that are invoked by actors to lead them through terrifying and bewildering situations? Uncertainty cannot be avoided altogether and so one seeks ways to minimize or manage it. Button writes that uncertainty 'does not simply exist – it is produced, and the production of uncertainty can result in new political, economic and social formations' (2010: 11). While the new social formations that are gradually being generated in the wake of disaster, such as new patterns of fishing labour, village relocation plans, etc., are outside the temporal scope of this volume, it is worth noting that as uncertainty is produced, it is also encountered, negotiated, and addressed by individuals and groups positioned in different ways at different points in society and disaster. Relations of power can produce patterns of vulnerability, along old or new fault lines, chronic and maybe familiar, or not yet recognized at all. Unequal power balances may occur at the micro-level of family relations, but it could also be argued that the whole of Tohoku, as a neglected part of Japan, exploited as a source of labour and resources, is collectively subject to these prejudices and suffers materially because of it. To ethnographically capture these requires a finely grained analysis, one that allows for some unfolding in space and time, that does not always rely on interview or survey, one that includes but does not solely depend upon narrative, to capture the features of everyday life, the practical logics and tactical manoeuvres, that come with varying degrees of conscious reflection, intentionality, and efficacy. While this does not tell the whole story, and must be triangulated with past and future developments, only close ethnography, close to the disaster events, can capture this.

Telling the stories, as they are, now

No chapter in this collection is the result of a planned research project. There were no proposals made or funds applied for. Many of us were already doing volunteer work in the area before research could even be contemplated. Like the survivors, we saw what was in front of us, what was needed, and then took notes when possible, what Hoffman and Oliver-Smith call 'applied research' (1999: 10). Often, it was the local residents who helped us see the importance of writing this up as research. As a result, the positionality of the researcher as participant-observer was often tilted to the participant end. What methodological and ethical issues does this raise? It certainly has a significant effect on the sorts of relationship we had with our informants. There is nothing new about an ethnographer being of some utility to the people he or she is writing about, but when that utility involves providing basic survival services in such a dire situation, the degree and nature of engagement will inevitably affect one's relationships and research. Does it obscure the ability of the researcher to see what is around them? Or does it allow insight not accessible under less extreme situations? Later researchers, in the controlled situation of retrospective interviews, years or decades later, will not face the same problems that are characteristic of our situations, and they will be better able to judge these issues from that perspective. Our research situation has been daunting at times, and we have had to do the best we can. We hope these chapters will be of value, located somewhere between field reports and theoretical case studies. Each of us in this volume was differently situated within this field, and while none of us except Ikeda include ourselves as a central feature in the analysis itself, we have each tried to make it clear in what sort of capacity we were involved, and to clarify the effect our own positionality might have had on the story we offer.

The papers gathered here are defined by their close proximity to the event, and by their focus on the micro-tactics of getting by. While it is true that the longer we wait, the more data we collect, this also begs the question of when we might be able to decide that we have collected 'enough' data, or what that would even mean. Of course, the more we know, the more of the structural effects we will be able to see. Things may turn out very differently from how they look today, as described in these pages. Perhaps strife-torn communities will find resolution; relationships between local and national aid organizations will shift; mothers will once more feel happy to send their children outdoors to play; and fishermen will restore their shattered industry. We all look forward to updating the studies included in the present volume. For now, our goal is not to produce the final analysis of 3.11. Rather it is to document the struggles and experiences of those people and groups with whom we came into direct contact during an intensely traumatic period. Amid those struggles we glimpse the use, transformation and reassertion of cultural schema, and the effects such uses had on the people involved. This is what we wanted to pass on.

We are principally motivated by the views of our own informants, the people whose voices you read on these pages. They wanted their stories told because they often felt unheard, and they wanted them told sooner rather than later, 'so people won't forget'. Convinced that the struggles of individuals and communities were significant and relevant to others, we also felt a need, even an obligation, to publish these studies. We have already published a Japanese-language edition, whose *obi*[6] reads, '3.11 is not over'. We wanted to remind readers, in Tokyo and beyond, that more than 350,000 people are still displaced and unable to return home, that fishing and farming is still impossible in many places, and that communities and even families remain widely scattered to this day as a result of the events of 11 March 2011. This volume is an attempt to help understand how individuals and communities have tried to cope with a continuing calamity.

References

Adams, Vincanne (2013). *Markets of Sorrow, Labors of Faith: New Orleans in the Wake of Katrina.* Durham: Duke University Press.

Adachi Kiyoshi, Ohara-Hirano Yuko, Pauline Kent, and Nomiya Daishiro (eds) (2012). 'Introduction', *International Journal of Japanese Sociology*, 21(1), 2–5.

Adelstein, Jake, Michael Cucek, Kurokawa Kiyoshi, and Philip Brasor (2013). *Reconstructing 3.11.* Seattle: CreateSpace Independent Publishing Platform.

Akasaka Norio (2000). *Tōzai nanboku kō: Ikutsumo no Nihon e* (Thoughts on directions: Towards a multi-faceted Japan). Tokyo: Iwanami Shoten.

——(2009). *Tōhokugaku: Wasurerareta Tōhoku* (Tohoku studies: Forgotten Tohoku). Tokyo. Kōdansha.

——(ed.) (2012a). *Chinkon to saisei: Higashi Nihon daishinsai, Tōhoku kara no koe 100* (Requiem and rebirth: Great East Japan Earthquake, 100 voices from Tohoku). Tokyo: Fujiwara Shoten.

——(2012b). *3.11 kara kangaeru 'kono kuni no katachi': Tōhokugaku o saiken suru* (Thinking about 'the shape of this country' through 3.11: Reconstructing Tohoku studies). Tokyo: Shinchōsha.

Anderson, Kathryn, and Dana C. Jack (2006). 'Learning to Listen: Interview Techniques and Analyses'. In Robert Perks and Alistair Thomson (eds), *The Oral History Reader*, pp. 157–171. New York: Routledge.

Birmingham, Lucy, and David McNeill (2012). *Strong in the Rain: Surviving Japan's Earthquake, Tsunami, and Fukushima Nuclear Disaster.* Basingstoke: Palgrave Macmillan.

---

6 A paper band put around a book with PR material written on it.

Blogos Henshūbu (Blogos Editorial Office) (2012). 'Rainen rokugatsu ni wa dete itte kudasai: Fukushima kasetsu jūtaku no genjitsu (Please leave here by June next year: The situation of Fukushima temporary housing)', *Blogos* (blog entry), 17 May 2012. <http://blogos.com/article/39223/> accessed 6 June 2013.

Blue Shoe (2011). 'Big One!' *Just Another Day in Japan* (blog entry), 11 March 2011. <http://www.jadij.com/2011/03/big-one.html> accessed 8 June 2013.

Button, Gregory (2010). *Disaster Culture Knowledge and Uncertainty in the Wake of Human and Environmental Catastrophe.* Walnut Creek, CA: Left Coast Press.

Corbett, Steve (2011). 'Driving Away from a Tsunami'. In Jeff Kingston (ed.), *Tsunami: Japan's Post-Fukushima Future.* Washington, DC: Foreign Policy Magazine, 22–33.

de Certeau, Michel (1984). *The Practice of Everyday Life.* Berkeley: University of California Press.

Digital Archive of Japan's 2011 Disasters. <http://www.jdarchive.org/en/home> accessed 5 June 2013.

Gakuranman (2011). 'Great Tohoku Earthquake 1'. *Gakuranman: Illuminating Japan* (blog entry), 11 March. <http://gakuran.com/great-tohoku-earthquake-1/> accessed 8 June 2013.

Hamada Jinzaburō (2011). 'Kasetsu shigaichi, kasetsu shūraku-zukuri' (Temporary urban spaces, temporary settlement building). In Satō Shigeru, ed., cited below, 73–98.

Hatanaka Akihiro (2012). *Saigai to yōkai: Yanagita Kunio to aruku Nihon no tenpen chi'i* (Disaster and monsters: Walking with Yanagita Kunio through natural disasters of Japan). Tokyo: Aki Shobō.

Hayashi Isao (2010). *Shizen saigai to fukkō shien* (Natural disaster and recovery support). Tokyo: Akashi Shoten.

'Higashi Nihon Daishinsai: News Tokushū (Great East Japan Earthquake: News Selection)'. *Asahi Shinbun Digital* <http://www.asahi.com/special/10005/> accessed 6 June 2013.

Hirose Takashi (2011). *Fukushima Meltdown: The World's First Earthquake-Tsunami-Nuclear Disaster.* Seattle: CreateSpace Independent Publishing Platform.

Hoffman, Susanna M. (1999). 'The Worst of Times, The Best of Times: Toward a Model of Cultural Response to Disaster'. In Anthony Oliver-Smith and Susanna M. Hoffman (eds), *The Angry Earth: Disaster in Anthropological Perspective,* pp. 134–155. New York: Routledge.

Hoffman, Susanna M., and Anthony Oliver-Smith (eds) (2002). *Catastrophe & Culture: The Anthropology of Disaster.* Santa Fe, NM: School of American Research Press.

Hommerich, Carola (2012). 'Trust and Subjective Well-being after the Great East Japan Earthquake, Tsunami and Nuclear Meltdown: Preliminary Results', *International Journal of Japanese Sociology*, 21(1), 46–64.

Iryō Gabanansu Gakkai (Academic Association of Medical Governance). 'Ishinomaki-shi Ogatsu-chō no genjō: Jūmin fuzai no kenchiku seigen ni yori machi ga kieyō to shite iru (Current situation of Ogatsu-chō, Ishinomaki: Building restrictions that ignore residents are killing the town)', *Blogos* (blog entry), <http://blogos.com/article/26237/> accessed 6 June 2013.

JCEJ (ed.) (2013). *Life after the Tsunami Vol.1: A Collection of the Otsuchi Mirai Shinbun News Reports.* Japan Center of Education for Journalists.

Kahoku Shinpōsha (2011). *Kahoku Shinpō no ichiban nagai hi: Shinsaika no jimoto-shi* (The longest day of Kahoku Shinpō: A local newspaper under a state of disaster). Tokyo: Bungei Shunjū.

Kanebishi Kiyoshi (ed.) (2012). *3.11 dōkoku no kiroku: 71-nin ga taikan shita ōtsunami, genpatsu, kyodai jishin* (Record of lament 3.11: 71 experiences of the tsunami, nuclear incident and massive earthquake). Tokyo: Shinyōsha.

Kelly, William W. (2012). 'Tohoku's Futures: Predicting Outcomes or Imagining Possibilities?' *The Asia-Pacific Journal: Japan Focus.* <http://www.japanfocus.org/-William_W_-Kelly/3703> accessed 28 June 2013.

Kimura Shūhei (2012). 'Lessons from the Great East Japan Earthquake: The Public Use of Anthropological Knowledge', *Asian Anthropology*, 11(1), 65–74.

—— (2013). *Shinsai no kōkyō jinruigaku: Yure to tomo ni ikiru Toruko no hitobito* (Public anthropology of disaster: Turkish people living with tremors). Kyoto: Sekai Shisōsha.

Kingston, Jeff (ed.) (2012). *Natural Disaster and Nuclear Crisis in Japan: Response and Recovery after Japan's 3/11.* London: Routledge.

Kinoshita Isamu (2007). *Wākushoppu: Jūmin shutai no machizukuri e no hōhōron* (Workshop: Methodology towards residents-centered city building). Kyoto: Gakugei.

Kondo Yoshiya (2012). *Hisaichi kara no tegami: Furomu Iwate* (Letters from Tohoku: From Iwate). Tokyo: Inochi no Kotobasha

Mainichi Shinbun. 'Higashi Nihon Daishinsai (Great East Japan Earthquake)', *Mainichi Jp.* <http://mainichi.jp/feature/20110311/> accessed 6 June 2013.

Matanle, Peter and Anthony S. Rausch (2011). *Japan's Shrinking Regions in the 21st Century: Contemporary Responses to Depopulation and Socioeconomic Decline.* London: Cambria Press.

Nihon Keizai Shinbun. 'Daishinsai hisaichi kara: Tokushū (Great Disaster, from Tohoku: Special Issue)'. <http://www.nikkei.com/news/special/top/?uah=DF110320117140> accessed 6 June 2013.

NPO Urato Fukushikai, *Miyagi-ken Shiogama no NPO Urato Fukushikai no burogu (Higashi Nihon daishinsai no kyūen katsudō yō)* (Blog of NPO Urato Welfare Association of Shiogama, Miyagi (For relief activities of Great Eastern Japan Earthquake)). <http://ameblo.jp/npo-urato/> accessed 6 June 2013.

Numazaki Ichiro (2013). 'Too Wide, Too Big, Too Complicated to Comprehend: A Personal Reflection on the Disaster that Started on March 11, 2011', *Asian Anthropology*, 11(1), 27–38.

Okada Hiroki (2012). 'An Anthropological Examination of Differences between the Great East Japan Earthquake and the Great Hanshin Earthquake'. *Asian Anthropology*, 11(1), 55–63.

Oliver-Smith, Anthony (1986). *The Martyred City: Death and Rebirth in the Andes.* Albuquerque: University of New Mexico Press.

—— (1996). 'Anthropological Research on Hazards and Disasters', *Annual Review of Anthropology*, 25, 303–328.

Oliver-Smith, Anthony and Susanna Hoffman (eds) (1999). *The Angry Earth: Disaster in Anthropological Perspective.* New York: Routledge.

Our Man in Abiko (ed.) (2011). *2:46: Aftershocks: Stories from the Japan Earthquake.* London: Enhanced Editions.

Rieken, Bernd (2010). *Schatten über Galtür? Gespräche mit Einheimischen über die Lawine von 1999. Ein Beitrag zur Katastrophenforschung* (Shadow over Galtür? Conversations with locals on the 1999 avalanche. A contribution to disaster research.) Münster: Waxmann.

Saijō Takeo and Funbarō Higashi Nihon Shien Project Otayori-han (Hang On East Japan Relief Project, Correspondence Team) (2012). *Hisaichi kara no tegami, hisaichi e no tegami: Wasurenai* (Letters to Tohoku, letters from Tohoku: Never forget). Tokyo: Daiwa Shobō.

Samuels, Richard J. (2013). *3.11 Disaster and Change in Japan.* Ithaca, NY: Cornell University Press.

Satō Shigeru (ed.) (2011). *Higashi Nihon daishinsai kara no fukkō machizukuri* (Community building towards recovery from the Great Eastern Japan Earthquake). Tokyo: Ōtsuki Shoten.

Shibuya 246 (2011). 'Earthquake Evacuations, Tokyo', *Shibuya246: Japan Living* (blog entry), 11 March 2011. <http://shibuya246.com/2011/03/11/earthquake-evacuations-tokyo/> accessed 8 June 2013.

Shimizu Hiromu (2003). *Funka no kodama: Pinatubo Aeta no hisai to shinsei o meguru bunka kaihatsu NGO* (Echoes of the eruption: The survival and rebirth of the Pinatubo Aeta and their relationship with culture, development and NGOs). Fukuoka: Kyushu University Press.

Slater, David H., Nishimura Keiko, and Love Kindstrand (2012). 'Social Media, Information, and Political Activism in Japan's 3.11 Crisis', *The Asia-Pacific Journal: Japan Focus.* <http://www.japanfocus.org/-Nishimura-Keiko/3762> accessed 28 June 2013.

Sone Eiji (2010). *Genkai shūraku: Ware no mura nareba* (Marginal settlement: If it were my village). Tokyo: Nihon Keizai Shinbun.

Suzuki Itoko and Kaneko Yuko (2013). *Japan's Disaster Governance: How was the 3.11 Crisis Managed?* New York: Springer.

Thompson, Christopher S., and Dawn Grimes-MacLellan (eds) (2012). 'The Great East Japan Earthquake One Year On: Reports from the Field', *The Asia-Pacific Journal: Japan Focus.* <http://www.japanfocus.org/-Christopher-Thompson/3702> accessed 5 July 2013.

Ueda Kyoko and Torigoe Hiroyuki (2012). 'Why do Victims of the Tsunami Return to the Coast?' *International Journal of Japanese Sociology*, 21(1), 21–29.

Wolf, Eric (1990). 'Facing Power: Old Insights, New Questions', *American Anthropologist*, 92(3), 586–596.

Wood, Donald C. (2013). 'Tremors in the "Contact Zone" and Challenges to Anthropology Following the Great East Japan Earthquake: The View of a Foreign Resident Anthropologist', *Asian Anthropology*, 11(1), 39–53.

Yamada-machi Daishinsai Kinenshi Henshū I'inkai (Yamada Township Memorial History Editorial Committee) (ed.) (2013). *Ano hi kara ashita ni mukatte: Higashi Nihon Daishinsai Yamada no kiroku* (From that day towards tomorrow: Reports of the Great East Japan Earthquake in Yamada township). Tokyo: Dentsūkan.

Yamagata Yuka and Minami-Sanrikuchō kara no Tegami Seisaku Iinkai (Letters from Minami-Sanrikuchō Production Committee) (2012), *Minami-Sanrikuchō kara no tegami: Higashi Nihon Daishinsai, sorezore no ano hi* (Letters from Minami-Sanrikuchō: Great Eastern Japan Earthquake, individual experiences of the day). Minami-Sanriku: NPO Mirai Minami-Sanriku.

Yamashita, Shinji (2012), 'The Public Anthropology of Disaster: An Introductory Note', *Asian Anthropology*, 11(1), 21–25.

Yamashita Yusuke (2012). *Genkai shūraku no shinjitsu: Kaso no mura wa kieru ka* (The truth of the marginal village: Will depopulated villages disappear?). Tokyo: Chikuma Shobō.

Yomiuri Shinbun (2011). 'Higashi Nihon Daishinsai: Tokushū (Great East Japan Earthquake: Special Issue)', *Yomiuri Online.* <http://www.yomiuri.co.jp/feature/eq2011/> accessed 6 June 2013.

PART I

Coping with Life after the Tsunami

BRIGITTE STEGER

Solidarity and Distinction through Practices of Cleanliness in Tsunami Evacuation Shelters in Yamada, Iwate Prefecture[1]

On about the tenth day of shelter life, the operators of a spa in Toyomane, a few miles inland, opened up the bath for us. They provided a bus so we could take a bath there. Actually, it was sooner than I had expected. I had assumed we would have to go even longer without a bath. That bath felt so great! I was really relieved (*hotto shimashita*). Shortly after that, electricity and water were reconnected at the shelter. When I could wash my hands again, and when I could drink the water again, I finally began to feel a little less anxious (*hajimete hito anshin*). Then daily life started to improve.

— TODA HARUKO[*2] (36), staying at the Minami Elementary
School shelter

How do people react during a major crisis? How do they co-operate and when do they refuse to co-operate? How do social hierarchies and power relations, including gender roles and relationships, develop when a large number of people of diverse backgrounds suddenly share the fate of destroyed homes and abruptly smashed community?

1 An earlier and longer version of this paper was published online in *Japan Focus* on 17 September 2012. <http://www.japanfocus.org/-Brigitte-Steger/3833>. I would like to thank all the people in Yamada who shared their experiences with me, in particular my host at the shelter, head priest Shimizu Seishō, as well as Keiko Morrison, John Traphagan, Jerry Eades, Lodewijk Brunt, Sen Hiraizumi, Rika Morioka, Johannes Wilhelm, Mary Anketell and Barry Plows, as well as an anonymous reader for comments and editing advice on earlier versions of this chapter.
2 Asterisks indicate pseudonyms.

For people staying at tsunami evacuation shelters in Yamada, a coastal town in Iwate prefecture, one of the important ways in which people in this region tried to regain control over their lives after losing their houses was by cleaning – both their own bodies and their environment. Toda Haruko's comment illustrates how their first bath after the disaster of 11 March 2011 not only washed away the accumulated dirt, but also started the process of recreating social order and stability. I will show what challenges they faced in overcrowded shelters lacking basic facilities, and how they sought to avoid contamination by infectious diseases. (People hardly mentioned the fear of radiation; some 200 miles north of the nuclear disaster and protected by mountains, they had more immediate concerns.) I discuss how dirty, barely usable toilets affected their sense of stability and shame. However, while the difficulties in taking care of personal hygiene after the disaster were unsettling, people initially put up with unwashed clothes and body odour remarkably easily. Sharing the experience of dirty conditions showed that they were 'all in this together' and thus became a source and a sign of solidarity. Survivors soon re-established hygienic conditions in the shelters by resorting to the *han* (group) structures they had experienced at school. By working together for a clean environment, they tried to make sense of their situation and get a grip on the anxieties they were facing.

There are only a few anthropological studies investigating life in shelters after major disasters (e.g. Blinn-Pike 2006), and I have found none that deals with the basic issues of cleanliness and hygiene, so scope for international comparison is limited. Earlier studies, however, show an interesting divergence on the topic of what happens to social norms after a disaster, especially those relating to gender. In countries with low socio-economic standards, women are usually more affected by disaster than men are, due to their restricted access to resources (Arai 2012: 1), but how about highly industrialized countries? Studying the 1997 Red River Valley Flood, which affected the Canadian province of Manitoba and the states of North Dakota and Minnesota in the US, Linda Jencson (2001: 51) concludes that coping with disaster enhances community identity and blurs gender distinctions. Stories of survivors 'reflect gender equity and reversal of gender roles'. By contrast, Susanna Hoffman (1999: 174) finds that in the wake of the 1991 Oakland firestorm 'what appeared first among the survivors [...] was not the reconstitution of the life lived immediately prior to the conflagration but rather the regeneration of old, deeply rooted cultural patterns'. This was true particularly for gendered roles and division of labour, going hand-in-hand with a cultural division of public and private arenas. Many women lost or gave up their jobs to concentrate on taking care of other family members and getting their household up and running again.

For Jencson, disaster seems to force people to improvise new, potentially progressive ways of life. For Hoffman, it seems to send people back to older, more gender-differentiated ways. With these two North American cases in mind, let us now turn to Japan. Since cleaning practices are sharply gendered in everyday life, focusing on cleanliness in the shelters provides an opportunity to look into the impact of major disasters on social structures, in particular gender relations and the gendered division of labour.

Yamada and the 3.11 disaster

The central and coastal areas of Yamada were badly hit by the earthquake and tsunami of 11 March 2011. A total of 3,346 residential buildings (55.5 per cent) were damaged by the tsunami and fires that followed, and 2,789 of them were completely destroyed. The death toll reached 734.[3] I visited Yamada from 1 to 13 June and from 15 to 25 July 2011, to conduct ethnographic research in the evacuation shelters (*hinanjo*). I stayed at Ryūshōji, a Sōtō-shū temple,[4] as a guest of the head priest (*jūshoku*), Shimizu Seishō (68), and his wife Noriko (60). The temple had narrowly escaped both

---

3   Data as of 19 December 2011; they exclude the district of Toyomane, a village further inland that had merged with Yamada in 1955. <http://www.town.yamada.iwate.jp/saigai/kouhyou12-19.pdf> accessed 28 December 2011. Yamada had about 20,000 inhabitants before the earthquake; on 1 October 2011 there were only 17,735 registered. <http://www.town.yamada.iwate.jp/01_gaiyou/jinkou/2011_1001jinkou.pdf> accessed 7 October 2011.

4   Sōtō-shū is a branch of Zen Buddhism. <http://www.ryushotemple.sakura.ne.jp/index.html> accessed 9 June 2013.

the tsunami and fire and had become a shelter for some twelve to fifteen evacuees, whose lives I temporarily shared. The priest also provided me with contacts, an occasional driver and a quiet room for interviews – an invaluable asset as I talked to people who had lost their homes. My second main research site was Minami Elementary School,[5] although I was not allowed to enter the sports hall, where about a hundred people were dwelling. I also visited a few other shelters. Once I had established contact with a former high school teacher and my research project had been introduced by the local newspaper *Iwate Nippō* (4 June 2011), recruiting willing interviewees posed no problem. I conducted more than thirty in-depth interviews with people staying at shelters and a few who had restored their flooded house and moved back in again. In addition to these interviews, which each lasted between one and four hours, I also had many informal conversations at the temple, accompanying a doctor on house calls, or simply walking around town. People were very open with me, some saying that it helped them to clear their heads (see Steger 2011). They also had more time than usual and seemed happy to help me, as they depended so much on the support of others and saw this as one way of creating a balance of exchange (see Slater in this volume).

There was, however, one methodological challenge I had not anticipated: most people had suffered from a period of 'amnesia'. While they told me the stories about the first hours during and after the earthquake and tsunami in detail, they found their memories of the following days or even weeks had blurred or completely disappeared. They had a very unreliable sense of time and filled the gaps in their memories with stories they had heard from others or read in the newspaper. Shimizu had warned me that some survivors would tell other people's stories as their own. Such reactions are common in people who have lived through traumatic experiences (Elzinga and Bremner 2002), and I will further explore this phenomenon in a forthcoming book on shelter life. For the purpose of this article, I would like to emphasize its methodological consequences, as it complicates the reconstruction and interpretation of events and means that some of the gaps cannot be filled.

---

5   *Minami Shōgakkō* or Southern Elementary School; hereafter, Minami Elementary.

Taking off shoes: Marking the shelter as *uchi*

TV images showed Japanese evacuees taking off their shoes in shelters and neatly lining them up at the entrance. Foreign media admired this sign of Japanese orderliness and composure. Initially, however, chaos and anxiety were prevalent. When the people who had escaped the tsunami and had gathered at the grounds of Minami Elementary were told to get inside the sports hall on the evening of 11 March, the thought of taking their shoes off never crossed their minds. The practical reasons for this are obvious: in a crowded and dark building, people would not have found their own shoes again if they had taken them off. It was also too cold to walk around without footwear in the hall. More importantly, I suggest, people did not regard the sports hall as their own or anybody else's home (*uchi*). Nobody imagined they would stay there for long. My informants all assumed that they would be able to return after a few hours when the tsunami had receded, clean up their houses and get on with their lives.

After some time,[6] the evacuees at Minami Elementary realized that they would have to make themselves a temporary home in the sports hall. In my first group interview, Yamamoto Tomi (81), a former high school teacher who had been able to move back into her partially repaired house after spending a few weeks in the Minami Elementary sports hall, and the Inakawas, a couple who were still staying at the shelter, told me:

> At the beginning there were some 180 people staying at Minami Elementary. There was hardly any space to walk between people, and it was very dusty. As we had a medical care unit in the school, there were also many people coming in from outside with their shoes on. Nobody changed into slippers;[7] everything became very dirty. The dust was incredible. Now everyone has slippers – they were probably donated from somewhere. The other day we saw someone walking outside the house in slippers and were appalled. But then we realized that there was 'soto-yō' (for outside use) written on the slippers.

6   Due to the blurred memories of my informants, the timing of the following events, as well as the details, is unclear.

7   It is customary in Japan to change from outdoor shoes into slippers when entering a medical or dental surgery.

Everyone laughed at this. The initial horror of seeing someone walking outside in indoor slippers and presumably gathering dirt that would be taken into the living space was followed by the laughter of relief that things were in perfect order. Anthropologist Mary Douglas has pointed out the importance of the distinction between the clean inside or house (both words are conveyed as *uchi* in Japanese) and the dirty outside as a basic classification in any culture. The inside is vulnerable to dirt from the outside, brought in by shoes or unwashed hands (Douglas 2002 [1966], see also Ohnuki-Tierney 1994: 21–50). Miura Michiko (56), who sheltered at Minami Elementary, told me:

> In other places, illnesses were very common, but at our place (*uchi wa*) nothing spread. Even if someone caught a cold, it was dealt with very quickly. Also, when we had some cases of infectious bowel disease, these people were immediately isolated and treated (in the hospital). In terms of hygiene, Minami Elementary was probably the most sophisticated place. As soon as possible it was strictly forbidden to walk inside the sports hall with shoes on. When they came back in, people would thoroughly clean their hands with alcohol. ... We had nurses and public health workers teaching these things, but we also established it for ourselves. We decided on a shelter representative; he and the *hanchō* (group leaders) talked it over and decided we would no longer allow people to enter in shoes or boots. ... In the beginning when people went out to town (to look after their destroyed houses), they were really dirty. If they had come back in just like that, diseases would have spread.

Miura explains these cleaning practices by referring to the necessity of keeping germs and dirt outside to prevent the spread of disease. Much of the dirt is, however, not directly linked to germs and disease. Practices of cleanliness, particularly of the floor, served to classify the sports hall as a safe place.

People soon started to clean the floor of the school, initially with the help of volunteers and aid workers. Without electricity and running water, they drew upon 'traditional' techniques. They used wet newspaper shavings, spread them over the floor and swept them with a broom to get up the dust. This cleaning technique (originally with wet tea leaves) had been widely used in Japan before vacuum cleaners became commonly available in the 1960s and 1970s. A dust-free environment certainly helped people to feel more comfortable. However, the frequency and context in which dust is mentioned clearly shows that there is more to it. Dust (*hokori*) seems to be not only the tangible dirt that contains real germs, but also a symbol of all the other potential kinds of contamination that people cannot feel, see or smell. Moreover, there is also a spiritual dimension to thinking on cleanliness, which is most explicitly expressed by Tenrikyō, a so-called new religion (actually founded in the mid-19th century) which sees the self-centred ways of individuals as 'dust of the mind'.[8] By sweeping away physical dust with a broom – seen in many cultures as an instrument of power and control (Hildburgh 1919) – people also attempted to gain control over dangerous conceptual dirt.

If we follow Elizabeth Shove's (2003: 84) assessment that 'cleaning is at heart a matter of policing social boundaries and restoring order', then it is evident that by creating a distinction between the dirty outside and clean inside through cleaning techniques and changing shoes, the evacuees also worked towards creating a home for themselves, albeit a temporary one. This is why strangers were not allowed inside the school without scrutiny. The head of disaster relief in Yamada, Shirato Yasuyuki, whom I interviewed during my second visit, pointed out that it would be impossible to protect the people from disease and crime if any well-meaning researcher, journalist or volunteer were just to walk inside the shelter as he or she pleased. Restoring the cleanliness of the sports hall in the school was thus not only a matter of hygiene to avoid contamination with infectious diseases. It was most importantly an issue of marking the place as interior space, or even as a home, that provided some degree of comfort and safety, despite continuing aftershocks and existential fears caused by the destruction of the town and loss of loved ones, houses and jobs. Tsunami victims initially felt that they had lost control over their lives; by gaining some degree of

---

8   'If the cleaning is done promptly, dust can be cleared away easily. But dust accumulates quickly and, if we are negligent, the dust will in time pile up so high that the cleaning will be very difficult no matter how hard we attempt to sweep or wipe it away. Our use of the mind works in much the same way. The dust of the mind can accumulate and become habits of thought and conditioning even before we know it. To prevent this from happening, it is important to pay close attention to our use of the mind and watch for selfish mind states as we proceed through each day'. See <http://www.Tenrikyō.or.jp/eng/?page_id=129> accessed 9 June 2013.

control over the dirt in their environment, they were able to regain a sense of stability. I do not entirely agree with Mary Douglas when she writes: 'In chasing dirt, in papering, decorating, tidying we are not governed by anxiety to escape disease, but are positively re-ordering our environment, making it conform to an idea' (Douglas 2002: 2). Douglas' mistake is to treat the avoidance of disease and the ordering of the environment as two mutually exclusive motivations. Both issues are relevant (see also Kirby 2011: 115); and in a disaster situation both become much more urgent issues than in everyday life, which was the implicit backdrop to Douglas' theory. In Yamada, a major motivator for the avoidance of dirt *was* the anxiety to avoid disease. At the same time, re-establishing a sense of social order was also a central concern in the cleaning practices.

People who had evacuated to Ryūshōji always took off their shoes. They were apologetic and hesitated to enter the tatami-floored temple hall (*hondō*) in wet and dirty clothes. Despite the panic, people very much perceived their entry into the temple as equivalent to that of a guest entering a private house. In this context, the rule of taking off shoes was strictly observed.

Water and food hygiene

A central problem in dealing with matters of hygiene and cleanliness was the lack of running water and electricity. With the streets full of debris, the Self-Defence Forces (SDF) were unable to deliver water. Minami Elementary was one of the first places in the town to have its water supply reconnected. This took place on 19 March, only eight days after the disaster. In the memory of my informants, however, it took much longer than that. In the daily struggle for survival, time was perceived as passing very slowly. Luckily, people could collect spring water in the hills behind the town. For Shirano Takashi (29), a young fisherman staying at Ryūshōji, collecting water was his most important job immediately after the disaster:

> Since we had no tap water, securing water was one of our central tasks. Around Yamada, there are several sources of spring water, but the streets were impassable to traffic, so water had to be carried on foot. It was quite an effort. This was one of my responsibilities from the beginning. Later, a few others helped me. I always walked around with empty plastic bottles in my rucksack. Later, when the streets were cleared, the SDF water truck started coming to the entrance of the temple compound, so we only needed to go down there to fill our plastic bottles and canteens.

Minami Elementary remained accessible via a small mountain road, so the SDF water truck was able to begin visiting only a day or two after the disaster. A number of people who lived in private houses reactivated the wells in their gardens. They hesitated to drink the water after decades of not using or testing it, but at least they could use the well for non-drinking water. That was an enormous help with the drudgery of cleaning the house of sand, salt and mud, and also for laundry. Since drinking water was scarce and labour-intensive to obtain, it was crucial to use it very frugally and to boil it before consumption. Takashi's mother, Shirano Mikiko (51), explained:

> At the beginning we were very careful not to waste water. We covered individual rice plates with cling film and only washed them when we ripped it by accident.[9] We used disposable chopsticks, and for drinking we used paper cups on which we wrote our names, so that we could reuse them. Unlike now (mid June 2011), we did not have one little individual plate for each dish, but just put the big pots on the table, and we put the fish or vegetables onto the rice on our plates. This is how we ate, trying to reduce dish-washing as much as possible. It also helped that it was still cold, so even though we did not have refrigerators, the food did not spoil that quickly and it was easier to maintain hygiene. We usually drank tea, but even when we drank spring water, we always boiled it first to make sure we would not get sick.

Yamada's new hospital had been flooded by the tsunami, but medical care units were established in the large shelters and the town hall immediately after the disaster, so healthcare was available in the town. But lack of water, electricity and medical supplies meant that this care was limited to first aid,

---

9   After each meal, they would remove the cling film, wrapping any leftovers or sauce smears in it, and throw it in the rubbish bin, leaving the plate clean without having to be washed.

disinfection, emotional support and preventative care. Infectious, severe or chronic cases were evacuated to other areas. People took particular care not to catch infectious diseases, knowing they could not be hospitalized locally. Water was heated mainly with gas stoves, fuelled by small propane tanks, and initially also with outdoor wood fires. Several people recalled frequent visits from public health workers and nurses who gave guidance on how to maintain food hygiene. They also brought antibacterial hand sanitizer.

As the wife of the priest at Ryūshōji, Shimizu Noriko also felt responsible for the people using the temple as a shelter and emphasized the importance of hygiene, especially in the kitchen. Public-health training is highly developed in Japan; even toddlers are aware of the necessity of fighting germs by hygienic practices through stories based on their favourite animation character, Anpanman.[10] It was not difficult to convince people to adopt hygienic behaviour such as boiling water, wrapping food and washing hands with anti-bacterial hand sanitizer. Many of them were already doing so, also wearing face masks or rubber gloves while cooking.

I did not observe any systematic usage of the white surgical mask. Masks were distributed at the shelters and although everyone was encouraged to wear one, some women would wear one while preparing rice balls, while others would not. However, it was not the case that these same women would always wear a mask when cooking. The priest told me to wear a mask when I went outdoors because of the dust, though he himself never wore one. In principle people used the mask both to protect themselves from germs and dirt (as well as radiation, although this was hardly an issue in Yamada) and to avoid allowing their own germs to contaminate food.[11]

---

10   *Anpanman* (first published in 1973) is one of the most popular cartoon and animation characters for young children in Japan. In the stories, the hero Anpanman (Bean-paste Bread Man, so called because his head is full of health-giving sweet bean-paste) fights against the villain Baikinman (Germ Man), helped by others who use weapons, including soap and toothpaste.

11   Burgess and Horii (2012) trace the use of the white mask in everyday Japanese life back to the outbreak of the Spanish flu in 1919. However, using the mask for protection against epidemics probably started in Manchuria, where the Malay-born, Cambridge-trained Chinese doctor Wu Lien-Teh (1879–1960) developed and systematized it for

Toilet troubles

Although hardly ever discussed in public, toilets were a crucial issue for people affected by the tsunami. The topic came up frequently in interviews. The sanitary facilities at schools used as shelters were not meant to serve so many people, especially without running water and electricity. Moreover, toilets for elementary school children are small. Toda Haruko* (36), mother of a toddler and an elementary school child, described the precarious situation:

> As we did not have running water, the hygiene situation at Minami Elementary declined more and more. First of all, there were the toilets. We carried many buckets of water from the school's swimming pool to put into the toilets' tank and to use for flushing, but we could not get them clean. Without electricity the sewage pumps do not work. So, very soon all the toilets were overflowing and could not be used anymore. People who had to empty their bowels were told to go into the hills or to use the school garden, where holes had been dug. But afterwards you couldn't wash your hands properly. Buckets of water were provided, but that water was rather disgusting. After changing my son's nappies, I could not wash my hands either. It was really, really filthy. Occasionally I used hand wipes, but they were scarce, so we had to use them very sparingly. In the end I caught a bowel infection and had to be taken to hospital in Miyako by ambulance. I recovered quickly and was only kept in one night, but even in the hospital I could not take a shower, as they did not have enough water.
>
> I was really, really desperate and anxious. How long would this go on? What other troubles were in store for us? It was very, very stressful and I was extremely exhausted. Not surprisingly, we couldn't sleep properly. Even if I fell asleep, I would wake up again immediately. I could not think clearly at all; everything was spinning around in my head.

Toilets were a central concern not only due to the risk of infectious diseases. It was only during my second lengthy interview with Toda that she told me about her bowel infection. She was clearly ashamed of the consequences

---

use in a pneumonic plague epidemic in Harbin in 1911. He later advocated the use of the white gauze mask through the WHO; cf. Wu (1926). See also Ohnuki-Tierney 1994: 25–6; Kirby 2011: 116.

of unhygienic behaviour, even though she could not do anything about it. Loss of control over ones environment caused anxiety and insomnia; losing control over one's own bowel movements became a question of shame.[12]

The authorities were able to restore public safety relatively quickly, but most people could hardly get any sleep during the first few days and nights. Many strong aftershocks, worries about relatives and friends, fear for the future, the close presence of strangers and physical discomfort kept them awake. They had to visit the toilet more often at night. Outside it was cold, dark and unfamiliar. Even at the temple, where the toilets were indoors, nocturnal visits were a challenge for some.

Among the children, such insecurity sometimes manifested itself in bed-wetting. Yamanishi Shiho* (36) told me that her eight-year-old son started to wet his bed at the shelter. This was embarrassing for him and his mother, since he had already passed the age for bed-wetting. Since washing machines were not available, washing the bedding was also a practical problem. His mother dealt with the problem by helping him to secretly put on his two-year-old brother's nappies underneath the futon.

Considering that many young women in normal life in Japan find it embarrassing to use public toilets (because the person in the neighbouring cubicle might hear them urinating or defecating),[13] it is easy to understand that this toilet situation added to the discomfort and tension experienced by evacuees at Minami Elementary. Luckily for people at Ryūshōji, the facilities there did not depend on electricity and running water. As Satō Tatsuya (43) recalled:

12   None of the women talked about menstruation, either because they were too shy to do so or they could not remember. However, according to Fukushima Yūko (2012: 61–64), a midwife who volunteered in several shelters in Iwate starting in mid-March 2011, the lack of sanitary towels was also a major problem for many women.

13   In public toilets, it is common for women to flush the toilet just before using it to hide the sound of their excretions. To avoid water wastage, many companies, schools and universities use electric flushing sound devices. A friend told me that during the electricity-saving campaigns in summer 2011, some companies switched these devices off, only to realise that water consumption went up rapidly as women reverted to flushing while using the toilet. These women appear to feel embarrassed that one of their most intimate activities is being overheard by strangers.

The temple does not have flush toilets, so in terms of toilet use we had 'peace' (laughs). In places with flush toilets the situation became really bad. Once I visited a different shelter and saw a note with instructions on how to use the toilet: 'If you have to empty your bowels, put some paper into the toilet pot, and when you have finished, wrap it up and throw it in the bucket provided'. It must be terrible, if you have to do that every day. At that shelter there were several hundred people. You can imagine how the situation must have been before they put up that note. But the temple toilet is disaster-resistant. This alone probably made a big difference to how we felt. We were a bit worried about what to do if the toilet waste tank became full. It's an everyday issue, and you need to be clean. Fortunately, that problem did not arise.

For many reasons, including this toilet situation, it was noticeable that people at Minami Elementary were far more stressed by their inability to wash themselves properly than those at Ryūshōji. Thus, for them the first bath was a much more emotional and significant event, despite the fact that they did not have to wait as long as the people at the temple.

The bath

First baths were prominent events in people's personal accounts and in the media. The Japanese are known for their love of a daily hot bath, not only for personal hygiene, but also as a way to relax, and to warm body and soul (Clark 1994). After their dramatic escape from the tsunami, their first bath was often the first event people remembered clearly. As the statement quoted at the beginning of this article makes clear, the first bath marked the transition from a state of helplessness, sleeplessness, amnesia and angst, back to normality, especially for people at Minami Elementary. Until this bath, the sense of time is very unreliable; most people regardless of age believed they waited much longer for this event than they actually had (Toda, quoted above, is one example). The sensory tension before the first bath was also recognizable in their relative insensitivity to dirty bodies. People were worried about hygiene and contamination, but uncharacteristically lax about body odour and unwashed clothes. My interviewees explained this by saying that hygiene problems would have been much worse in the summer, when they would have sweated more. I suggest that there was another reason for the increased tolerance: the overwhelming post-traumatic stress placed on the senses and emotions, which clouded people's sense of time, also made them relatively insensitive towards dirt and body smell. Ueno Noriko (70) told me that although she normally washed her hair every day, much to her surprise, she did not even sense itching after more than a week of it being unwashed. My interviewees also commented that they were 'all in this together'. As Shirano Mikiko (51) recalled:

> We were all in this together and we were lucky that everyone in our family had survived. People who have not lost their house, even those who lived nearby, probably cannot understand our feelings properly. Just a few days after the disaster, when we were all still unwashed and wearing the same clothes day and night, a woman came to the temple in full make-up. 'That can't be true!' (*uso deshō*), I thought.

Shirano felt strongly that in the midst of the debris, showing off a made-up face, something that would be expected under normal circumstances, was an affront to all the victims of the tsunami. Sharing dirty conditions had become a sign of shared suffering and understanding, and a source of communal solidarity.

Restoring cleanliness and order

Reinstating toilet hygiene at Minami Elementary was an essential step towards regaining control over daily life. The handling of the 'toilet problem' is also a prime example of the techniques and social structures that enabled people to re-establish a sense of normality, cleanliness and order. Initially it seems to have been mostly volunteers, town officials or the SDF who took care of cleaning, as the victims needed all their energy to hold on to their lives. But gradually, as Satō Katsumi (61) explained, some evacuees started to think they should take care of things themselves:

> After a while I thought we needed to get organized. So on 1 April, I became the shelter representative (of Minami Elementary) and we created a *han* (group) structure responsible for cooking and cleaning on a weekly rota basis.

The *han* structure is commonly used in Japanese schools and other institutions to assign certain tasks, including cleaning. At Minami Elementary, people were sleeping (and living) in four long rows in the sports hall, each divided into two *han*, making eight in total.[14] A few more people were sleeping by the wall, away from the main rows. They were allocated to *han* according to their gender. This was because, as Satō explained, if a *han* consisting mostly of men were put in charge of cooking, the food would have been terrible. (During my stay I did not hear of any male evacuee cooking in any shelter.) Each *han* had a leader (*hanchō*) and a deputy (*fuku-hanchō*). They coordinated tasks within the *han* and represented the group in daily meetings, along with the representative of the shelter and town officials responsible for the shelter. These posts rotated. There were no elections. *Hanchō* 'naturally emerged' through volunteering, as people explained to me; they often had to be persuaded to emerge by someone senior. Being a *hanchō* meant a great commitment of time and energy. Initially most of the group leaders were men, but when more men went back to work, many women took up leading roles. Here the shelter was a microcosm of Japanese society generally, where posts in the smallest local administrative units used to be held almost exclusively by men, but are now frequently held by women as wage work at distant locations cuts into the time available for men to participate in the local community.

Miura Michiko (56), herself a *hanchō* at the time of the interview, told me that they made great efforts to respond to people's often contradicting demands and to reduce stress. Many people found shelter life a severe test of endurance (*gaman*). Endurance is supposed to be a common cultural trait of people in north-eastern Japan, but in fact individuals differed greatly in deciding when to ask the *hanchō* for help and when to endure in silence. Noda Tokiko*, a single mother in her thirties, whose baby was

---

14   By June, the eight *han* had been reduced to four, as people departed to return to their homes or to live with relatives.

six months old in March 2011, was excused from community cleaning and
cooking duties, as were many elderly people. She also requested a room for
breastfeeding, and she and another woman with an infant were allocated a
classroom in the school building for their own use. By contrast, Yamanishi
Shiho* (36) slept with her extended family in the sports hall. She found her
cramped sleeping space very stressful, especially as there was no partition
between sleeping places. The absence of partitions meant that Yamanishi
had to constantly prevent her toddler son from violating other people's
space. When I asked her what she wished for most, she answered, 'walls'.
Nevertheless, even when her own father was *hanchō*, she did not feel that
she could make demands. Most large shelters, on the recommendation of
experts, installed partitions between individual sleeping places. The recently
amended 2005 Basic Plan for Disaster Prevention incorporates specific
support for women, such as providing a room for changing clothes and
for breastfeeding, the distribution of sanitary items, and the introduction
of privacy partitions (Saito 2012: 267). Officials tried to introduce such
partitions at Minami Elementary as well, but shelter representative Satō
Katsumi told me that he himself decided that they wouldn't need any, com-
menting that 'we are like a family'. Shirato, the town official, also confirmed
that his attempt to introduce partitions had been rejected by the people
in the shelter. On the positive side, he thought the lack of privacy might
have discouraged sexual harassment.[15]

In shelters in Yamada, kitchens were run exclusively by women. Women
and men alike took it for granted that women would do the cooking; this
was also the case in other shelters. The women I talked to did not complain
about this, though at other shelters some were frustrated that they were
not paid for cooking and other household chores that contributed to the
community (see Saito 2012: 269). Miura put her mother forward to be the
'head chef' of their *han*, as she had professional experience. The women
always drew up the menu, based on the food deliveries from the town hall.
The main meal in all shelters was breakfast, generally taken around 6.00

---

15   Although a few people mentioned the topic, I did not hear of any incident of sexual
      harassment at either of the shelters in Yamada.

or 6.30 am, to make sure everyone could get to their workplace on time.[16] As a result, being in charge of cooking meant early rising. Nevertheless, as Miura said, they aimed to create a cheerful (*akarui*) atmosphere. Toda*, who was in the same *han*, confirmed that the women enjoyed preparing meals together, even though it was a lot of work. Men did the heavy work (*chikara shigoto*), such as carrying cooking pots and water or, in the case of small shelters like the Ryūshōji, going to pick up food from the town hall.

At Japanese schools both boys and girls generally have to take turns in cleaning the toilets. Accordingly, at Minami Elementary men cleaned the men's facilities and women cleaned theirs. Shelter representative Satō Katsumi (61) remembers that he took his turn at the beginning, although as a 'traditional' husband he had never done this at home before. He introduced some unique strategies to reduce dirt:

> Nowadays we all use Western toilets at home, but at the school there are no such toilets, and the elderly don't have enough muscle strength to squat,[17] so the toilets were really dirty. Since I cleaned the toilets, I was very much aware of this and I suggested to a former teacher who had taught sumo wrestling that we might introduce some squatting exercises. So, at our shelter we did the radio callisthenics programme,[18] followed by squatting exercises. The old ladies were really into it; and with stronger thighs, they were able to use the toilets properly. After a while, I was liberated from my duty of cleaning the toilets.

Preventative measures needing a high level of co-operation were thus introduced (and maintained) to handle the toilet crisis. These examples show how communities used cleaning to enhance social integration through

16   Though many workplaces in the centre of Yamada had been destroyed by the tsunami, by June most men and many women could either return to their workplaces further away or were given temporary jobs in cleaning up or rebuilding the town or in social work.

17   Traditional Japanese toilets involve squatting over a hole in the ground. Today, most people have heated toilet seats with bidet function and are no longer used to squatting. At the elementary school, however, the majority of the toilets were in smaller sizes for children, thus required squatting.

18   Radio callisthenics were introduced to Japan in 1928. To this day, every primary school child is supposed to participate in early morning radio gymnastics during the summer holidays. Many elderly people also take part regularly.

collaboration in avoiding dirt, establishing structure and order, and increasing personal comfort. It also makes clear that although some people had creative ideas to tackle problems, they mostly relied on received social structures and habits. They were highly aware and well-trained in hygienic practices even before the disaster.

Similarly, at Ryūshōji, negotiating and sharing household duties helped create a community. The small group of evacuees had no officials or volunteers to assist them, since the temple was not initially granted formal recognition as a shelter. The priest and his wife organized food and other supplies, but they were also extremely busy counselling the bereaved and conducting funerals and other community services. Thus, they mostly left household chores to the evacuees themselves. One of them, a 37-year-old woman called Sasaki Mami, commented thus:

> This is a small shelter with nice people; so when there is something to decide, someone makes a suggestion, and we come to an agreement. It's different from other shelters, where they divide themselves into *han*, and you often hear, 'You can't do this, you can't do that'. We get along very well – that's good, isn't it? It's rather rare in a shelter. ... I'm usually at work during the day, so I can't help much with the cooking and cleaning, but I do all the toilets in the morning before breakfast. Downstairs at the temple hall, I clean once a week, more often when there are funerals; upstairs I do every other day, so that it's always clean. I also help after breakfast, doing the dishes and preparing the rice balls, but during the day, I leave things to Kon Rumiko and Shirano Mikiko. It's quite a lot of work for them.

In this 'household-sized' shelter, where people had the feeling that the division of labour had emerged 'naturally' (*shizen ni*), cleaning was mostly done by women. There were exceptions, though. Shirano Takashi (29) was in charge of cleaning the bathroom every day (encouraged to do so by his mother), and one weekend, when he was away, his father stepped in:

> We live here as a group, so everyone has to help out. At first I mainly carried water around, but this is not necessary anymore. The women do the cooking for us, so I help to set the table, and I also clean the bath every day. I did that at home as well.

Carrying waste bags to the collection site was also a job for men, in this case for the retired Saitō-san (73) and, on his free days, also Sasaki-san (65). In the temple, it was obvious that everyone made an effort to contribute to group life and avoid conflicts in order to show gratitude to their hosts, though problems did occasionally arise (see Steger 2011). In larger shelters where there was no host comparable to the priest and his wife, not everyone seems to have felt that way, as I gathered from small hints in my conversations with people staying at Minami Elementary.

At both shelters, each family took care of its own laundry. Single men did their own laundry; otherwise it was women's work. Washing machines were available once electricity and water had been re-established, but there were only three machines for a shelter of 100 people. Yamanishi Shiho* said she often had her husband drive her fifteen miles to Miyako to use the coin launderette there because she had too much laundry. (As an epileptic she was not able to drive herself.) With a bed-wetting child, she may also have preferred using an anonymous facility rather than hanging up her laundry at the shelter. In addition, she may have been reluctant to hang out her underwear at the shelter. Many young Japanese women will avoid hanging out their underwear in public, because they are intimate articles of clothing associated with male sexual fantasies, and are sometimes stolen by 'underwear thieves' (*shitagi dorobō*).[19] No woman mentioned such a concern during interviews. However, revisiting the interview transcripts, I find that almost all the women under the age of forty I talked to actually said that they were doing their laundry either at a friend's or relative's home or in a public launderette rather than at the shelter. A fact-finding mission in April and May 2011 by the Tokyo-based NGO Human Rights Now (HRN) found that 'little safe space is secured to hang out female laundry, so women have little choice but to use their underwear once and throw it away, and the supply of underwear is limited' (Human Rights Now 2011). This confirms that hanging out women's underwear in public spaces was indeed considered a problem in shelters and that, despite much talk of 'living together like a family', shelter life increasingly demanded measures to maintain privacy. Increasing cleanliness and order also meant an increasing social differentiation.

Children and teenagers were hardly ever involved in household tasks. Adults were very concerned about the psychological stress to children

19   I am grateful to Keiko Morrison for her insight on this point.

caused by the disaster, and were generally very indulgent. Older children concentrated on studying: they struggled to find a quiet place to finish their work before the 9pm curfew and would often sit in the corridor to study after that. Thus, men, women and children living in the shelters all concentrated on what they perceived to be their core responsibilities, based on practices learned in everyday life before the disaster.

Conclusion

Re-establishing cleanliness and orderliness was a central way for evacuees to get a grip on life after the disaster. It helped them to regain some structure in their lives and a sense of normality, familiarity and emotional security. Practices demarcating the clean, safe interior or *uchi* from the dirty, dangerous exterior or *soto* marked the shelter as an – albeit temporary – home. A safe and clean place makes the home. Or, put the other way around, to turn an emergency gathering-place into a home, it is necessary to clean it.

Joy Hendry (1984: 219) suggests that from early childhood onwards 'the enormous ritual distinction made between the inside of the house and the outside world, recalled at least at a subconscious level each time shoes are donned or removed, creates a system of classification predisposed towards further dichotomies in behaviour based on the difference between a public and a private self'. In the shelter, people created a sense of community and solidarity by sharing and solving hygiene problems. Immediately after the disaster, unwashed bodies and clothes became a symbol of shared suffering. With time, shelter inhabitants succeeded in creating solidarity through shared efforts to keep their living space comfortable and safe. Likewise, maintaining hygiene and organizing household duties at the shelter helped create a social structure that held the community together. By cleaning their hands, taking off shoes, wearing masks, cleaning the toilets and the bath, and by preventing contamination of food, people established clear standards for right and wrong behaviour.

Traditional gender roles were re-emphasized. Everyone took it for granted that women had the main responsibility for cooking and cleaning. Shirano Mikiko (51) told me that everyone helped out with household tasks. When I asked her whether she meant 'all women' or 'all evacuees', she laughed at the question. Of course, only women would work in the kitchen, she said. Sharing responsibilities among fellow women helped them to gain some sense of normality and solidarity. Gender roles in rural north-eastern Japan were much more clearly divided than in urban areas even before the disaster (Rosenberger 2006; see also Saito 2011: 267). However, confirming Hoffman's findings introduced at the beginning of this article and contrasting with Jencson's views, I found that far from being radicalized, gender relations and social structures reverted to older and deeper-rooted patterns. Far more women than men lost their jobs after 3.11, and they found it harder to re-enter employment.[20] Without jobs, women were automatically expected to bear the brunt of household responsibilities unpaid, including care of children and elderly as well as cooking and cleaning.

Cleanliness and order in the shelter reflected social norms and morals. As the toilet issue has shown most poignantly, not being able to keep oneself and one's home clean is also a question of shame. Women were affected more than men; they had to protect their underwear from the male gaze and felt uncomfortable using communal toilets. While the shared experience of being dirty before the first bath brought a feeling of shared suffering and solidarity to shelter inhabitants, with increasing levels of cleanliness, social distinctions within the shelter became more pronounced. Over the months, the sense of solidarity that marked the first phase of life in the shelter started to fade. Many evacuees felt an increasing need to have partitions between themselves and others and eagerly anticipated the move into temporary housing, which happened sometime between late June

---

20 This is partly because women tended to be employed locally and on a temporary or part-time basis. Most of the local small businesses were destroyed by the tsunami. Moreover, government programmes to create employment after the disaster concentrated on the construction industry. But informants indicated that men were also advantaged in relatively gender-neutral areas of employment such as retailing.

and late August for most people. The need for privacy increased. The same shared hygienic norms that brought people together and made shelter life possible, now drove them apart, as the equation between cleanliness and privacy gradually outweighed communitarian norms. The need to be clean, and to appear clean in the eyes of the community, helped people maintain standards of hygiene in the shelters. But maintaining those standards was a growing burden, and a source of friction and psychological stress among evacuees, that might well have undermined the community had not the temporary housing units finally been completed in August 2011.

References

Arai Hiroko (2012). 'Saigai, fukkō to danjo kyōdō sankaku: Josei ga shutai to natte iku koto' (Disaster, reconstruction and the plan for gender equality: Women becoming main subjects). In Murata Akiko (ed.), *Fukkō ni joseitachi no koe o: '3.11' to jendā.* (Women's voices for reconstruction: '3.11' and gender), pp. 1–9. Tokyo: Waseda University Press.

Blinn-Pike, Lynn (2006). 'Shelter Life after Hurricane Katrina: A Visual Analysis of Evacuee Perspectives', *International Journal of Mass Emergencies and Disasters* 24(1), 303–330.

Burgess, Adam and Horii Mitsutoshi (2012). 'Risk, Ritual and Health Responsibilisation: Japan's "Safety Blanket" of Surgical Face Mask-wearing', *Sociology of Health and Illness* 34(8), 1184–1198.

Clark, Scott (1994). *Japan, A View from the Bath*. Honolulu: University of Hawaii Press.

Douglas, Mary (2002 [1966]). *Purity and Danger: An Analysis of the Concepts of Pollution and Taboo.* London: Routledge.

Elzinga, Bernet, and J. Douglas Bremner (2002). 'Review: Are the Neural Substrates of Memory the Final Common Pathway in Posttraumatic Stress Disorder (PTSD)?' *Journal of Affective Disorders*, 70, 1–17.

Fukushima Yūko (2012). 'Saigaiji, josei no karada o dō mamoru ka' (How can we protect women's bodies at times of disaster). In Murata Akiko (ed.), *Fukkō ni joseitachi no koe o: '3.11' to jendā* (Women's voices for the reconstruction: '3.11' and gender), pp. 61–64. Tokyo: Waseda University Press.

Hendry, Joy (1984). 'Shoes: The Early Learning of an Important Distinction in Japanese Society'. In Gordon Daniels (ed.), *Europe Interprets Japan*, pp. 215–222. Tenterden, Kent: Paul Norbury Publications.

Hildburgh, Leo Walter (1919). 'Some Magical Applications of Brooms in Japan', *Folklore* 30(3), 169–207.

Hoffman, Susanna (1999). 'The Regenesis of Traditional Gender Patterns in the Wake of Disaster'. In Anthony Oliver-Smith and Susanna Hoffman (eds), *The Angry Earth: Disaster in Anthropological Perspective*, pp. 173–191. London: Routledge.

Human Rights Now (2011). (Statement) 'Regarding the establishment of evacuation centres with due consideration of the various needs of residents, including those of women'. <http://hrn.or.jp/eng/activity/area/japan/regarding-the-establishment-of-evacuation-centres-with-due-consideration-of-the-various-needs-of-res/> accessed 9 June 2013.

Iwate Nippō (2011). 'Yamada de hinanjo seikatsu chōsa. Kenburijji dai kenkyūsha' (Cambridge University researcher conducts study on life in shelters in Yamada), *Iwate Nippō*, 4 June, p. 27.

Jencson, Linda (2001). 'Disastrous Rites: Liminality and Communitas in a Flood Crisis', *Anthropology and Humanism*, 26(1), 46–58.

Kirby, Peter (2011). *Troubled Natures: Waste, Environment, Japan*. Honolulu: University of Hawaii Press.

Kuwayama Takami (1996). '"Gasshuku" Off-campus Training in the Japanese School', *Anthropology and Education Quarterly*, 27(1), 111–134.

Ohnuki-Tierney, Emiko (1994). *Illness and Culture in Contemporary Japan: An Anthropological View*. Cambridge: Cambridge University Press.

Rosenberger, Nancy (2006). 'Young Women Making Lives in Northeast Japan'. In Christopher Thompson and John Traphagan (eds), *Wearing Cultural Styles in Japan: Concepts of Tradition and Modernity in Practice*, pp. 76–95. New York: State University of New York Press.

Saito Fumie (2012). 'Women and the 2011 East Japan Disaster', *Gender & Development*, 20(2), 267.

Shove, Elizabeth (2003). *Comfort, Cleanliness and Convenience: The Social Organization of Normality*. Oxford: Berg.

Steger, Brigitte (2011). 'Secrets in a Tsunami Evacuation Center', *Anthropology News*, 528, 14 November, 43.

Wada Hideki (2011). *Shinzai torauma* (Disaster trauma). Tokyo: Besuto Shinsho.

Wu Lien-Teh (1926). *Treatise on Pneumonic Plague*. Geneva: League of Nations.

NATHAN J. PETERSON

Adapting Religious Practice in Response to Disaster in Iwate Prefecture

> In tears, at the edge of the sea, we must remain:
> Going by sea, waist-deep in the water,
> We move forward with difficulty.
> — THE KOJIKI

> The muddied waters flow on,
> clearing as they go.
> — TANEDA SANTŌKA[1]

The tsunami that hit north-eastern Japan on 11 March 2011 overwhelmed nearly all the defences protecting coastal communities, inundating areas several kilometres inland that were once thought to be safe from flooding. The disaster challenged long-held assumptions about public safety in Japan. People are questioning scientists' ability to predict the scale of natural disasters and protect the public from them. Some Japanese were already critical about their government's ineffectiveness, and now they are uncertain about how their country should handle the trillions of yen worth of destruction caused by the disaster. Veteran journalist Ishizuka Masahiko

---

1   These epigraphs relate to two turbulent eras of Japanese culture during the eighth and twentieth centuries respectively. This section of the *Kojiki* details mourners rushing into the sea in order to follow the deceased prince Yamato Takeru after he transformed into a white bird (Philippi 1968: 252–253; Akima 1982: 492–493). The priest-poet Santōka, on the other hand, found solace in nature when wandering the countryside with meagre provisions and inadequate shelter (Abrams 1977: 274).

wrote: 'the recent catastrophe has unleashed a flood of profound soul-searching over the state of the nation – past, present and future. A key question is the moral and spiritual impact of this massive disaster, which was beyond the scope of conventional social and scientific wisdom' (*Nikkei Weekly*, 25 April 2011).

The tsunami destroyed entire neighbourhoods throughout the Sanriku[2] region, disrupting ordinary life for years to come, and it triggered a nuclear crisis comparable to Chernobyl. In Iwate prefecture, my main area for field studies, around 6,500 people died. The city of Rikuzen-Takata suffered the worst casualties of any city in the prefecture, with over 1,500 people dead. Three months on from the disaster, on 11 June 2011, around 21,183 evacuees from 34 communities in this prefecture were living in shelters or temporary housing (*Iwate Nippō*, 11 June 2011).

In Sanriku, the disaster is referred to as *Heisei no Sanriku Ōtsunami*, literally meaning the Great Sanriku Tsunami of the Heisei era.[3] Many compare it to the Sanriku earthquake and tsunami of the year 869 (*Nikkei Weekly*, 25 April 2011). Natural disasters like these can provide 'opportunities to examine aspects of social structures and processes that are hidden in everyday affairs' (Stallings 2002: 281). In this paper I will focus on what the disaster tells us about religious or spiritual beliefs and values in contemporary Japanese society.

Traditional religious practices such as visiting shrines and temples can be important coping mechanisms after a disaster, but people also convey their emotions through temporary memorials. Sometimes that is their only option, because the religious centres in their communities have been destroyed. The participants at these memorials can 'alter both the physical and social landscape' surrounding them (Thomson 2011). The variety of

2   Sanriku is a coastal region facing the Pacific Ocean, extending from southern Aomori prefecture through Iwate prefecture and northern Miyagi prefecture. It had been hit by devastating earthquakes and tsunamis many times, most famously in 869, 1896 and 1933, prior to the disastrous tsunami of 2011. See Wilhelm and Delaney in the present volume.
3   The Heisei Era began in 1989 with the ascent of Emperor Akihito to the Chrysanthemum Throne. The year of the disaster, 2011, was also Heisei 23.

ways of commemorating the disaster shows the plasticity of memories, life stories, and social roles within the Sanriku communities, where people were already battling with broader social problems such as the ageing population and ailing rural economy – problems exacerbated by the disaster.

The syncretism of Japanese religions can offer people latitude in expressing their faith. Differentiating between various religions' practices in Japan can be difficult because of their overlapping beliefs. People have freedom in the way they remember 3.11, and both rituals and popular culture influence their attitudes. Their neighbourhoods experienced the destruction of traditional religious centres such as Buddhist temples, Shinto shrines, and cemeteries. The tsunami destroyed some famous Shinto shrines along the Iwate shoreline, such as the Hachidai Riyūō Shrine at Hitachihama in Miyako. In this chapter I hope to show how residents of the disaster areas in Iwate prefecture adapted religious practice to the disorder brought by the catastrophe.

Niisato Masaya is a citizen of Kamaishi, a small city on the Sanriku coast. On 11 March he took shelter at the city's Osaki Shrine. He hopes that his community will be able to recover in ten years. He returned to the shrine and made offerings on 8 July when his family reopened their business, located about 500 metres south of the shrine in Kamaishi's Minatomachi district (Niisato, personal communication). Other people affected by the disaster are demoralized, such as 75-year-old Sekiguchi Yoshikazu. He retired after losing both his home and shoe store located in the Lower Kuwagasaki district of Miyako. He was dismayed by the destruction of his neighbourhood when returning on 3 July: all the local religious centres had been destroyed except for the Kumano Shrine where his neighbours sought shelter during the tsunami (Sekiguchi, personal communication). These people's hardships will last for many years, and the effect of the tsunami will stay with them for the rest of their lives.

Buddhist temples and cemeteries are normally built further inland than shrines and on hillsides, but some of them too suffered extensive damage because the tsunami reached so far inland. Predominant religions in Japan such as Buddhism and Shinto can provide the Japanese ways to cope with their loss, but they must adjust to the ruins of their communities. 'New religions' (*shinkō shūkyō*), offer alternatives to people affected by the disaster. Examining the religious response of people living in Iwate prefecture, particularly in the communities surrounding the city of Miyako, shows how religious culture can be adaptive to crisis. Aesthetics are influencing the residents of these communities, regardless of their personal religious beliefs, because 'our personal involvement adds to the perceptual intensity of such situations' (Berleant 1992: 170). The disaster areas, therefore, function like sacred sites in their communities, accessed by people in order to make offerings and remembrances. These areas, however, will inevitably transform as communities slowly regroup, redevelop their cities, and build lasting memorials for future generations to see.

Shinto and community involvement

A Shinto shrine in Japan can represent the vitality of its neighbourhood, community and region. Shrines organize one's 'social reality' (Nelson 2000: 23–24), serving as a physical point of reference linking people together through history, politics, and business. In Miyako, a person who visited the Kuromori Shrine just as the first shock hit the city on 3.11, wrote in the worship register that a great earthquake had just occurred, that a power outage had crippled the city, and that phone service was interrupted. He concludes that 'our lifelines have been cut off' (*raifu rain ga todaeta*). The person writing this entry, lacking any means to communicate with the outside world, used the register as a way to engage the deities of the shrine. He does not mention the tsunami, which suggests he wrote this entry before it reached the shore.

This register openly invites visitors to write their 'prayers, wishes, and thoughts, etcetera'. Both residents of Miyako and volunteers from across Japan came to this shrine, located on a forested mountainside over two kilometres from downtown, during the initial months after the tsunami. The average number of entries per month nearly doubled after the disaster, from an admittedly low base, peaking at 14 entries written between

10 August and 12 September. At the end of December 2011, the register had over 25 entries written by locals compared to five by people from other parts of Japan since 3.11. Most of the entries directly pertain to people's hopes and needs during the recovery. The volunteer Kohiyama Ichirō from Kyoto visited the shrine on 21 May, writing in the register: 'I pray that the people affected by the disaster will one day soon regain their former lives'. These inscriptions were coping mechanisms during the crisis, emphasizing the contribution of religious centres to a community's support system.

Religious centres during the initial recovery

Kōzan-ji is a Buddhist temple located in the Kanehama district of Miyako. It still serves the community, despite the tsunami having flooded its inner sanctum. It is located on a hillside less than 200 metres from the shore. The tsunami destroyed all the homes and businesses 500 metres inland that surrounded this temple. Residents of Kanehama, however, are still able to worship at the temple. Volunteer Iioka Michiko goes there once a week to clean the grounds. During the tsunami, she fled from downtown Miyako to seek shelter at the hospital. She started volunteering at Kōzan-ji about three months after the disaster (Iioka Michiko, personal communication). The grounds of this temple are distinct from the abandoned, overgrown homesites in the neighbourhood. Michiko's brother, Iioka Taidō, is a parishioner (*danka*) of the temple. He escaped to the nearby mountains just before the tsunami swept away his home on the temple grounds. He now lives in a small house on a nearby hillside. He still routinely worships at the temple, and he organized the Bon Festival in August when residents could return to Kanehama and pray for the dead. He believes that more than a decade will pass before the community fully recovers. He is deeply concerned that he may die before his beloved temple is fully restored (Iioka Taidō, personal communication).

As well as destroying places of worship, the tsunami also carried away countless cultural artefacts such as statues, masks, or costumes for ceremonial performances unique to Sanriku, whose very survival was put at risk. The government's Cultural Affairs Agency estimates that the tsunami has affected at least 500 designated national treasures and cultural assets. Folk traditions unique to Sanriku were also at least temporarily suspended (*Mainichi Daily News*, 17 May 2011). Religious groups such as Shinto associations lost members, worship centres, and funds for ceremonies. The association for the Kurosaki Shrine in the Uiso district of Miyako, for example, cancelled its annual festival in June 2011 because of insufficient funding.

Between them, the loss of cultural assets and the disintegration of communal ties threaten tremendous harm to Sanriku. Folklorist Hashimoto Hiroyuki from Morioka University is concerned about losing the 'intangible properties' of these local treasures that are important to people's livelihoods (Hashimoto, personal communication). His work, through funding provided by the Japan Foundation, promotes performance art such as the Tiger Dance (*Toramai*) held in disaster-struck Kamaishi on 17 July. These events can help in restoring communities torn apart by the tsunami.

Hashimoto is worried that the disaster will sweep away the customs of these coastal communities. He works with the Misawa Aviation Museum in Aomori prefecture to preserve the traditions of the area. On 4 September 2011, he videotaped the Kuromori Kagura performance, a Shinto dance unique to Miyako that recounts the myths of this community and is renowned throughout Japan. Around 60 people attended this event at the Yamaguchi community centre, fewer than expected by organizers. The musicians and performers, nonetheless, encouraged audience participation. Elementary students Nakano Takuto and his younger brother Kenta played significant roles during the dance of Ebisu, the god of fishing and commerce. Takuto ran in front of the stage holding on to an elusive fish, while Kenta helped a masked performer catch it. Involving these brothers, whom their mother said were stranded at school during the tsunami (Nakano Yukie, personal communication), is part of re-establishing the community's support system through local customs. The dancers and musicians of the Kuromori Kagura represented their community by touring Russia from 29 September to 5 October. Upon returning to Miyako, their performance at the Yamaguchi community centre on 4 December attracted over 70 people and national media coverage. The Nakano brothers, who came on their own for this performance, participated once again in these time-honoured dances.

The tsunami also affected centres for alternative religious movements, sometimes called 'new religions', such as Tenrikyō and Sōka Gakkai.[4] These religions are less popular in rural Tohoku than in urban areas, and are regarded with some suspicion. Nonetheless, they too responded to the needs of communities in the disaster area. The Tenrikyō branches in Miyako hosted around 30 volunteers who stayed for a week on average.[5] The priest, Takahashi Kuniyuki, estimates that 150 people worship at Tenrikyō branches in Miyako out of 58,000 people living there before 3.11. His congregation in Atago district lost five members during the tsunami, leaving some twenty survivors (Takahashi, personal communication).

The 'new religions' quickly responded to distressed people in Sanriku. However, their worship centres affected by the tsunami face long-term problems such as rebuilding and reengaging the community. The Tenrikyō church in the Sokei district of Miyako led by Kudō Toshinori suspended its services for over eight months because nearly two metres of water flooded its sanctuary. Horiuchi Akira from the Sōka Gakkai centre in the city's Sentoku district explained that his church was too preoccupied with counselling members to organize community events (Horiuchi, personal communication). Overall, these religions either maintained or lost members rather than gaining new ones during the initial months following the tsunami. The growth of these groups will depend on their engagement with devastated communities in the coming years, and both Takahashi and Kudō hope to apply lessons they have learned from the disaster to increase their influence in Miyako. Kudō, in particular, envisions his congregation

4   Tenrikyō (a monotheistic religion with emphasis on charity) was founded in 1838 and Sōka Gakkai, a lay Buddhist movement, in 1930. They are sometimes called 'old new religions' to distinguish them from the many religions that emerged after World War II.

5   Not many when compared to the 18,264 volunteers registered with the recovery centre in Miyako as of 31 October 2011.

building a mountain retreat in response to the disaster (Kudō, personal communication). His church, however, is only of marginal relevance to the broader community of Miyako.

Many communities throughout Iwate prefecture were in great need of assistance even six months after 3.11. The city of Ōtsuchi, which lost over 1,400 people, was engulfed in flames as the tsunami moved inland. The flood and fire damage is extensive throughout this community, and people living there face a difficult rebuilding process. Ogawa Fumi'ichi came to Ōtsuchi from Nagoya in central Japan after the tsunami in order to volunteer and promote awareness of Ōtsuichi's plight. In September 2011, he was living in a home-made tent in an insurance company's parking lot, where he survived a major typhoon. Ogawa is dedicated to rebuilding Ōtsuchi so that the city can withstand any future tsunami, and has designed plans for a new tsunami wall to protect the city. At his urban campsite he had already built a small altar with a statue of Hotei (one of the Seven Lucky Gods, a vaguely Buddhist pantheon revered in Japanese folklore) dedicated to the people of Ōtsuchi. He burned incense, lit candles, and offered refreshments branded with images of the famous Nebuta festival held at Hirosaki, Aomori prefecture. Behind the parking lot, he had positioned a cushion with a message tacked onto it praying for the dead and missing of Ōtsuchi. Living and working in the ruins of the city, he was unsure where he would live during winter. He explained, however, that his concern for the community outweighed his own needs (Ogawa, personal communication). By late February 2012, he had developed his campsite into a place of elaborate rituals with instructions for honouring the dead at separate shrines devoted to adults and children. His continued presence showed a measure of acceptance from the troubled community.

In the months after the disaster, the populations of Fukushima, Miyagi, and Iwate prefectures dropped by 25 per cent overall. Coastal cities affected by the tsunami experienced a 46 per cent decrease in population (*Iwate Nippō*, 26 September 2011). Survivors in charge of shrines and temples faced great difficulties when ministering to their communities. In Ōtsuchi, priest Matsubashi Tomoyuki lives at the Kozuchi Shrine located nearly three kilometres from the harbour. Both his house and the shrine were almost completely destroyed. A sacred tree to the west of the main sanctuary was lost to fire. Even so, residents participated in the shrine's festival in late September 2011.

A cemetery located next to the Kōgan Temple in Suehiro district sustained tremendous damage. This temple and cemetery complex is located closer to the harbour than the Kozuchi Shrine, and a smaller shrine closer still to the harbour in Suka district was completely destroyed. The community improvised its own memorials to cope with the loss of these religious centres. In front of the Kozuchi Shrine in Ōtsuchi the place where the Usuzawa family's house once stood had an arrangement of flowers, rocks, and fragments of cinder block, for the remembrance of family members lost to the tsunami, and it functioned like a gravesite for survivors to visit (*ohaka-mairi*) while the local cemetery is in disrepair.

Memorials in the disaster area are also built in honour of those missing after the tsunami. Across the street from the Kozuchi Shrine an anonymous person had erected a memorial at the Fujiwara household. The original homeowner is still alive, but a neighbour said he had no idea of his whereabouts. The memorial at the Fujiwara household had a vase of flowers, a statue of a bodhisattva, an offering of tea, and the Japanese *Hinomaru* (Rising Sun) flag. This memorial showed support for the residents of Ōtsuchi while demolition crews cleaned up the debris. The presence of the flag is somewhat controversial because many Japanese people associate it with wartime nationalism and reject it as a symbol of their identity. But despite widespread scepticism about the government's handling of the disaster, we have probably seen the Rising Sun flag displayed somewhat more often since 3.11, along with mildly nationalistic slogans such as *Ganbarō Nippon* (Come on Japan!). Like the Shinto religion, also tainted by its role in wartime fascism, patriotism may have offered a modicum of comfort to some disaster victims.

Neighbourhood shrines at risk

Neighbourhood shrines and temples are extensions of the community involving everyone living there. Fujiwara Ritsuko, who lives in the Orikasa district of Yamada, recalls how a family shrine located behind her childhood home was once called Okuman-sama. However, this shrine was nameless when I visited because tsunami damage was considered to have made it impure for the deity to inhabit. Debris cluttered the grounds of this shrine nearly five months after 3.11, which is atypical because usually caretakers rigorously clean Shinto shrines. Ritsuko believes the residing *kami* left the shrine, just as her family left the neighbourhood after the tsunami. In Japanese folklore, *kami* or sacred spirits[6] can be viewed as being 'divine strangers' (Ohnuki-Tierney 1987) who periodically visit humans but might leave if pollution is a threat. This small shrine has ceased to be a vessel in which a deity may reside, and its restoration is precluded because her family members that once took care of it have moved away. Without anyone to worship the *kami*, Ritsuko explained that the former shrine had been transformed into an ordinary building and that she was too preoccupied to care for it herself (Fujiwara personal communication). This shrine was still in disrepair nine months after 3.11 during *hatsumōde* celebrations in January 2012. The physical damage to the shrine and the collapse of the community that once worshipped at it has dissolved its sacredness. This building's change from holy vessel to temporal object may be reversed, but its restoration is contingent upon the revitalization of the neighbourhood. That may never happen, however, because local residents are wary of rebuilding at this location, less than 500 metres from the sea.

The disappearance of kinship networks in devastated communities puts family shrines at risk of being demolished. A small shrine in the Lower

---

6   The word *kami* is often translated as 'god' or 'Shinto god', but in truth it is a more elusive idea, referring to the spirits of ancestors, heroic individuals, and certain animals, trees, rocks, etc. A sub-group called *ujigami* are the tutelary deities of communities and reside in the local shrine. See Gill in this volume (p. 206).

Kuwagasaki district of Miyako is also nameless after 3.11. The tsunami splintered the *torii* of this shrine and washed away parts of its foundation. The damage to this shrine has caused it to be shuttered up indefinitely during the recovery. The key unlocking the shrine doors, furthermore, was apparently swept away by the tsunami. Apparently the Sawauchi household used to care for this shrine, but neighbours were still unaware of the family's whereabouts six months after 3.11. Most neighbours still living in Lower Kuwagasaki have ignored the shrine altogether, despite its proximity to the Hishiya Saké distillery where saké brewing restarted by the end of 2011. The father and son who run the nearby Kawabe liquor store are unaware of either its name or which *kami* resided there before the tsunami. School superintendent Sasaki Hisashi, who lived in the neighbourhood before the tsunami, believes that the shrine is now nameless and nonreligious because of the damage. This 'idiosyncratic shrine' (*koseiteki-na jinja*), as he explains, lost its sacredness after the death and displacement of the families that once worshipped there, suggesting that both physical and spiritual pollution affect the block where the shrine is located. He doubts the shrine will be restored because most people are hesitant to rebuild their homes in this neighbourhood (Sasaki personal communication). Unless a family reclaims the plot of land adjoining the shrine to build a home, he thinks neighbouring Shinto associations like the Konsei Shrine in Hikage district might dismantle it as plans move forward for redeveloping the neighbourhood. Pollution resulting from death, decay and other 'complexities' (Boyd and Williams 2005) are a source of anxiety for residents. This abandoned shrine is symptomatic of the decline in social embeddedness that its neighbourhood has experienced since the disaster (Kaniasty and Norris 1995: 96) – something that threatens communities throughout the disaster zone.

Family altars as temporary memorials

Memorials built in the disaster zones in place of family altars can promote togetherness when social networks are weak. Participants at these memorials 'transform and redefine' these sites just as their interaction with the memorials redefines them (Thomson 2011). An altar built at the home of Hikage Yuzō in the fishing hamlet of Otobe, on the coast of Miyako, is a site where people prayed for the dead. Hikage and his wife died on 3.11 despite their house being close to a tsunami evacuation shelter. Six cinder blocks formed the entire structure of the altar built on the destroyed homesite. Bouquets of flowers were positioned inside the cavities of the lateral blocks. The middle block had two glasses of water next to an open bottle of tea. An oval ceramic bowl served as an incense burner, and to its left were two candles. A necklace made of seashells rested upon the interior block on the left side, and a damaged statue of the deity Daikokuten (like Hotei, one of the Seven Lucky Gods) and a metal spoon were on the far right block. The position of the middle block corresponded to the vestibule of the demolished house. This interior location is important because sacred places offer 'the feeling of getting into the inner part' (Tada 1983: 425); the house was gone, but the sacredness of the interior was still acknowledged. Unlike the shattered shrines, the site of the former Hikage house had been neither polluted nor profaned in the eyes of the local community.

This improvised altar helped friends and family cope with the deaths of Hikage Yuzō and his wife. Candles, incense burners, flowers, and statues are all common objects found at altars. The seashell necklace, on the other hand, was an unusual addition, possibly referencing the suffering that came from the sea in the form of the tsunami. Middle school teacher Ōhodo Asako explained that the Hikage memorial was a Buddhist altar (*butsudan*) rather than a Shinto one (*saidan*). She recognized that this altar was dedicated to the deceased members of the Hikage family because it resembled a decorated altar inside a Buddhist temple (Ōhodo personal communication).

The memorials in the disaster area, whether influenced by Buddhism or Shinto, were temporary structures built out of immediate spiritual need. The cinder blocks at the Hikage household, for example, were all that remained of the altar six months after the tsunami. The cleaning up and dismantling of these memorials marked a new phase of the recovery process that gradually distanced communities from the events of 3.11.

A few blocks from the Hikage household is a memorial dedicated to Yamamoto Satoshi, who also died during the tsunami. He was the first cousin of Ōhodo Asako's brother-in-law, Tanaka Washichi. Several bottles of saké, a traditional offering called *kumotsu*, stood underneath large boulders resting beside the homesite. A bottle of perfume stood atop one boulder, while several bouquets of flowers adorn the foundation. The Yamamoto memorial appeared to have crumbled into disorganized rubble four months after the disaster. Piles of dirt had accumulated around the foundation, which was overgrown with weeds. Scattered debris was spread across the entire site. Distinguishing the offerings left at this memorial from litter was difficult by then. Two months later, however, the site had been transformed by volunteers and clean-up crews working in this neighbourhood. A relative of the family, a patrilineal cousin (Ōhodo, personal communication), had also maintained the homesite by cleaning around the foundation, replacing old bouquets with fresh ones, and reorganizing the *kumotsu* offerings. The transformation of the Yamamoto memorial shows how such memorials can symbolize the survival of family and community ties after the disaster.

Another memorial, in the hamlet of Tategemori in Tarō, another formerly independent township now incorporated into Miyako city, corresponds to resident Sasaki Akira's lost family members. Before the tsunami, his wife Emiko left the building of the fishing cooperative to take their seven year old grandson Fūta home from elementary school. They were swept away by the tsunami, a block down the road from the schoolyard. Akira explains that rescue workers found Emiko days later covered in sludge that he called 'blue oil' (*aoi abura*), and it took two days' work by three people to clean up the body. He has routinely placed flowers, fruits and refreshments at that site in remembrance of his loved ones. He said his plan was to place offerings at this site along the road on the eleventh day of each month and during *shōgatsu* (the New Year holiday season) for the first year after the disaster (Sasaki Akira, personal communication). After the first year, he would continue to place offerings there twice a year because, as he says, 'I will never forget this place' (*kono basho o wasure-nai*). He planned to make similar offerings at both his family's plot at the cemetery run by the Jō'un Temple and at his family's altar at home. The latter was surrounded by gifts, such as a water heater and several wrapped boxes for Emiko and toys for Fūta, nine months after the tsunami. His efforts tie together his personal loss with those of others through religious activities – and not just locally. He also made a trip with some other Tohoku people across the disaster areas along the coast to participate in a memorial service for victims of the Hanshin earthquake in Kobe. There he was interviewed by the media, and openly discussed his personal loss, though adding that 'few people can understand our circumstances' (*Asahi Shinbun*, 17 January 2012).

Akira's roadside memorial has been a welcomed presence in the neighbourhood, and others sometimes added their own offerings alongside his. The Morimoto family owns a grocery store opposite Akira's memorial, and they keep flowers in stock for Akira and others after tirelessly working to reopen their store. Priest Takahashi Eisei of the Jō'un Temple has also been in close contact with Akira during this time. He held a memorial service (*hōyō*) on 31 December 2011, during which Akira and his neighbours remembered their lost ones. He even organized services during O-Bon, regardless that his temple sheltered 300 people during the tsunami and housed 80 people for a month. As a pivotal figure in the community, Takahashi believes 'there is no going back to the days before the tsunami' (*tsunami no mae ni modoranai*) and that the recovery is a day-to-day process of cleaning up and moving forward (Takahashi personal communication). However, he said that he did not feel much stress throughout the time since the disaster, having been helped by listening to the music of Eric Clapton in his temple.

Debris and relics

The clean-up of Tarō has been difficult because most of the houses were close to the sea walls designed to protect the community from tsunamis, and were destroyed when the walls were breached on 3.11. Evacuees must travel a considerable distance to get to Tarō from the temporary housing complexes. Residents whose homes are still habitable struggle to make repairs. Sasaki Eiji, for example, finds the recovery phase to be isolating (Sasaki Eiji, personal communication). He and his wife walk their dog through the ruins every evening, but few neighbours remain with whom they can converse. After 3.11, little remained standing in Tarō, so landmarks were hard to find. A half-metre tall statue of Kannon, the bodhisattva of mercy, stood amid the wreckage beside the tsunami wall in the hamlet of Kawamuki in Tarō, perhaps retrieved by the Self-Defence Forces. People could make coin offerings and say a prayer at this site, as at the nearby Jō'un Temple. Resident Harako Chōichi recognizes the spiritual importance of this statue located a few blocks from his old house. He explains how residents of Tarō, soldiers in charge of the clean-up, and volunteers alike can all pray to Kannon (Harako, personal communication). The difference between relics and debris found in the communities across the disaster zone is complicated. Some scholars (e.g. Boyd and Williams 2005; Namihira 1987) have noted a loose relationship between 'clean' and 'polluted' objects. The location and arrangement of this statue of Kannon can show someone's choice to distinguish it from the rubble, suggesting that its meaning is interpreted through this choice and by the coin offerings left in front of it. As with the memorials described above, however, this relic was used only as a temporary memorial during the clean-up and later was properly disposed of by local volunteers.

The tsunami upended gravestones at the cemetery next to the Dewa Shrine located near the wharf of Tarō. Several of these gravestones were positioned upright among the group while the shrine and cemetery were in disrepair. Two flower vases (*hanatate*) marked the front of this group while a toy rested upon a broken stone, creating a triangular composition with the vases at the base and the toy at the top. This toy was a doll version of Hamtaro, the well-known animé hamster. Arranging this toy with the vases and gravestones creates a memorial that a person may use to pray for the dead. The toy, therefore, functions as a votive statue. There may even be a hinted play on words, with Tarō being part of the cartoon character's name as well as the name of the locality.

Toys, dolls and stuffed animals often feature in ad-hoc disaster memorials. One worshipper at the Jōan Temple at Miyako, for example, placed a Winnie the Pooh doll beside an altar venerating the arhat known in Japanese as Binzuru – in Buddhist mythology, one of the four enlightened ones who asked to remain behind on Earth to continue the Buddha's teachings. The tenderness of this doll contrasts with the intense stare of the arhat, but the juxtaposition is fitting because the Japanese believe that Binzuru has healing powers and watches over the health of babies (Frédéric 1995: 101–102). Stuffed dolls were found elsewhere in Miyako before the demolition was finished. A couple of dolls were placed at the entrance of the Kanasawa residence located in Minatomachi district. Several mementos such as a photo of a high school athletic team and student registration cards were also placed on the central axis of the entrance, allowing people to feel that they had accessed an inner sanctum located among the ruins of their neighbourhood.

During the demolition phase in coastal cities across Iwate prefecture, clean-up crews left alone objects in destroyed houses that might hold personal symbolism. Photo albums and family documents often would be placed in baskets and left to the discretion of family members and religious organizations. Sorting through the debris to find symbolic objects is exhausting, and some people were unable to retrieve these mementos. Ogasawara Takahiro and his family, who moved to Morioka, the prefectural capital of Iwate, after the tsunami, left behind everything at their old house in the Kōganji district of Miyako except a statue of Kannon. They told me of the difficulty of seeing the remnants of their household after living there for 14 years (Ogasawara, personal communication). The objects left behind at the site of their destroyed home, were considered not as discarded junk but as symbolic of their lives before the tsunami. Leaving behind their old crockery in what used to be the kitchen and dining area, furthermore, can be interpreted as one way of worshiping the *kami* of the house (Ishino 1992: 199). The volunteers of shrine associations cleared a portion of the remains from these homesites by mid-July, but many ceramic utensils were left resting upon the foundations even seven months after the tsunami. These objects, according to Hamazaki Makoto, an elderly local volunteer, must eventually be burned because the *kami* disapprove of trash due to its impurity (Hamazaki, personal communication). This impurity, he argued, was the result of death, decay and destruction brought by the tsunami. The dismantling of these memorials was inevitable, but volunteers from shrine associations like the Yokoyama Hachiman Shrine in Miyako had to handle the objects with great care before they were incinerated. But these considerations slowed down the post-tsunami clean-up. Professor Hashimoto explained that six months on from 3.11, local municipalities were becoming impatient with the mass of people's unclaimed possessions (Hashimoto, personal communication). As of September 2011, he was searching for temporary storage places for these possessions so that people could return to reclaim them if they wanted. Otherwise, he planned on storing as many of the objects as possible at the Misawa Aviation Museum. Otherwise, they were at risk of being dumped in landfills across Japan.

The improvised memorials at wrecked houses organize the devastated landscape so that people may access these sites to make offerings and remembrances. Hamazaki Makoto, furthermore, considers them to be private temples (Hamazaki, personal communication). Many homesites display bottles of alcohol recovered from the debris and used as offerings, as well as other objects such as rusted tools that can be considered slightly less orthodox offerings. Such offerings and the household *kami* Daikokuten were found at the Akanuma household in Lower Kuwagasaki district. Underneath these objects, however, was a pile of adult magazines left undisturbed by the clean-up crews. These magazines, rather than being immediately discarded, were left at the homesite for nearly four months because of their significance to the deceased homeowner. While adult magazines might seem to violate the holiness of this site, sacred and profane 'are not seen as categorical opposites in Japanese society' (Nelson 1996: 148). Scholars, moreover, have shown a close link in the past between shrine festivals, female shamans and prostitution (Hori 1985; Nakayama 1993). The adult magazines among the offerings found at the Akanuma household, evidently, were considered as part of the memorial rather than a violation of sanctity. Otherwise, clean-up crews would have quickly disposed of them in the massive dump at the nearby Rias Harbour.

The religious culture of Japan values individual expression, as seen by the shrines built in the disaster areas. These shrines are poignant and heartfelt, but another form of expression at the Sannōiwa rock formation at Tarō may strike some as vandalism. This park is famous for three massive cretaceous rocks that give good luck to visitors. Someone had spray-painted the graffito '*Ganbarō Tarō*!' (Come on Tarō!) on a wall beside the sidewalk. The park had been closed since the tsunami heavily damaged it, but someone felt compelled to mark the site with an encouraging slogan. The graffito may seem to deface the park, but then again, Japanese people have written inscriptions at spiritual sites throughout history. The graffito expresses the same wishes we found written in the worship register of the Kuromori Shrine. Inscriptions at spiritual sites permit individuals to express their identity and prayers. The graffito at Sannōiwa, therefore, should be perceived as a sign of support rather than vandalism. In the wharf nearby the park, further evidence suggesting that whoever wrote this inscription wishes for the recovery of this community is the graffito 'I love' written at the wharf of Tarō, a few metres away from the rock formation.

Conclusion

3.11 has brought challenges to religious practice in communities struggling with loss, economic troubles, and destroyed infrastructure. Religious practice and ceremonial performances are integral to culture in the Sanriku area, as seen through entries in the worship register at the Kuromori Shrine in Miyako. Interacting with the *kami* of this shrine was an immediate response to the earthquake. People repeatedly visited this shrine during the aftermath of the tsunami, expressing their prayers and wishes during a stressful time. On 7 September, Suzuki Akimi returned to Miyako and wrote 'I visited because I was worried about the shrine, but I am relieved to find no sign of damage from the disaster. I will pray and then return to my own home'.[7] She was probably someone who had left Miyako before the disaster, whose desire to worship brought her back. People also express their hopes for recovery through events sponsored by religious organizations, often in tandem with secular associations. The Sansa Odori held in Morioka from 1–5 August 2011, for example, brought together corporations, student organizations, and Shinto associations. This festival, which is based upon the myth that the deity Mitsuishi banished a demon from Morioka, both celebrated local customs and gave encouragement to people affected by 3.11. The Dream Lantern festival, held in Miyako on the evening of 28 August, was a newly devised ceremony, a candlelight vigil during which people prayed for the repose of souls. Tokyo residents Fujinuma Kazunori and Fumiko made four lanterns out of old drink cartons for the festival and wrote messages on them expressing their prayers for the recovery and prosperity of Miyako. These lanterns, according to the regional newspaper *Iwate Nippō* (29 August 2011), 'float up into the darkness carrying prayers for recovery'.[8]

Many observers have found it paradoxical that although Japan has so many religious institutions, most Japanese people say they are non-religious when surveyed on the subject.[9] What does 3.11 tell us about Japanese religious attitudes? A Japanese proverb says that 'people turn to the gods in times of crisis'.[10] Many escaped to Shinto shrines and Buddhist temples during the disaster, though one could argue that they were motivated by survival since these sites often stand above residential areas – indeed, many are designated evacuation sites. At the same time, identities of the devastated communities are often based upon affiliations with these shrines and temples. Some of the religious sites affected by the disaster will be lost because people are wary of rebuilding in their old neighbourhoods. This may eventually threaten the link between civil and religious society.

7   *Shinpai de tazunete mimashita. Shinsai no eikyō nai yō de hotto shimashita. Sanpai shite kaerasete itadakimasu.*
8   *Fukkō e no negai o kome, yami ni ukabi agaru.*
9   See for example Ama (2005), a translation of his bestselling Japanese book (Ama 1996).
10 *Kurushii toki no kami-danomi.*

But the disaster shed light on personal, as well as communal, aspects of Japanese religiosity. Many victims of the disaster devised their own memorials. Sometimes they had no choice because local religious centres had been destroyed; but in other cases the personal memorial seemed to be a preferred choice. These personal memorials attempt to make sense of the disaster by altering chaotic spaces to include memories of the family or community.

'New religions' might have been expected to attract converts at this time of sudden loss, when people might seek new religious symbolization to find comfort in the disaster. In fact they seem to have struggled. The death, destruction, and displacement brought by the tsunami were major impediments to participation in communal religious activities. Kudō Toshinori, from the Tenrikyō church in Sokei district, still believes that the *kami*, rather than fleeing from the tsunami, are active in the affected communities both during and after the crisis. He explains that 'the *kami* saved us' (*kamisama ni tasukatta*) from the disaster (Kudō, personal communication). While this is obviously not the case for the 20,000 people who were killed, it does show the resilience of religious belief *in extremis*.

People living throughout Japan are having soul-searching conversations about 3.11. Tokyo governor Ishihara Shintarō was perhaps the only Japanese public figure to opine openly that the disaster was 'divine punishment' (*tenbatsu*) for the corruption of modern society, although similar comments were made by several foreign commentators.[11] No-one in the disaster area would openly express such a belief. Despite the scale of the disaster, the existential question 'why?' was not posed. No-one seemed to blame or question religious institutions. Their role was social, not philosophical, their job to restore social cohesion by defending and reviving the reassuring traditions and rituals that give people a sense of communal continuity even in the face of such a brutal interruption as this one.

---

11   See for example this ABC news item from 18 March 2011: <http://abcnews.go.com/
      Politics/japan-earthquake-tsunami-divine-retribution-natural-disaster-religious/
      story?id=13167670#.Txietvn7-No> accessed 10 June 2013.

For example, the Kurosaki Shrine Association in Miyako regrouped and held its annual festival on 10 June 2012 with help from performers from the Kuromori Kagura. Local fishermen, business owners and administrators from the neighbourhood schools all participated in prayer ceremonies held at the shrine complex, which had been inundated by debris that washed ashore a year before. This festival and one held in Tsugaruishi district of Miyako on 16 August 2012, included parading the *kami* in their portable shrines called *mikoshi* through neighbourhoods affected by the tsunami. High school and middle school students from Tsugaruishi performed traditional songs and dances during their first festival since the disaster.[12] These festivals are encouraging signs that communities in Tohoku are rebounding. Ritual practice, rather than theological doctrine, is what makes religion of continued relevance to these communities.

References

Abrams, James (1977). 'Hail in the Begging Bowl: The Odyssey and Poetry of Santoka', *Monumenta Nipponica*, 32(3), 269–302.

Akima Toshio (1982). 'The Songs of the Dead: Poetry, Drama, and Ancient Death Rituals of Japan', *Journal of Asian Studies*, 41(3), 485–509.

Ama Toshimaru (1996). *Nihonjin wa naze mushūkyō na no ka?* (Why are the Japanese non-religious?) Tokyo: Chikuma Shobō.

—— (2005). *Why Are the Japanese Non-religious? Japanese Spirituality: Being Non-religious in a Religious Culture*. Lanham, MD: University Press of America.

Berleant, Arnold (1992). *The Aesthetics of Environment*. Philadelphia: Temple University Press.

12   Videos of these performances and others such as the *Toramai* performed in Kamaishi are posted on YouTube by a blogger calling himself asaproabe. <http://www.youtube.com/user/asaproabe> accessed 10 June 2013. His blog in Japanese describes his efforts to create a library of Shinto dances and other folk arts. See <http://okuderazeki.at.webry.info> accessed 10 June 2013.

Boyd, James W., and Ron G. Williams (2005). 'Interpretation of a Priestly Perspective', *Philosophy East and West*, 55(1), 33–63.

Frédéric, Louis (1995). *Buddhism: Flammarion Iconographic Guides*. New York: Flammarion.

Hori Ichirō (1985). *Waga kuni minkan-shikō-shi no kenkyū* (Research on the history of folkloric thought in Japan). Tokyo: Tōkyō Sōgensha.

Ishino Hironobu (1992). 'Rites and Rituals of the Kofun Period', *Japanese Journal of Religious Studies*, 19(2/3), 191–216.

Isomae Jun'ichi (2005). 'Deconstructing "Japanese Religion": A Historical Survey', *Japanese Journal of Religious Studies*, 32(2), 235–248.

Kaniasty, Krzysztof, and Fran H. Norris (1995). 'Mobilization and Deterioration of Social Support following Natural Disasters', *Current Directions in Psychological Science*, 4(3), 94–98.

Nakayama Tarō (1993). *Nihon Miko-shi* (History of shrine maidens in Japan). Tokyo: Parutosu-sha.

Namihira Emiko (1987). 'Pollution in the Folk Belief System', *Current Anthropology*, 28(4) 65–74.

Nelson, John (1996). 'Freedom of Expression: The Very Modern Practice of Visiting a Shinto Shrine', *Japanese Journal of Religious Studies*, 23(1/2) 117–153.

——(2000). *Enduring Identities: The Guise of Shinto in Contemporary Japan*. Honolulu: University of Hawaii Press.

Ohnuki-Tierney, Emiko (1987). *The Monkey as Mirror: Symbolic Transformations in Japanese History and Ritual*. Princeton: Princeton University Press.

Philippi, Donald (1968). *Kojiki*. Tokyo: University of Tokyo Press.

Stallings, Robert A. (2002). 'Weberian Political Sociology and Sociological Disaster Studies', *Sociological Forum*, 17(2) 281–305.

Tada Michitarō (1983). 'Oku no kankaku' (The interior feeling). In Ueda Atsushi, Tada Michitarō and Nakaoka Yoshisuke (eds), *Kūkan no genkei: Sumai ni okeru sei no hikaku bunka* (Archetypes of space: Comparative culture of sacredness in residence), pp. 423–434. Tokyo: Chikuma Shobō.

Thomson, Charisma (2011). 'Roadside Memorials (Re)presented', *Anthropology News*, online edition. <http://www.anthropology-news.org/index.php/2011/09/14/roadside-memorials-\represented> accessed 3 October 2011. (Now archived and requires subscription).

JOHANNES WILHELM AND ALYNE DELANEY

No Homes, No Boats, No Rafts:
Miyagi Coastal People in the Aftermath of Disaster[1]

Introduction

This chapter explores the plight of two coastal fishing communities in Miyagi prefecture, as well as reconstruction efforts in the local fishery industry. We show how these people have been reconstructing their livelihoods in the wake of the tsunami that devastated the Sanriku coast on 11 March 2011. We are particularly interested in showing how governmental policies have evolved to aid them in their return to productive lives. The aftermath of the tsunami, and the new policies drafted in response, together constitute the new realities of life on the Miyagi coastline.

In some cases, the government moved relatively quickly after the disasters to set up programmes to aid fishers and their families. As we will show, such programmes included providing money to fishing cooperatives in payment for part-time work cleaning up the dock and harbour areas. In other cases, however, attempted changes in laws by politicians have left locals frustrated and confused, without any clear indication of what the future holds for them; this includes possible changes to fishing rights as well as changes limiting where people may be allowed to live.

1   This paper was written after fieldtrips by Delaney in Shichigahama (October 2011), and by Wilhelm in Ishinomaki (Ogatsu town and Yoriiso district), Kesennuma (Karakuwa town) and in Sendai (21 July to 30 August 2011, September 2012 and February 2013). We appreciate the generosity of the Austrian Research Association (ÖFG) for funding parts of our travel expenses. Alyne Delaney thanks the people of Shichigahama and Johannes Wilhelm thanks the people of Yoriiso, Ogatsu and Karakuwa for their kind cooperation under extreme stress.

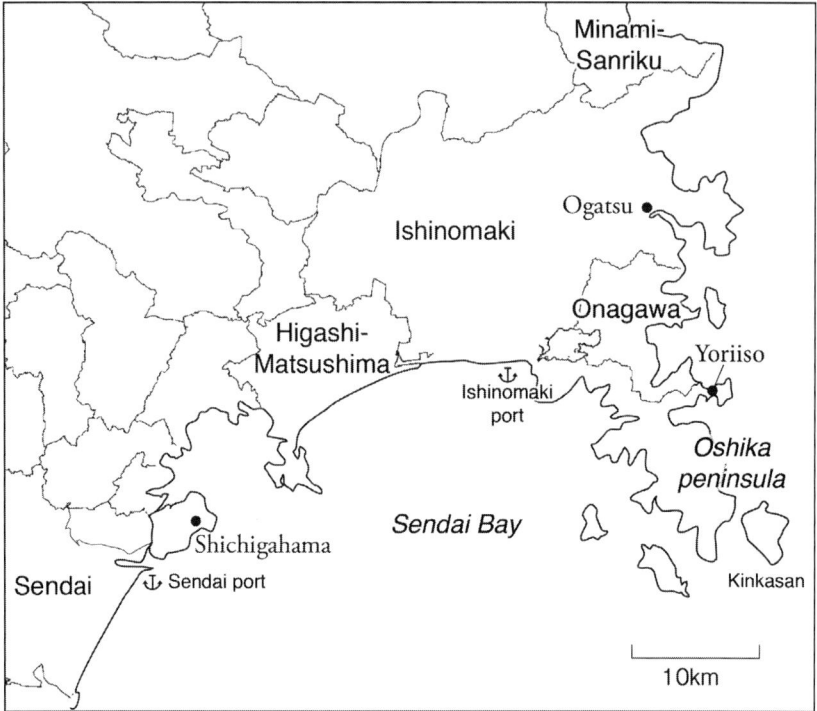

Figure 1 Map of Sendai bay and the Oshika peninsula showing locations of Shichigahama, Yoriiso and Ogatsu. Reprinted and translated from Gill et al., *Higashi Nihon daishinsai no Jinruigaku* (Jinbun Shoin, 2013), p. 332.

With a population of 20,000, Shichigahama is the smallest town (*machi*) in Miyagi in land area and is located just southeast of Shiogama, one of Miyagi's most important ports, and less than twenty kilometres from downtown Sendai. Shichigahama has both scenic, pine-covered hills and long, sandy beaches, making it popular with tourists. The name literally means 'Seven Beaches'; Shichigahama was created out of seven communities with beaches (*hama*) in 1889, being upgraded to a town in 1959. In terms of industry, the cultivation of *nori*[2] seaweed is the most important

---

2   *Nori* (*Porphyra* spp.) is a seaweed known particularly in the Western world as a wrapper for sushi rolls.

harvest, followed by flounder, abalone, shellfish and other fish species. In recent years, part of the town has turned into a dormitory town for commuters to Sendai, though the coastal neighbourhoods remain populated primarily by traditional fishing households.

Yoriiso, on the other hand, is a small settlement in a steep valley southeast of the Onagawa nuclear power plant (NPP) marking the northern tip of Samenoura bay on the eastern side of the Oshika peninsula. Since 2005 a part of Ishinomaki City, the settlement has approximately 400 people living in just under a hundred households. Agriculture in Yoriiso is impractical because of the harsh topography in this area. Consequently, fisheries, especially the cultivation of sea squirt[3] and scallop, have been the main source of income for local residents.

Shichigahama and Yoriiso (see Figure 1) are part of an important fishing region on the Sanriku coast.[4] That importance stems primarily from location: the warm, southern Kuroshio current crosses with the cold, northern Oyashio current here, making the waters off the coast of Miyagi extremely rich in marine resources. Another specific feature of Miyagi's shoreline is the divide in coastal fisheries between the sandy shore south of Shichigahama and the rocky shore in the north that is suited for cultivation of marine products like seaweed (especially *nori* and *wakame*), oyster, sea squirt and scallop. Yoriiso, on the other hand, represents a small, remote fishery settlement like many others along the devastated coastline of Sanriku. A structural characteristic of Sanriku's fishery sector is the predominance of aquaculture that is conducted inside the *ria* bays[5] along the craggy coast. These aquaculture activities, as in Shichigahama,

---

3   This species, *Halocynthia roretzi*, is known as *hoya* in Japanese and popularly called 'sea pineapple', too. It is eaten raw or cooked and is an ingredient of Korean *kimchi*.

4   Sanriku, literally 'three countries', refers to the three former provinces Mutsu, Rikuchū and Rikuzen which existed for a short period during the political and administrational time of unrest at the beginning of the Meiji period. The area focussed upon in this paper corresponds to northern Rikuzen as used in Wakamori (1969) and, the term Sanriku is used in a broader sense, i.e., a cultural area between Sendai (Miyagi) and Same (Aomori) as defined in Takimoto and Nasukawa (2004: 2–4).

5   *Ria* are narrow coastal inlets that were formed by submergence of riverine beds. Unlike fjords they were not formed by glaciers and are shallower and smaller.

are mostly operated by fishing families involving women's labour as well as men's (see Delaney 2011). About half of Miyagi's fishing population is over sixty years of age, so the 'greying' of the workforce is another severe structural problem in this sector. The 12th Fishery Census (2008) found that in Ishinomaki, 58 per cent of fishermen were over the age of 60 and only 3 per cent were under the age of 40. Wilhelm's field sites of Ogatsu and Yoriiso are formerly independent fishing villages, now incorporated into Ishinomaki, and they show even more dramatic ageing patterns. As for Delaney's field site of Shichigahama, 68 per cent were over 60 and only 1 per cent under the age of 40.

Delaney first began interviewing the wives of local fishing cooperative (FCA) members in 1991 and wrote a doctoral thesis discussing the connection between the health of the marine environment and the ways social ties became important for accessing marine resources (Delaney 2003). Wilhelm started fieldwork in Sanriku in 1998, focusing on fishery use rights among seaweed collectors. Later, his interest shifted towards the historical roots of informal institutions on the Pacific side of the Oshika peninsula and other places along the coast of Sanriku (Wilhelm 2009). Our history of working in this maritime region provided us with good connections and rapport with those directly impacted by the disasters, but also deeply affected us personally: we had worked and lived with people who later lived through the tsunami, and also with some who perished in it. Delaney's first trip to Shichigahama resulted in her breaking down in tears in the Shōbutahama neighbourhood. Though she knew what to expect, it was a completely different experience to be in such a familiar neighbourhood, and see absolutely nothing left; homes of friends had been swept away, leaving only the concrete foundations. Everything was gone, and all signs of life had been swept away, as if no one had ever lived in what was in fact once a lively neighbourhood.

Thus, in this chapter, we build upon our knowledge of the industries, politics and social networks in Shichigahama and Yoriiso, focusing on the impacts of government policies appear to have on the rebuilding of lives in coastal Miyagi prefecture.

Dimensions of disaster

Miyagi's coastal fisheries were most severely impacted by the tsunami of 11 March 2011. Nine out of ten fishing vessels were lost in the prefecture – 12,000 out of 13,500 boats. Some 452 members of Miyagi's Fishing Cooperative Association (FCA), Japan Fisheries (JF) Miyagi, lost their lives. More than 6,000 members' homes were destroyed or damaged – nearly two-thirds of the total. Moreover 162 processing facilities, 57,886 aquacultural rafts and 831 set-nets were washed away or destroyed, while aquaculture facilities for seaweed, oyster, sea squirt and scallop were completely destroyed (Funato 2011: 1).

In addition, the whole Pacific coastline sank up to 1.2 metres and moved about 5.3 metres eastward (Seibidō Shuppan Henshū-bu 2011: 19), leaving many fishing ports and landing piers under water. Most fishermen thus faced difficulties resuming their work although the majority (80 per cent) were in favour of returning to fishing and their former way of life.[6]

Another challenge was the incredible amount of debris in the water. Operating motorboats – in those few cases where boats are available – was difficult and sometimes dangerous given the high risk of becoming entangled in ropes and wires which were swept into the sea by the tsunami. Professional divers did their best to take apart and dismantle underwater debris at main ports such as in Rikuzen-Takata. After supper in one of the few inns that was open (on 23 August 2011 in Tsumoto at the tip of the Karakuwa peninsula), one of these divers said:

> There is lots of work for us below the water surface. ... Sometimes we spot clothes – a pair of trousers and a shirt pinned between some bigger stuff, and we know, those are *hotoke* (literally, a Buddhist spirit; hence, a dead person).

6   <http://www.kahoku.co.jp/spe/spe_sys1062/20110529_17.htm> accessed 29 May 2011.

Hatakeyama Shigeatsu, an oyster cultivator and founder of the famed Japanese ecological movement *Mori wa Umi no Koibito* (The forest is longing for the sea, the sea is longing for the forest) said in an interview at his home in Higashi-Mōne bay (Karakuwa peninsula, 24 August 2011):

> This catastrophe was the sort of thing that happens once in a thousand years, and we have to cope with that situation. ... Nobody blames the sea, and she is recovering well. However, I am concerned about possible effects of the incidents at Fukushima nuclear power plant on marine coastal fisheries ..., too. *Fūhyō-higai* (damage by rumour), you know what I mean ...?

The fears and rumours surrounding the safety of marine products after the Fukushima meltdown are referred to by many as the 'fourth disaster'. The safety of marine products was and remains a major concern for the fisherman in the disaster area along the Pacific coast. But there were many more practical and pressing things they had to cope with first, such as their day-to-day survival.

Some Miyagi fishermen left their communities immediately after the disaster, but returned several weeks later in an attempt to resume their traditional livelihood. However, they faced many challenges. One of the most contentious was the proposal to relocate settlements to higher ground. Though this plan was advocated by construction authorities, local municipal authorities could not develop final development plans because of issues with land property rights and planned modifications in construction laws at the time of writing. This issue looms especially large for communities in Sanriku, where building land is scarce.

One neighbourhood in Shichigahama has been completely cleaned up after the tsunami, down to bare foundations, yet no rebuilding has taken place yet. Here the land has sunk, leaving the area below sea level. Ms Wada described how some residents of this neighbourhood evacuated to a hilltop outside her home. As they watched the waves crash in, destroying all the homes below, she realized with horror that the hillside they were standing upon was not high enough to protect them. 'I yelled for everyone to run, to run away higher up the hill. But no one moved. Not one. They just stood still'. Neighbours and three of her family members were caught in the waves. Though her family miraculously survived being overrun by the waves, several of her neighbours died.

The surviving residents of the neighbourhood moved in with family members, into temporary housing, or into apartments outside the town borders. The new housing has great advantages over the cramped shelter conditions lacking privacy, and is especially well appreciated in Yoriiso, where temporary housing was not available until mid-September, so that people endured shelter life for far longer than in most parts of the disaster zone. But the way temporary housing units were allocated had the effect of tearing apart many coastal communities socially. A concern to give everyone an equal chance of getting rehoused early prompted local authorities to use a lottery system to allocate temporary housing. However, this meant that little or no attention was put to old neighbourhood structures; former neighbours ended up living far apart from each other and people could thus not rely on old neighbourhood support networks. Some people from little coastal hamlets, such as from the Pacific eastern coast of the Oshika peninsula, were moved to more urban areas up to 20 kilometres inland. This made it nearly impossible for them to fix things in their home settlements regularly, not least since many cars had been destroyed and in some cases roads had to be rebuilt or restored.

Long after the disaster, many still did not know the whereabouts or safety of acquaintances. On 20 October 2011, a young woman called Wagatsuma-san drove out with Delaney to see an area of Oku-Matsushima they had visited together ten years previously. During the drive she said she had not yet gone to see the area as she was afraid to know the truth. As they drove into the area, she said,

> Just as I feared, ah, there's nothing left. The guest-house was here, remember? With all those other houses ... and now there is absolutely nothing at all. Now I cannot find my friend; I no longer have his phone number and I do not know where he could be, or if he is all right.

Looking out over the destruction, she added,

> You know, 'unthinkable' is no longer a phrase in my vocabulary.

In Shichigahama, the peak wave of over 12 metres flooded almost one-third of the town. Though the town is quite hilly, over 1,000 homes were destroyed or severely damaged in the tsunami and another 3,000 moderately damaged. Almost a hundred residents died and over 6,000 were evacuated and living in shelters – in thirty-six different locations and with the aid of twenty independent disaster prevention groups. A useful account of events was published at an online news-site of Shichigama's sister city in the US, Plymouth Massachusetts (Mand 2012). Over a year later, the clean-up continues in Shichigahama. Further north on the Sanriku coast, Yoriiso remained the only bay-side settlement at the bay of Samenoura that was halfway spared by the tsunami due to its steep topography (similar to that of Shichigahama). In Ogatsu, however, the town's former centre was completely destroyed. Only settlements on higher ground around it, such as Mizuhama, had any buildings survive the disasters.

Recovery and reconstruction strategies

Within months, the Japanese government launched recovery efforts such as rebuilding infrastructure and buildings, and providing employment and income for those affected. As this section highlights, some of these policies and programmes have been a great help for locals trying to rebuild their lives; others, however, have left people frustrated and confused.

In Miyagi prefecture's reconstruction plan for fisheries, a part of the prefecture's reconstruction master plan, reconstruction is expected to take ten years (see Table 1). These ten years are divided into three step-by-step phases: the restoration phase (*fukkyū-ki*; three years, i.e. 2011 to 2013), the regeneration phase (*saisei-ki*; four years, i.e. 2014 to 2017), and the development phase (three years, i.e. 2018 to 2020). Each of these phases have specific objectives, such as removal of debris and *ad hoc* restoration of port facilities and fishing gear in the first phase emergency measures, while full-scale rebuilding of port facilities are planned during the second phase (Miyagi Prefecture 2011: 3).

Table 1 Reconstruction plan for Miyagi's fisheries

Restoration (3 years; 2011–2013)	Regeneration (4 years; 2014–2017)	Development (3 years; 2018–2020)
Reorganization and temporary reinstallation of harbours and landing facilities	Permanent reinstallation of harbours and landing facilities	Support for integration of 'base harbours' and 'collection harbours' through improved infrastructure
Cleaning up debris	Reorganization of releasing game*	Support of local, autonomous resource management
Emergency measures in aquaculture	Support to stabilize the fishing sector based on a reorganization of fishing licenses and rights	Consolidation of companies through product development
Provision of vessels, gear and fry; reinstallation of farming facilities	Consolidation of companies through mergers	Increased revival of municipal fishery areas
Emergency measures for cooling facilities and markets	Improvement and development of aquaculture facilities	Support of scientific fishery research
Introduction of new organizational structures	Reinstallation of markets and cooling facilities	Adaptation to situation at Fukushima No.1 NPP
Resumption of scientific research institutions	Adaptation to situation at Fukushima No.1 NPP	
Adaptation to situation at Fukushima No.1 NPP		

Source: Miyagi Prefecture (2011: 3). Spellings corrected from original document.
* This refers to release into the sea of fry (in case of fish) or small scallop or stones with *wakame*-spores etc. to cultivate them.

However, a number of problems arise immediately, as we can see in the discourse regarding 'special zones for reconstruction of fisheries' in the following section.

Recovery: Fisheries rights

Miyagi Governor Murai Yoshihiro, a former Self Defence Force (SDF) helicopter pilot, announced the idea of these special zones[7] (*tokku*) at the fourth meeting of the 'Earthquake Reconstruction Design Council' (ERDP) on 10 May 2011.[8] The initial idea was to simplify administrative priorities when assigning sectoral fishing rights. Opening these fishing rights up to outsiders would shift the assignment of sectoral fishing rights from local fisheries cooperative associations (FCA) to people who had no historical connection with the local fisheries. The idea was to encourage outsiders to bring in much-needed capital for rebuilding. Murai's initiative, however, was poorly prepared: he failed to consult with the local fisheries cooperative – JF Miyagi[9] – in advance of the meeting, which led to strong opposition by FCA members, who collected the signatures of 14,000 fishermen against the *tokku* plan. Fisheries *tokku* were included in the National Reconstruction Plan, but negotiations between the government and JF Miyagi have led to on-going opposition so far.

An important structural issue surrounding the *tokku* plan is the fact that sectorial fishery-use rights, good for five-year periods, were allocated in 2008, meaning the earliest point in time these new *tokku* rights could be put into practice would be in September 2013. Thus when implemented, it would actually be far too late for them to legitimately be considered as aid for immediate reconstruction, but would instead appear to be a backdoor change in the laws in the name of disaster relief. As of May 2013, only

---

7   These are commonly referred as *suisan tokku* (fisheries special zones) or *suisan-gyō fukkō tokku* (fishery industry reconstruction special zones). They are separate from the far broader program of *fukkō tokubetsu kuiki* (reconstruction special zones) or *fukkō tokku*, which cover 222 municipalities in eleven prefectures.

8   Earthquake Reconstruction Design Council (ERDC, *Higashi-Nihon daishinsai fukkō kōsō kaigi*) held its first meeting on 14 April 2011. Note that the 16 members of the main council included no fishery experts, and 19 members of the advisory board included just one – Baba Osamu, a professor at Tokyo University of Marine Science and Technology. <http://www.cas.go.jp/jp/fukkou/pdf/kousei.pdf> accessed 18 August 2013.

9   Japan Fisheries Miyagi, or *Miyagi-ken Gyogyō Kyōdō Kumai*.

one group of fishermen in Momonoura (on the western side of Oshika peninsula, Ishinomaki) had decided to introduce *tokku*.[10] If the *tokku* of Momonoura remains the only one realized by September 2013, no more can be created until 2018 when Miyagi's Sea-Area Adjustment Commission (*Kaiku gyogyō chōsei i'inkai*) will assign new fishery zones for the next time. In this sense, the clash of opinions during the introduction of *tokku* can be characterized as a ghost-debate that probably hindered the prefectural fishery administration's ability to focus on more relevant issues.

Miyagi's Reconstruction Plan for Fisheries, published in October 2011, states that 'Fishery special zones are a subject that will be adjusted by thorough discussions with fishermen and FCAs' (Miyagi Prefecture 2011: 6). Contentious debates escalated during the appointment of members for the Sea-Area Adjustment Commission in the summer of 2012. This powerful commission, whose members are chosen from administrators, fishermen etc., is responsible for the final assignment of fishing rights, territories and seasonal restrictions.[11]

Recovery: Fisheries infrastructure

Unlike the fisheries law talks, a programme to finance reconstruction in fisheries has developed smoothly. This scheme is a part of the 12 trillion yen Third Supplementary Budget which was submitted by the Cabinet to Parliament on 28 October 2011 and passed on 21 November 2011.

---

10 An informant whose family had been involved in the local fishery industry in Ishinomaki said: 'There are rumours that the introduction of the only special zone so far in Momonoura has been arranged between Murai and a good friend of his just to protect Murai's face in public over his futile efforts regarding *tokku*. Those guys in Momonoura do this just for show (*omote muki ni*), even they actually do not expect any benefits' (Ishinomaki, 21 September 2012).

11 A detailed outline and comparison of reconstruction plans in Miyagi and Iwate prefectures is provided by Wilhelm (2013).

This programme provides payments to rebuild fisheries following specific rules for several kinds of operators, gradually decreasing over several years as they return to independent operating. For example, one cooperative group of four *nori* cultivators in Shichigahama expected a deficit of 10 million yen in 2012 and 5 million yen in 2013. The government promised 9 million yen in 2012 and 4.5 million yen in 2012, while the four cultivators had to come up with 1 million yen (2012) and 500,000 yen (2013) through interest-free loans provided by the government (Japan Finance Corporation, JFC) and cooperative banks (JF Marine Bank).[12] The total amount earmarked for fishery reconstruction in the third supplementary budget was put at 499 billion yen as of November 2011.[13]

Recovery: Employment

Aside from these specific plans which are only available to certain groups meeting certain conditions, how can the affected fishermen generally make their living without a fishing income? Even in cases were fishing was part-time, seasonal work, it still provided vital income for families and fishers. Moreover, job opportunities outside the fishing industry were extremely rare along the Pacific coast after the disaster. Little more than half of local companies reopened in the first three months.[14] Local towns and cities currently face the difficult task of creating job opportunities to prevent people from leaving the area.

12   A full outline of reconstruction is provided by the Fishery Agency: <http://www. jfa.maff.go.jp/j/budget/23_hosei/dai3ji.html> accessed 5 November 2011. A simplified outline for fishermen can be downloaded here: <http://www.jfa.maff.go.jp/j/yosan/23/pdf/zenbun2_2.pdf> accessed 5 November 2011.

13   <http://www.jfa.maff.go.jp/j/budget/23_hosei/pdf/3jiyosan_gaiyo.pdf> accessed 12 August 2012.

14   <http://www.zaikei.co.jp/article/20110708/75608.html> accessed 3 July 2011.

One attempt to provide jobs for fishermen was a temporary support system to remove and collect debris from their fishing grounds, a kind of self-help programme for fishing villages financed by local governments. To apply for this program, at least five fishermen had to join together. Upon successful application, each member was paid a daily salary of 12,100 yen. Monetary support to rent vessels was provided (21,000 to 92,500 yen depending on tonnage of the vessel being used).

JF Miyagi and its branch FCAs served as agents for consultation and support during the negotiation and application of this administrative programme. In Shichigahama, FCA members were employed by the FCA itself to help clear and burn debris in the port areas. This work programme had two benefits: first, members were provided with much-needed income while they are unable to fish or cultivate. Second, through this work they were making the ports useable for the future. Thus the programme met both present and future needs. Some groups along the coast benefited to a modest degree from such programmes. This holds true for the long-term clients (*kokyaku*) of local distributors of fishery products, as well.

However, some other fishermen and local businessmen further north in Miyagi harshly criticized JF Miyagi. In their eyes, the cooperative is an old boys' club where regular members (often older men) monopolize decision-making power – this despite the fact that they are physically unable to do reconstruction work themselves. In Ogatsu, a fishing village administratively part of Ishinomaki, a group of younger fishermen calling themselves *Oh, Guts!* have tried to infuse local fishery structures with new ideas and throw out the old structures. This is particularly relevant in respect to structural problems inside local FCAs where the elders (many of them over 65 years) have full voting rights as full members (*sei kumiai-in*) whereas the younger junior members have no right to vote (Wilhelm 2009: 96–97). *Oh, Guts!* has been following an alternative approach with its *hitokuchi*-ownership system, in which people in local cities or elsewhere who want to support local fishermen and producers can do so through small investments, typically of 10,000 yen for one share (*hitokuchi*; literally, 'one mouth'). When shareholders wish to actively take part in reconstruction work the group supplies them with information on local inns and restaurants so that the bond between the local victims and supporters from elsewhere is strengthened and local businesses can also benefit. As one former fisherman in Mizuhama (a district of Ogatsu) said while working on his small field along a meandering road: 'Even though the local FCA helped us in former times, its members are too old to cope with this situation. Therefore, I very much appreciate the initiative of those young guys' (27 August 2011).

Recovery: The rise of 'self-help' groups

Being connected to partners, friends and regular customers across great distances is common among fishermen. Among the volunteers and supporters of the disaster relief efforts, many such friends reactivated their bonds and formed self-help groups. The Friends and Supporters of the Sea (FSS, or *Kaiyū Shien-tai*) is one such group. FSS was set up just a couple of weeks after the March disasters as a company by former high school friends in their fifties and sixties. Its members' relatively advanced age distinguishes this group from other – mostly younger – volunteers. The three core members all had successful careers as businessmen before the disaster struck and, now that their adult children have left home they have enough time and financial stability to focus on their new activities as experienced and locally respected persons. Based in central Ishinomaki, their activities focus on Samenoura bay.

Samenoura bay is where fishers from small ports such as Yoriiso harvest 80 per cent of Japanese cultivated sea squirt, a delicacy which has been successfully marketed even to South Korea and North America. FSS is primarily supported by *Oasis Life Care*, an international Baptist group based in Rifu near Sendai. Inai-san, who runs the FSS bureau, was a shopkeeper at a supermarket in central Ishinomaki when the tsunami struck. Another school friend involved in FSS is Watanabe-san, who married into Kanzaya, a Yoriiso-based merchant family for 300 years, running a company called Yamaboshi. He is sometimes referred to as 'Dr Sea Squirt' (*hoya hakase*) inside and outside of Yoriiso. As a local businessman from a traditional *amimoto* (literally 'net-owner', thus a local merchant family) in Yoriiso,

Watanabe-san feels responsible for the villagers' fate and gave a strong push to inculcate commercial virtues in FSS, such as planning, accounting and company leadership. By August 2012, FSS had managed to acquire 1,600 *hitokuchi* supporters (Anonymous 2012: 120). However, acquisition of new supporters has become harder with the passage of time.

In Yoriiso, two thirds of the residents make their living from cultivating sea squirt or scallop. Twelve people died in Yoriiso during the disaster. The local elementary school atop a hill served as a shelter for many people until mid-September 2011. As building land is scarce, not all homeless inhabitants could get temporary housing in or near the village. In adjacent Maeami, a small settlement of a hundred people, the official shelter was washed away by the waves, so that refugees had to find shelter in a single house on a hill-top in the settlement. The home's lack of official status as a shelter meant that people struggled with confused local authorities and were greatly hampered in efforts to get help.

FSS is trying hard to rebuild the local cultivation fisheries. They also care of people's practical needs by providing vacuum cleaners, renting out forklifts, etc. They are also conscious of their cultural heritage, and see festivals as an important factor to strengthen community bonds. For example, the Daikoku dance performed during New Year's ceremonies by the local boys' group (*kodomo-gumi*) went ahead in 2012 after FSS presented it with new ceremonial clothes to replace those washed away by the waves. Interestingly this ceremony was carried out jointly by children of Yoriiso and the neighbouring settlement of Maeami, whereas the two communities had separate groups before 3.11. Also, girls joined in for the first time in local history. As all related records and documents of the ceremony were also lost and the former advisor of the children's group left Yoriiso after 3.11, a new, yet, inexperienced person (Endō Ken'ichi, alias Daikichi) took over responsibility. Wilhelm was able to provide texts, photographs and other information on the ceremony he had collected during previous fieldtrips. Most people from Maeami found shelter in temporary housing on a small spot at Gobaisawa in Yoriiso, and it is worth noting that several other ceremonies and festivals formerly carried out separately have been done jointly by residents of Yoriiso and Maeami since 3.11. Disaster seems to have brought the two communities closer together.

In Yoriiso, not all elder fishermen are willing to shoulder the financial risks of resuming their fishery activities, as they will be far too old to work by the time reconstruction is finally completed and some of them lack successors in their families. Endō Hitoshi, a younger fisherman and producer of seaweed and scallop, managed to make use of government financial aid to build a processing facility near the former site of the Yoriiso FCA, employing twelve people initially. In July 2012, Endō-san resumed shipments of *wakame* seaweed and scallops. He was able to resume production rapidly by using fry donated by fishermen from Hokkaidō in 2011.

After resuming operations in March 2012 the marine fishery fleet in Yoriiso is facing many problems. They first went out to catch krill (*okiami*) but it turned out to exceed official levels for radioactive contamination (100 bq/kg) and so could not be sold. Later they caught sandfish (*kōnago*), but although they passed radiation tests they still could not find customers because of damage by rumour (*fūhyō-higai*). Then, in early summer, the fleet caught squid, yet the catch was poor compared to previous years. An interesting saying in context with tsunamis is *iwashi de korosare, ika de ikasareta* ('killed by sardine and living with squid'), referring to an oral tradition common throughout Japan that huge amounts of sardine are caught before a coming tsunami and squid in the aftermath (Kawashima 2012: 95–97). Unfortunately, the latter did not hold true for Yoriiso this time.

In Yoriiso, 33 marine cultivators produced *hoya* and scallops using 150 rafts before 11 March 2011. Data collected in spring 2013 shows that the number of cultivators was down to just 19. Some 90 cultivation rafts were restored for use in autumn 2011 and 2012 and another 52 were planned for June 2013 (see Table 2). This means that although the absolute numbers of cultivators and rafts decreased, each cultivator will eventually have nearly double the share of access to marine resources compared to the time before disaster struck.

Table 2   Marine cultivators and rafts in Yoriiso as of 31 March 2013

Marine cultivators	sea squirt	scallop
19*	15	11

	sea squirt rafts	scallop rafts	Total
Autumn 2011	16	22	38
Autumn 2012	30	22	52
Plan for June 2013	30	22	52
	76	66	142

Note: There were 33 marine cultivators using 150 rafts before 11 March 2011.
Source: FSS personal communication.
* Many of these cultivate both sea squirt and scallop.

As other settlements (Yagawa, Ō-Yagawa and Samenoura) on Samenoura bay were completely destroyed and will probably not be reset-tled in the near future, the weight of rebuilding fisheries in the bay lays heav-ily on Yoriiso, which was assigned the status of 'base harbour' (*kyoten-kō*) by Miyagi officials in December 2012. The nearby Yagawa elementary school was totally destroyed and formally closed in March 2012 after being effectively merged with Ōhara elementary school. The future of Yoriiso's elementary school, which dates back to the Meiji period, is uncertain since only fourteen youngsters were still attending classes as of September 2012, about half the pre-disaster enrolment. Keeping younger generations within Yoriiso greatly depends on the survival of the school, yet, its principal, Sugawara Susumu, was worried about its future in a personal communica-tion on 23 September 2012:

> The future of this school is in the hands of Ishinomaki's board of education. Many elementary schools in remote places were closed after amalgamation in 2005. ... For now, the city's authorities cannot even provide housing for teachers over here in Yoriiso. I have to commute every day from central Ishinomaki, so communication with local residents has been limited since I took up office in March 2011. The school has been virtually operated by the PTA of these villagers for a long time and they surely wish it to remain that way.

Kimura-san, another prominent distributor of fishery products in Ishinomaki city, fears losing his loyal customers during the period he is unable to supply them. He commented in an interview how in the past they often acted as 'lone wolves' (*ippiki ōkami*) before, but feels that now 'it isn't possible to rebuild alone. That's why people came together after the disaster. However, it's quite difficult to coordinate all their opinions and pleas ... reconstruction efforts require leadership'.

When pressed as to whether he saw the situation as a chance to change the status quo, he responded, 'Our ties with our customers can be deepened through an investment system to participate in reconstruction (i.e. the *hitokuchi* system). We have to be careful not to lose our customers during the period until we're able to deliver the goods again'.

Recovery: Cooperation

Meanwhile, the situation in Shichigahama provides an example of how cooperative work can be practiced. Coastal neighbourhoods are populated by long-standing residents who tend to be fishers, farmers, and the self-employed, while the inner part of the town has been filled in the last few years with 'bedtowns' for commuters working in the neighbouring cities of Sendai, Tagajō, and Shiogama.

The local self-employed farmers and fishers were disproportionately affected by the disaster. In Shichigahama, over 90 per cent of the farm-land was inundated by seawater and all the ports were damaged, whether through the destruction of seawalls or the sinking of land, leaving parts of them permanently under water (Shichigahama 2011b). Over 600 homes were completely destroyed, over 400 severely damaged, and almost 4,000 others moderately damaged (Mand 2012). Initially nearly a quarter of the population was in shelters; after seven months, 2,000 remained in temporary housing in Shichigahama or in apartments outside the town (Shichigahama 2011b).

According to official Shichigahama town hall statistics (Shichigahama 2011a), 91 residents and nine outsiders died in the tsunami, the remains of two dead people are unidentified, and five residents were never found. These statistics show that Shichigahama, as a town, suffered fewer deaths per capita than many other communities in Miyagi along the Sanriku coast. It fared much better than the coastal settlement of Ogatsu, for example, discussed above. Crucially for rebuilding, though several municipal buildings, including a gymnasium and one school, were destroyed by the earthquake, the town hall was located above the tsunami-hit area and only one town hall employee died in the disaster. Consequently, most of the town's human capital and records remain, and these have put Shichigahama in a better position than towns which lost both.

Shichigahama, therefore, has relatively good potential for recovery. We may, however, see a fundamental alteration in the way of life of Shichigahama *nori* cultivators. *Nori* cultivating households were fiercely independent prior to the disaster and most never considered working cooperatively. There were 75 independent households cultivating *nori* on the day of the tsunami. By November 2011 there were only five. Another thirty households plan to begin cultivation again, but in groups, not independently.

As with most fisheries, the start-up of cultivation following the tsunami was slow. There are a number of important reasons behind the delay in beginning harvesting *nori* again, beyond the obvious destruction. *Nori* cultivation requires the entire summer for preparing the nets and rafts. The crop is seeded in September, transplanted in October, and harvesting begins in November (for details see Delaney 2011). Even among those cultivators who still had equipment and boats, very few were able to get everything together in time for seeding. So it is quite impressive that even five households managed to produce *nori* in the 2011–2012 season.

Andō-san was one of them. He had already re-built his home and workshop by the summer and had a new boat; and he was able to use seeded nets stored in freezers. Even so, he is only growing one-third the crop of the previous year. Most of his competitors are producing nothing. The expense of rebuilding and re-purchasing equipment, doubts as to whether they will be allowed to rebuild by officials, fears over the security of their cultivation rights, and advanced personal age are all limiting factors.

As mentioned previously, the government (through the Fisheries Agency, *Suisanchō*) is addressing some of the issues in a way that is helpful for some locals (while potentially hurting others). Yet some of these plans require fiercely independent households to work cooperatively together and form work groups as Hashimoto-san, a *nori* cultivator, explained on 18 October 2011.

> Before the quake, there was almost no cooperative work. There was quite a bit of competition among the fisher-folk in this area. The most important thing was to look after Number One. After the tsunami, well, people have changed. They know that, compared to doing it alone, doing it together will enable us to stand on our own feet faster ... those feelings have resulted from the tsunami.

Of course, there are a number of positive, practical reasons for working cooperatively on the government projects, including receiving a steady salary, having days off work, and receiving government grants enough to pay for 90 per cent of investment in new machines, buildings, and materials.

Nevertheless, through autumn 2011, some FCA members planned to remain independent operators. As Hayashi-san from the Matsushima Bay coast commented, 'Before the tsunami, I had no thoughts of working cooperatively, none at all. My machines are still all right, I still have my boats. But, if you work alone, there is no support (aid from the government) forthcoming' (19 October 2011).

He acknowledged that there are disadvantages to the cooperative groups, especially since it is difficult to guarantee everyone will do their fair share of work, but he believes his own group can overcome those problems. He pointed out that there were problems with the management of the only cooperative work group in the town prior to the tsunami. But he says that, 'we will be okay in our group. Everyone will work hard' (21 October 2011).

As Hayashi-san pointed out, there are, at most, four or five *nori* cultivators in Shichigahama who will remain independent rather than joining cooperative work groups. They are those lucky enough to still have their machines and boats, and they can still use their local ports. Thus they do not need to work cooperatively. Though small in numbers, their case is significant because it shows that joining cooperative work groups is a forced choice rather than reflecting a new, post-tsunami sense of togetherness.

Those who have not lost everything have not seen the need to change their way of working and living. But in Hayashi-san's case, his harbour has sunk below sea level and so he can no longer work out of that port. There are many in a similar predicament.

With his change of heart, he is thinking of the positive aspects of group work, rather than the negatives, and says he does not think his life will change that much. He points out that 'the expenses are covered by the group, so we will not have personal expenses. And there will not be any need for repair of the machines. And we will not have to pay for entering other fishing grounds' (see Delaney 2003 for a detailed description of the practice of renting/trading fishing ground access).

He also pointed out the positive side of having fewer cultivators in the future, 'In Sendai there is no one left anymore on the coast, so no one can do *nori* cultivation there, the sea is wide open, so we can rent the cultivating space from the Sendai cooperative. ... and there are fewer here at home, so there is more space available for those of us who remain'. In the Sendai Yuriage area, even prior to the tsunami, most seaweed cultivators had retired and thus Shichigahama *nori* cultivators have long rented sea space from Sendai.

Many like him can see the benefits of working cooperatively. Yet what do the lower numbers of members mean for the fishing cooperative? Will it be able to survive as an institution? Less than half of Shichigahama *nori* households plan to return to cultivation.[15] Will this be enough? The assistant head of the Shichigahama cooperative stated that 'the cooperative will be all right, even though our numbers are lower. *Nori* was always the most valuable harvest, though fishers were greater in number' (21 October 2011). And he pointed out that he believes the cooperative groups will be able to produce more than individual households since they will have fewer non-cultivating days.

Shichigahama FCA members are making the best of a bad situation. Once a path is set, these people are ready to dive in full force. They are ready to believe that this plan will benefit themselves and their community. As

15   Personal communication, Assistant Head Shichigahama FCA.

in the old days, '*nori* cultivators thrive on the enjoyment of "what could be"; you never know how much you can make, but you can always hope/dream' (Delaney 2003: 216).[16]

Recovery: Rebuilding

In addition to policy recommendations regarding employment, there has also been a great deal of discussion in Japan on where people may live and work in the future. Many recovery plans (e.g. Shichigahama 2011b) include proposals which would remove people from their ancestral homes and move them inland to higher elevations which are believed to be safer. Such plans are contentious and it remains to be seen if and when they will be approved. Yet there is some precedent for such actions in Miyagi. Following the 1933 Sanriku earthquake, for example, Iwate and Miyagi prefectures used prefectural funds to relocate over 2,000 homes in Iwate and 800 in Miyagi (Noh 1966: 5).[17]

These rebuilding strategies call for making large coastal areas into buffer zones. In most cases, small neighbourhoods would become parks and green spaces. In Shichigahama, the greatest change would take place in the Shōbutahama and Hanabuchihama neighbourhoods,[18] which suffered the greatest loss of life and infrastructure (see Figure 2).

16 Spoken by a town council member and retired *nori* cultivator.
17 Yamaguchi Yaichirō, a cultural geographer and student of Yanagita Kunio, published valuable studies on the relocation of settlements after the tsunami of 3 March 1933 (Tanakadate and Yamaguchi 1936, Yamaguchi 1943 and Yamaguchi 1972 [1964–1965]). Briefly, the relocation strategies after the 1933 tsunami eventually failed due to resettlement of the profitable areas near the sea by fishermen from middle and western Japan. A well-crafted summary and acknowledgement of Yamaguchi's studies can be found in Kawashima (2012: 37–59).
18 These are two of the seven 'beaches' (*hama*) of Shichigahama.

Cross section of area near Shōbutahama harbour

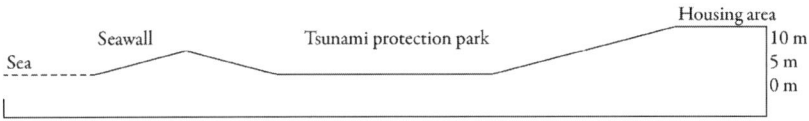

Tsunami protection park

Housing area

Seawall

Sea

10 m
5 m
0 m

Cross section of area near Sasayama Hanabuchihama

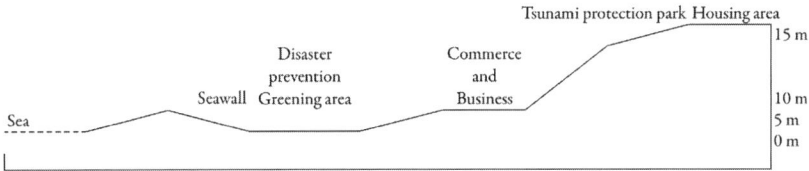

Tsunami protection park Housing area

15 m

Disaster
prevention
Seawall Greening area

Commerce
and
Business

Sea

10 m
5 m
0 m

Figure 2 Diagram of rebuilding plans in the Shōbutahama and Hanabuchihama
districts of Shichigahama. Source: Shichigahama (2011b: 21).

The 'tsunami protection park' displayed in the diagram for Shōbutahama, and the 'disaster prevention greening area' for Hanabuchihama are both in areas hitherto occupied by residential communities. These coastal communities will effectively be banned from rebuilding in the danger zone and forced to move elsewhere. One female resident was distraught at the thought of forced removal, despite the severity of the destruction, including the destruction of her own home. 'I have nowhere else to go; this is my home. Where else can I go?' (18 October 2011) Others seemed resigned. As Wada-san commented, 'The land here has sunk below sea level so they are talking about making it a park ... I do not know where my parents will live'. It remains to be seen how the plans pan out. People interviewed in Shichigahama were quite divided: some fishers wanted to rebuild, and in fact one had already done so, while others wanted to move. This same split of opinion can be found up and down the Sanriku coast.

Conclusion

Fishermen along the Sanriku coast of Miyagi prefecture are resuming their ways of life and getting back their occupations which, in many cases, stretch back generations. Though the scale of the disaster was nearly unprecedented, the Sanriku coast is hit by tsunami approximately three times during the average person's life span. These people know the dangers of work at sea. They know the danger signs of tsunami at the water's edge. This knowledge saved many of them from the waves. But their situation now requires more than traditional knowledge.

The people who really need to move now are the politicians and administrators who hold the purse strings for aid. It is they who will set the stage for reconstruction. If adjustments are made to the fisheries law, they need to be made on a temporary basis for the true good of the people in rebuilding, and not as a backdoor way to change the law for the benefit of a few outside investors. True, some people think the law is outdated, but that debate should be treated separately from the issue of reconstruction.

The authorities will have to listen carefully to the people's needs and demands on a case-by-case basis rather than simply following a master plan to get business done. Generational problems such as the unwillingness of elderly people to take financial risks for reconstruction with no successor to their business, and the survival of remote schools to keep younger people in the local communities, must be part of any comprehensive revival of Sanriku fisheries. On the other hand, reconstruction after disaster also generates new opportunities for fishermen trying to rebuild their livelihood (*nariwai*). This topic, however, deserves extensive discussion and thus must be saved for another article.

Over a million people have been directly affected by the disaster. Tens of thousands have lost their homes and/or their livelihoods. Some say it could take a decade or more to overcome the destruction. But the most heartening thing we found was the strong morale of so many people in the disaster zone. These people are known for perseverance in the face of adversity, a trait which has grown out of hundreds of years of droughts, famines, earthquakes, and tsunami (see, e.g. Hane 1982; Nishida 1978; Wilhelm 2009). Though this trait can come across as a stereotype, the experiences of our post-disaster fieldwork show it is real. Such perseverance is more than a simple acceptance of fate – it is a call of defiance. As was posted in the window of a destroyed home in the Hanabuchihama neighbourhood of Shichigahama, 'We refuse to lose, and we must get through it together' (*Maketara-akan, tomo ni yaru shika nai*).

Such perseverance is one of the keys to recovery; a willingness to work together in cooperation is a second. Supportive and inclusive government programmes and policies would be the third key to recovery. Here the issue of special fishery zones will be a litmus test. It is intensely controversial because many in the national and prefectural governments see opening up fisheries to outside interests as the only way to secure long-term revival, whereas many local fishermen see such moves as yet another threat to their livelihoods on top of what they have already had to endure.

References

Anonymous (2012). 'Ishinomaki meisan no hoya to hotate no fukkō o mezasu (Targeting the revival of Ishinomaki's famous products: scallop and sea squirt)', *Enishi*, 3, 120–121.

Delaney, Alyne Elizabeth (2003). *Setting Nets on Troubled Waters. Environment, Economics, and Autonomy Among Nori Cultivating Households in a Japanese Fishing Cooperative*. PhD thesis, Faculty of Arts and Sciences, University of Pittsburgh, Pittsburgh, PA.

—— (2011). 'Algal Management through a Cultural Lens: Examining the Roles of Women and Households in Japanese *Nori* Cultivation', *CBM – Cahiers de Biologie Marine*, 52, 527–533.

Funato Ryūhei (2011). 'Gyogyō-sha, chi'iki no tame no fukkō o: fukkō no samatage ni naru suisan tokku kōsō wa tekkai o (Reconstructing for fishermen and the local area: retract the idea of special fishery zones that are harmful to rebuilding)', *Nihon no shinro* (Japan's path forward), 227 (July), 11–13.

Hane Mikiso (1982). *Peasants, Rebels, and Outcastes: The Underside of Modern Japan*. New York: Pantheon.

Kalland, Arne (1995). 'Culture in Japanese Nature'. In Bruun, Ole, and Kalland (eds), *Asian Perceptions of Nature: A Critical Approach*, pp. 243–257. Richmond, Surrey: Curzon Press.

Kawashima Shūichi (2012). *Tsunami no machi ni ikite* (Living in a tsunami town). Tokyo: Fūzambō International.

Mand, Frank (2012). 'Shichigahama by the numbers: Vice Mayor provides first detailed look at 2011 earthquake'. *Old Colony Memorial Newspaper, Wicked Local Plymouth*, 11 August. <http://www.wickedlocal.com/plymouth/features/x866123310/Shichigahama-by-the-numbers#axzz23Px2YV8w> accessed 9 June 2012.

Miyagi Prefecture (ed.) (2011). *Miyagi-ken suisan fukkō puran* (Reconstruction plan for the fisheries of Miyagi prefecture). <http://www.pref.miyagi.jp/uploaded/attachment/68807.pdf > accessed 9 June 2013.

Nishida Kōzō (ed.) (1978). *Minami Sanriku saigai-shi. Tsunami, kasai to shōbō no kiroku* (A history of disasters in Minami Sanriku: A record of tsunamis, fires and fire-fighting). Kesennuma: NSK Chihō Shuppan.

Shichigahama (2011a). *Municipal Disaster Relief Headquarters, Earthquake reconstruction information (No.95)*, 31 October.

—— (2011b). *Shichigahama Municipal Disaster Relief Headquarters, Shichigahama Municipal Disaster Plan (2011–2020). First Stage Plan (2011–2015)*.

Seibidō shuppan henshū-bu (ed.) (2011). *Chizu de yomu Higashi-Nihon daishinsai*. Tokyo: Seibidō Shuppan.

Takimoto Hisafumi and Nasukawa Itsuo (eds) (2004). *Sanriku-kaigan to hamakaidō* (The Sanriku coast and its coastal highways). Tokyo: Yoshikawa Kōbunkan.

Tanakadate Hidezō and Yamaguchi Yaichirō (1936). 'Sanriku-chihō ni okeru tsunami ni yoru shūraku idō' (Relocation of settlements in tsunami-hit Sanriku region), *Chiri to kikai*, 1(3), 302–311.

Wakamori Tarō (ed.) (1969). *Rikuzen hokubu no minzoku* (Folklore of northern Rikuzen). Tokyo: Yoshikawa kōbun-kan.

Wilhelm, Johannes Harumi (2009). *Ressourcenmanagement in der japanischen Küstenfischerei* (Resource management in Japanese coastal fisheries). PhD Dissertation, Rheinische Friedrich-Wilhelms-Universität Bonn, Philosophische Fakultät. Norderstedt: BoD.

—— (2013). 'Der Wiederaufbau der Fischerei Sanrikus zwischen Sonderzonen und Fischereigenossenschaften', *Asiatische Studien / Études Asiatiques*, 67(2), 625–650.

Yamaguchi Yaichirō (1943). *Tsunami to mura* (Tsunami and villages). Tokyo: Kōshunkaku.

—— (1972). 'Tsunami-jōshū-chi Sanriku engan chi'iki no shūraku idō (Tsunami-hit areas in the Sanriku region and the relocation of residents)'. In Yamaguchi Yaichirō, *Nihon no koyūsei o motomete* (Looking for the Uniqueness of Japan), pp. 323–430. Tokyo: Sekai bunko. (PhD thesis, originally published in four papers of *Ajia daigaku sho-gaku kiyō* between 1964 and 1965.)

PART 2

Coping with Life after the Nuclear Disaster

DAVID MCNEILL

Them versus Us: Japanese and International Reporting of the Fukushima Nuclear Crisis

On 7 April 2011, as Japan tottered back to its feet after the 11 March calamity, I chaired a press conference at the Foreign Correspondents' Club of Japan (FCCJ) held by Higashikokubaru Hideo, then a candidate in Tokyo's gubernatorial election. A famous comedian before he entered politics, Higashikokubaru was uncharacteristically sombre as he discussed what Japan must do to recover from the terrible damage inflicted by the disaster. A major problem, he intoned, was the non-Japanese reporting of the nuclear crisis in Fukushima. 'Do you think we foreign journalists have done a bad job of reporting the disaster?' I asked him and he turned, unsmiling, to face me full on for the first time. 'Yes, I do', he replied.

That stinging rebuke in the venerated sixty-year-old home of the foreign press in Japan epitomized criticism of American and European journalists in the month after 3.11. Japan's Ministry of Foreign Affairs led the criticism of 'excessive' coverage in April, singling out the *Blade*, a local US newspaper from Toledo, Ohio, that ran a cartoon depicting three mushroom clouds, one each for Hiroshima, Nagasaki and Fukushima.[1] *Newsweek Japan* was one of several publications to take up the cudgel against shrill, alarmist *gaijin* (foreigner) reporters (Yokota 2011). 'The foreign media in Japan ... has been put on a pedestal as the paragon of journalism, and was viewed as a source of credibility. The Great East Japan Earthquake shattered that myth', thundered editor Yokota Takashi. 'The Western media failed to fulfil its mission during the disaster, hitting new lows with shoddy journalism as reporters were overtaken by the news and lost their composure'.

1   'Japan Criticizes Foreign Media's Fukushima Coverage'. *Asahi Shinbun*, 9 April 2011.

Yokota accused foreign journalists of gross sensationalism after the first explosion at the Fukushima No.1 nuclear plant, condemning them in *Newsweek Japan* for turning the story into 'Japan's Chernobyl' – a week before the Japanese government officially raised Fukushima to INES[2] Level 7, which is in fact the same as the 1986 Ukraine disaster. *The Wall Street Journal* also noted the 'gulf' that Fukushima opened up in reporting, noting that while local journalists gave the sense that the 'situation will be resolved', their foreign counterparts focused 'on the other side – that this is getting out of control' (Sanchanta 2011). In the week after the nuclear crisis erupted, Japan-based bloggers assembled a 'wall of shame', citing dozens of foreign crimes against journalism, including an infamous report in the UK tabloid *The Sun*, calling Tokyo a 'city of ghosts' (Wheeler 2011).[3] *The Sun* reporter had never set foot in Japan.

Such hyperbolic reporting was not all imported. One of the most criticized examples was Japanese: *AERA* magazine's famous 19 March cover story showing a masked nuclear worker and the headline 'radiation is coming to Tokyo' was controversial enough to force an apology and the resignation of at least one columnist (though the headline was technically correct).[4] Moreover, once the dust from the crisis settled, weekly Japanese magazines quickly sank their teeth into the nuclear industry and its administrators far more aggressively then the foreign media ever did. *Shūkan Shinchō* dubbed the management of Tokyo Electric Power Co. (TEPCO) *senpan* (war criminals). *Shūkan Gendai* named and shamed the most culpable of Japan's elite pro-nuclear scientists, calling them *goyō gakusha* (government lackeys) and *tonchinkan* – roughly meaning 'blundering idiots'. Other magazines turned their critical gaze on the radiation issue, exposing government malfeasance and lies. *AERA* also revealed that local governments manipulated public opinion in support of reopening nuclear plants.

2   The International Nuclear Event Scale, introduced in 1990 by the International Atomic Energy Agency (IAEA). It is a logarithmic scale, similar to those used to measure earthquakes.
3   For the 'Journalists Wall of Shame' see <http://www.jpquake.info/home> accessed 7 June 2013. See also McNeill 2011a.
4   See '"Hōshanō ga kuru" no hyōshi ni hihan, *AERA* ga shazai', *The Yomiuri*, 21 March 2011. <http://www.yomiuri.co.jp/national/news/20110320-OYT1T00786.htm> accessed 7 June 2013.

The Fukushima disaster revealed one of the major fault lines in Japanese journalism, between the mainstream newspapers and television companies – hereafter 'big media' – and the less inhibited mass-market weeklies and their ranks of freelancers. Both these branches of the Japanese media have massive audiences, but the daily papers and TV stations are heavily dependent on briefings by government and big business to get their daily coverage, whereas the weeklies tend to look for scoops in unofficial places and are therefore less beholden to the powers that be.

The subject was new but the debate it amplified on the influence of the press club system had been going on for decades. As Laurie Anne Freeman (1996, 2000) and others (Hall 1997; DeLange 1998) have noted, the system means that Japan's big newspapers and TV companies channel information directly from the nation's political, bureaucratic and corporate elite to the media and the public beyond; in this case from the government, TEPCO and the Nuclear Industrial Safety Agency (NISA). The system's critics say it locks Japan's most influential journalists into a symbiotic relationship with their sources and discourages them from investigation or independent analysis and criticism. That certainly seemed to happen here. Foreign correspondents of course had no such restrictions, but neither did they have direct access to key sources.

The large swathe of journalism outside this official system is a different matter entirely. As Gamble and Watanabe have pointed out in a harshly critical survey of Japan's weekly media, the weeklies developed after the war partly in response to the feeling among Japan's growing urban middle class that they were getting a selective, pro-establishment line from the big media (Gamble and Watanabe 2004). One of the key distinctions across the fault-line is that unlike their big media counterparts, magazine journalists are not generally allowed access to the press clubs.[5] The consequences of this distinction would become clear in reporting on the Fukushima aftermath, as I will show later.

---

5   Some magazines are owned by big newspaper companies – *AERA* by *Asahi Shinbun*, *Sunday Mainichi* by *Mainichi Shinbun* etc. Here a journalist with access to the Press Club via the newspaper may also write for the magazine. However, controversial content may bring down official wrath on the newspaper as well as the magazine, so a degree of control remains.

130navigationnavigationnavigationnavigationnavigationnavigationnavigationnavigationnavigationnavigationnavigationnavigation

One problem with the foreign media was its lack of knowledgeable personnel in Japan. After the disaster many journalists were dispatched to Japan who had no knowledge of the country. The resulting inaccurate or unbalanced reporting was criticized by local foreigners as well as by Japanese. Jeff Kingston, director of Asian studies at Temple University's Japan Campus, was one of several critics who cited the 'many egregious instances of … exaggeration and misrepresentation', fuelled by what he called 'parachute journalism'.[6] For years, Japan's dreary, protracted economic decline had been a turnoff to distant editors, and the country had fallen off the media radar, eclipsed by fast-rising China. FCCJ hacks sometimes joked darkly that it would take a major disaster to revive Japan's newsworthiness. Disaster had duly arrived, and there weren't enough reporters to cover it.

It is also worth pointing out that many foreign journalists praised their Japanese counterparts. Washington Post correspondent Chico Harlan singled out public service broadcaster NHK's restrained, almost 'adjective free' coverage in a widely circulated opinion piece: 'Anchors do not use certain words that might make a catastrophe feel like a catastrophe', he wrote. '"Massive" is prohibited' (Harlan 2011). Martyn Williams, a former president of the Foreign Correspondents' Club of Japan, favourably noted the more sober domestic coverage, adding that Japan's media had 'a duty' to avoid causing panic. 'You can bet some of the media running the scare stories about Japan wouldn't handle a similar disaster in their own country in the same way'.[7]

By far the most unrestrained criticism of Japanese journalism came from Japanese commentators. Author and freelancer Uesugi Takashi was one of several who accused the local media of colluding with the government and Tokyo Electric Power Company (TEPCO), operator of the stricken nuclear plant, of lying and hiding information. 'TEPCO is a client of the media and the press clubs, being one of their biggest advertisers – so the press won't … say certain things', he said, citing their blackout of the meltdowns that occurred in reactors 1 to 3, and the fact that the

6   Personal interview with the author, 29 March 2011.
7   Personal communication, 3 April 2011. For an overview of foreign reporting of Fukushima, see Johnston 2011.

latter contained a large quantity of lethal plutonium. Such statements were enough, he claimed, to get him banned from TBS Radio in April.[8] Former Washington TBS Bureau Chief Akiyama Toyohiro, who owned a farm in Fukushima, made a similar assessment. 'The mass media, it seemed to us, was just acting as a mouthpiece for the government and the power company' (Wakiyama 2011).

It is obviously misleading to suggest that the government, TEPCO and big media were all huddled in the same room plotting to keep the Japanese public in the dark. Prime Minister Kan Naoto had several well-publicized disputes with the utility company and indeed was the victim of an attempted smear when TEPCO said his 12 March inspection of the Fukushima plant had delayed venting and caused the hydrogen explosions. And journalists at TEPCO's televised press conferences were often sharply critical of the company in the weeks after the crisis began.

Nevertheless, there is strong evidence for claims of structural bias. Japan's power-supply industry, collectively, is Japan's biggest advertiser, spending 88 billion yen (roughly US$1 billion) a year, according to the Nikkei Advertising Research Institute.[9] TEPCO's 24.4 billion yen alone is roughly half what a global firm as large as Toyota spends in a year. Many supposedly neutral journalists were tied to the industry in complex ways: senior *Yomiuri* editorial and science writer Nakamura Masao, for example, was an advisor to the Central Research Institute of Electric Power Industry (*Denryoku Chūō Kenkyūjo*); journalists from the *Nikkei* and *Mainichi* news-papers have taken post-retirement jobs with pro-nuclear organizations and publications (Koizumi 2011). Before the Fukushima crisis began, TEPCO's largesse may have helped silence all but the most determined of potential critics. According to *Shūkan Gendai* magazine, the utility spent roughly $26 million a year on advertising with the *Asahi* newspaper. TEPCO's quar-terly magazine, *Sola*, was edited by former *Asahi* writers.[10] That industry

---

8   See Uesugi's own website on <http://uesugitakashi.com/?p=677> accessed 20 June 2013.

9   <http://www.nikkei-koken.com/> accessed 3 October 2011. Confirmed by personal communication with NARI, 23 July 2012.

10   *Shūkan Gendai*, 'Skūpu repōto: Saidai no tabū, Tōden manē to *Asahi Shinbun*' ('The biggest taboo: TEPCO's money and the *Asahi* newspaper'), 22 August 2011.

financial clout, combined for decades with the press club system, surely helped discourage investigative reporting and kept concerns about nuclear power and critics of dangerous plants like Hamaoka and Fukushima off the media radar (cf. Hirose 2011). This is not to suggest that the Japanese media ignored nuclear power, just that the odds were heavily tilted against a balanced discussion.

As a stringer for two daily European newspapers (*The Independent* of the UK, and *The Irish Times*), I was often singed from the heat in this debate. In the course of four trips to Fukushima, writing over 100 newspaper articles and giving dozens of radio interviews in the month after the crisis began, I struggled like all other correspondents to give my audience a clear picture of the nuclear crisis, while avoiding the twin traps of complaisant and alarmist reporting. Every story on Fukushima or the fallout was followed by angry comments and letters demanding more 'balanced' reporting, often coming from diametrically opposed positions. Consider for example the response to an article I published about radiation fears in Tokyo in the 16 March edition of *The Independent*, in which I mentioned the widespread rumour that the emperor had left Tokyo for Kyoto and quoted a taxi-driver who said he was more concerned about where to buy petrol.[11] This drew 34 comments, including the following:

> Comment 1: 'This article is scaremongering, possibly more aimed at strengthening UK readers' opposition to nuclear power rather than painting an accurate picture of what's happening in Tokyo'.
> Comment 2: 'I live in Tokyo. Shibuya is exactly as the article says … The danger is not just a big earthquake, it is the very real possibility of complete nuclear meltdown at the plant in Fukushima which will most definitely be a catastrophe of a magnitude that will impact Tokyo citizens'.

---

11   'Thousands Flee Tokyo as Experts Try to Calm Radiation Fears', *The Independent*, 16 March 2011. <http://www.independent.co.uk/news/world/asia/thousands-flee-tokyo-as-experts-try-to-calm-contamination-fears-2242992.html> accessed 7 June 2013.

Comment 3: 'You lying pommie bastards. The emperor has not left Tokyo. There are no thousands fleeing Tokyo either. Of course you "journalists" are masking the lies you make up as "somebody heard" or similar weasel words'.

Comment 4: 'All the top-boy journalists have found a wonderful opportunity to make themselves a nice bit of cash by peddling yet more sensationalist crap. No matter how "independent" a media source is, there is always someone, somewhere trying to push their own agenda and make money from the misery of others'.

Comment 5: '"Making money out of the misery of others." You must be talking about the politicians and the owners of the nuclear plants that were poorly constructed in a known earthquake zone, within range of a tsunami. How many paid stooges is the nuclear industry using to blanket the news with lies and deception in order to keep the power flowing and the money coming?'

Despite their bitterly opposed viewpoints, these comments share a smouldering resentment and urge to apportion blame – a widespread response to the nuclear disaster. Accusations of rumour-mongering were partly a product of restricted access. As Uesugi notes, unlike their Japanese counterparts, foreign reporters were denied press time with the government's top figures: Prime Minister Kan Naoto, chief cabinet secretary and government spokesman Edano Yukio, and nuclear crisis minister Hosono Gōshi. Even *New York Times* reporter Tabuchi Hiroko was among those who were swatted away. 'We constantly asked for an interview with Kan, especially when we were criticized for misreporting. We said: 'OK then, so give us the top man and let us know what's going on'. We finally got Hosono after two months'.[12] Foreign reporters could watch Edano daily on Japanese TV but they could not ask him questions.

In Fukushima itself, however, at least until the government made it illegal in late April to enter the 20-km irradiated evacuee zone, access was almost unlimited. On the morning of 12 March, less than 24 hours after

12   Personal interview, 9 October 2011.

the earthquake struck, I set off with two colleagues before we knew any-thing about the nuclear accident. When we learned that Japanese reporters were able to travel the closed expressways along with Self-Defence Force troops and emergency relief workers, we negotiated with the police a pass that allowed us toll-free access to the whole north-east. In the following month, I reported from Iwaki, Iitate, Sōma, Minami-Sōma, and from the gates right in front of the Fukushima No.1 nuclear plant, all without being stopped by a single policeman. In early April, when I drove around the almost abandoned town of Futaba, 2 km from the plant, talking to local people who had stayed behind, masked policemen in patrol cars asked me to leave 'for my own safety' but otherwise left me alone. This was the only way to understand life inside the irradiated zone of the world's worst nuclear crisis in 25 years, and locals there told immensely poignant stories, expressing bewilderment and anger at their fate at the hands of a plant that didn't deliver a single watt of electricity to Fukushima.[13] Like the victims of Bhopal or Chernobyl, they felt they had been manipulated, lied to and finally abandoned by the company responsible and by the government. Still, some were determined to stay rather than abandon houses and farms that had been in their families for generations, in some cases since the nineteenth century.

I have tried in this brief sample of the voluminous coverage of the dis-aster to show how reporting was shaped by structural rather than national or international factors, and that analysis or commentary that simply con-demns 'foreign' or 'Japanese' reporting is off the point. Shut out from official sources and not subject to the discipline or constraints of employment with Japan's big media, Japanese freelancers and non-Japanese journalists were forced to report in very different ways. I will attempt to show this in more detail now by recalling the reporting I saw and did on the nuclear crisis while in Fukushima Prefecture, focusing on two key stories: the fate of Minami-Sōma and the evacuation of the 20-km exclusion zone around the nuclear plant.

13   Fukushima's electricity is supplied by Tohoku Electric rather than TEPCO.

Reporting Minami-Sōma

Minami-Sōma has the administrative status of a city, though it is more like a collection of small towns merged together by bureaucratic fiat. Its centre lies about 25 km north of the 20km exclusion zone, which cuts into its natural hinterland to the south. More than 71,000 people lived in the city before 11 March. By the end of the month there were fewer than 10,000. The earthquake and tsunami killed or left missing about 920; the remainder fled from the threat of radiation, according to Mayor Sakurai Katsunobu, who recalled looking out of the fourth-floor window of the city offices on 14 March, hours after a hydrogen explosion ripped apart the outer building of the No.3 reactor at the Fukushima No.1 plant. 'Cars clogged the street below as everyone packed up and left. I thought it was the end of the town.'[14]

Two days before, after the first hydrogen explosion in reactor No.1 on 12 March, journalists working for Japan's big media quietly pulled out of the town *en masse*. The evacuation included all the major newspaper dailies and broadcasters, including the *Mainichi*, *Asahi* and *Yomiuri*, as well as the Sendai-based *Kahoku Shinpō* newspaper. The journalists pulled back to Sendai, Fukushima city and other areas considered safe from the (then unconfirmed) radiation fallout. None thought to inform the mayor. They returned some forty days later, by which time a steady stream of foreign and freelance reporters had been to see the town (Agence France-Presse was the first to arrive, on 18 March). 'The Japanese journalists informed us later that their companies told them to leave, and they stayed away until the government and their companies said the radiation had fallen to safe levels', said Sakurai.[15] He added that the decision significantly worsened the situation for the town. 'We were abandoned so there was no way to tell the country or the world what was happening'.

14 Personal interview, 9 October 2011.
15 Personal interviews, 4 April, 9 October 2011.

After 12 March, regular deliveries of food and fuel began to dwindle and the citizens of Minami-Sōma were slowly left to fend for themselves. Information about the state of the power plant was gleaned from the television, mainly NHK, which relied on openly pro-nuclear experts to explain what was happening to its six reactors. The most prominent and heavily rotated was Sekimura Naoto, a vice dean of the Graduate School of Engineering at the University of Tokyo and a consultant with the Advisory Committee on Energy and Natural Resources at the Ministry of Economy, Trade and Industry (METI). Sekimura had previously written reports verifying the structural soundness of the Fukushima plant (his job was to assess the impact of ageing and seismic stress), and had signed off on a ten-year extension for the No.1 reactor (McNeill 2011b). The comments of other pro-nuclear scientists were also heavily reported, notably those of Madarame Haruki, the chairman of the Nuclear Safety Commission of Japan – to the exclusion of alternative voices.

Most of Sekimura's on-air comments reflected his close ties to the industry and were, he admitted later, regurgitated from his contacts inside TEPCO. 'Residents near the power station should stay calm', he said on 12 March, shortly before the first hydrogen explosion. 'Most of the fuel remains inside the reactor, which has stopped operation and is being cooled'. In fact, as TEPCO would admit two months later, the uranium fuel inside reactor No.1 had by this stage already completely melted. 'A major radioactive disaster is unlikely', Sekimura said. A short time later, the hydrogen explosion destroyed the concrete building housing reactor No.1, irradiating the surrounding countryside and sea, and eventually forcing the evacuation of at least 80,000 people. 'The people of our town didn't believe what they were hearing or seeing on TV', Mayor Sakurai recalled six months later. 'They made up their own minds'.

In an October post-mortem of NHK's March/April coverage, Ōgi Noriyuki, head of broadcasting during the Tohoku disaster, said of the nuclear crisis:

> Overwhelmingly the problem was lack of information. Even TEPCO and the government didn't know the whole picture. We didn't have enough time to evaluate their reports and so we didn't know how far we should go in telling the dangers of the situation. We were relying on TEPCO and the government and because they were not sure, we were not sure. (Ōgi 2011, author's translation)

Ōgi said NHK had gone above and beyond the call of duty:

> On the afternoon of 12 March, the police only reported that the sound of an explo-
> sion had been heard. TEPCO, NISA and the government said nothing. Looking at
> the screen, our reporter noticed what was happening and said, 'Just in case, anyone
> who is outside please go inside and stay out of the rain'. Even though we didn't have
> any proof, we went further than we needed to.

Thus he commended the initiative of a reporter who saw an explosion at a
nuclear power plant and advised people to take cover without being told
to do so by the government. That he felt the urge to do so tells us a little
about how rare such displays of initiative are in the big media of Japan.

He added, however, a crucial, if obscurely worded note of self-criticism.
'It is being asked whether it is really OK for our newsgathering system to
depend so exclusively on government sources' (Ōgi 2011). Others have
expressed much sharper criticism about how nuclear critics were excluded
from the analysis. 'It was very clear how NHK brought out pro-nuclear
professors in force after the earthquake struck', said Anzai Ikurō, a radiation
specialist and former professor at the University of Tokyo's nuclear engineering department. 'Critics like myself were not called on at all during the
crisis'. Eventually, he and other long-term critics such as Kyoto University
researcher Koide Hiroaki[16] would gain a large following among the public,
some recompense perhaps for being so long ignored by the mass media.

In the week after the crisis erupted, in fact, there was just one notable
appearance on TV by an academic who speculated that a meltdown had
occurred. Fujita Yuko, an ex-professor of physics at Keio University, told
Fuji TV on the evening of 11 March he was 'very concerned' that the reactors were in a 'state of meltdown'. He was never asked back. 'I speculate that
it was because the station management thought Fujita spoke too much on
the danger of the nuclear accident', said Itō Mamoru, who has published
a book surveying media coverage of the nuclear crisis (Itō 2012; see Arita
2012 for an interview with Itō).

---

16   See for example <http://www.youtube.com/watch?v=HTx942kwh94> accessed 7
     June 2013.

Immediately after the 12 March explosion, Mayor Sakurai and his staff watched Edano host a press conference. 'Even though the No.1 reactor building is damaged, the containment vessel is undamaged', the Chief Cabinet Secretary told reporters. 'In fact, the outside monitors show that the (radiation) dose rate is declining, so the cooling of the reactor is proceeding' (Hirose 2011: 42). Any suggestion that the accident would reach Chernobyl level was, he said, 'out of the question'. Author and nuclear critic Hirose Takashi noted afterwards: 'Most of the media believed this and the university professors encouraged optimism. It makes no logical sense to say, as Edano did, that the safety of the containment vessel could be determined by monitoring the radiation dose rate. All he did was repeat the lecture given him by TEPCO'. As media critic Takeda Tōru later wrote, the overwhelming strategy throughout the crisis, by both the authorities and big media, seemed to be reassuring people, not alerting them to possible dangers (Takeda 2011: 7).

Mayor Sakurai was left reeling from the impact of the nuclear disaster. His remaining constituents, including many elderly and bedridden people, faced starvation. Television reporters occasionally called from Fukushima city or Tokyo for updates but with so many other stories clamouring for attention, there seemed no way to impress on them how desperate the situation was. There would be no direct word from TEPCO on the state of the Fukushima No.1 plant for 22 days. The CEO of Second Harvest Japan, Charles E. McJilton (2013: 36–37) describes being rebuffed by Sakurai's staff when his organization offered food aid to the city, an incident we can interpret either as an indicator of the reflex response to foreign 'charity' among Japanese organizations, or simple bureaucratic disorganization. In any event, late at night on 24 March the mayor sat in front of a camcorder in his office and recorded an 11-minute video that was uploaded to YouTube with English subtitles. 'We are not getting enough information from the government and Tokyo Electric Power Company', said the exhausted-looking Sakurai. 'Convenience stores and supermarkets where people buy everyday goods are closed. Citizens are almost being driven to starvation … I beg you to help us'.[17] The video, perhaps the most striking attempt of the entire Tohoku disaster to bypass the mainstream media, registered more than 200,000 hits in the following week and attracted tons of aid. It also drew a stream of freelance Japanese and foreign reporters who made Sakurai an emblematic figure of the grassroots challenge to blundering and incompetent officialdom during the disaster.

When I arrived on 4 April, Sakurai was still stinging from his experience with the Japanese media. 'I appreciate that there were dangers but we had many people who stayed behind and in my view the journalists should have stayed too. They completely ignored us and left to protect themselves. That's not the mission of journalism' (Personal interview, 4 April 2011). What struck him about the Minami-Sōma episode was how the Japanese journalists acted together, like a retreating army. Speaking anonymously, a reporter for one of the major newspapers told me he and his colleagues were left with no choice once they were told to leave. 'There was some discussion but in the end we agreed that it would be safer to report from Fukushima city'. There was no conscious collective decision. It happened almost by osmosis. When they returned, he added, Mayor Sakurai had berated them. 'He said "the foreign media and freelancers came in droves to report what happened. What about you?"'

The reporting of the Minami-Sōma story demonstrated some striking differences in how foreign and large Japanese media organizations operated, particularly the discipline and homogeneity of the Japanese press corps. Masuyama Satoru, a director with NHK's Science and Culture Division, explains the decision to pull out of Minami-Sōma thus: 'It's a case of individual responsibility versus corporate responsibility. Reporters at a Japanese company will not take risks by themselves; they will wait for instructions. And the company will not send its workers off without proper preparation or protective gear. It's a nuisance but that's how it is'.[18] Many critics would later question why none of the big media broke ranks in the

---

17   See Fackler, Martin, 'Japanese City's Cry Resonates Around the World', *New York Times*, 6 April 2011. Also, McNeill 2011c.
18   Personal interview, 24 November 2011.

interests of their readers. One was Uchida Tatsuru, a professor at Kobe College, who told the *Asahi*:[19]

> I subscribe to four major national newspapers, but I cannot tell which newspaper I am reading in relation to articles about the nuclear accident. Not only is there no attempt to bring out a unique angle, there is also a sense of fear at reporting something different from the other papers and the feeling of security from running the same articles. That has led to anger among readers who see a repeat of what happened during World War II.

Reporting inside the 20 km evacuation zone

By late March, the war in Libya had knocked Japan from the front pages of the world's newspapers, but there was still one story that was very eagerly sought after: life inside the 20km zone around the power plant. The government had steadily strengthened this zone from advising evacuation on 11 March to ordering evacuation for 70–80,000 people later that week, while another 136,000 people in the zone 20–30km away were told to stay indoors. The government directive was widely criticized by Fukushima residents and some sections of the media as arbitrary and unscientific. Eventually, several highly irradiated villages outside the zone would also be evacuated, such as Iitate (see Tom Gill's paper in this collection). Most of those people had fled their homes, many of them leaving behind pets and farm animals that would eventually die. Animal corpses had been left to rot. Even more alarming were reports that hospitals had abandoned patients.[20] A small number of mainly elderly people stayed behind, refus-

---

19 'Barriers to coverage: High hurdles blocked reporting of Fukushima nuclear accident', *The Asahi Shimbun*, 13 July 2011. <http://ajw.asahi.com/article/0311disaster/analysis/AJ201107134358> accessed 21 June 2013.

20 See 'Families want answers after 45 people die following evacuation from Fukushima hospital', *Mainichi Daily News*, 26 April 2011. <http://mdn.mainichi.jp/features/archive/news/2011/04/20110426p2a00m0na006000c.html>.

ing to leave their ancestral homes. Not surprisingly, there was enormous global interest in their story and its disturbing echoes of the Chernobyl catastrophe 25 years earlier.

In late March, a trickle of foreign journalists braved radiation to report from inside the zone. *Newsweek*'s Joshua Hammer described it as '*The Twilight Zone* crossed with *The Day After* – an apocalyptic vision of life in the nuclear age' (Hammer 2011). Daniel Howden, from my own newspaper, *The Independent*, drove right to the gates of the plant, encountering deserted homes, stray pets and nervous nuclear workers along the way (Howden 2011). But he was unable to find interviewees inside the zone, so a few days later I followed him and talked to several holdouts (McNeill 2011d). None of us encountered a single Japanese reporter inside the exclusion zone, despite the fact that it was not yet illegal to be there. Some would begin reporting from the area much later, after receiving government clearance – the *Asahi* sent its first dispatch on 25 April when its reporters accompanied the commissioner general of the National Police Agency.[21] Later, they would explain why they stayed away and – with the exception of approved government excursions – continued to stay away. 'Journalists are employees and their companies have to protect them from dangers', explained Satō Keiichi, a deputy editor with the News Division of Nippon TV. 'Reporters like myself might want to go into that zone and get the story, and there was internal debate about that, but there isn't much personal freedom inside big media companies. We were told by our superiors that it was dangerous, so going in by ourselves would mean breaking that rule. It would mean nothing less than quitting the company'.[22]

Here we come to some important structural differences between Japanese and overseas news organizations. Outside Japan, foreign correspondents are increasingly retained by newspapers on casual contracts or as stringers, reflecting both shrinking budgets and the declining importance of all but a handful of must-have global stories. Of the foreign reporters I worked with in March, I can think of only a handful who were staff correspondents. Reporters like Hammer and Howden, brought over from their

21   Source as for note 19 above.
22   Personal interview, 28 November 2011.

normal beats (in the Middle East and Africa) because of their reputation for skill and bravery in difficult assignments, are under a lot of unspoken pressure to justify the expense of getting them there. They are expected to use their skills of interpretation and analysis in situations where they don't always know what is going on. In addition, their stories are by-lined, bringing a certain amount of individual glory in the event of a scoop. That background, the reporters' lack of specific knowledge about nuclear power and their unfamiliarity with Japan, helps explain sensationalist dispatches of the kind that so upset Higashikokubaru.

In contrast, reporters for Japan's big media are generally staffers, usually embedded in organizations with a strict line of command and lifetime employment. As Jochen Legewie points out, the emphasis at these companies is on a descriptive, fact-based style relying on official sources. Investigative reporting is limited and the individual reputation of each reporter is considered less important than those of their Western counterparts. Most of the stories carried in the Japanese newspapers are not by-lined. In practice, this means that the best investigative reporting in Japan is often done by free-spirited freelancers, such as Watai Takeharu and Kamata Satoshi (Arita 2011). Watai and three others co-directed one of the best documentaries of the disaster, *311*.[23] Kamata has emerged alongside Nobel prize-winning author Ōe Kenzaburo as a champion of the anti-nuclear movement. Before 3.11, he was already a sharp critic of nuclear power (Kamata 2011).

Later in 2011, a scandal involving hidden losses at the camera and optical equipment-maker Olympus further exposed the structure of the Japanese media. The scandal was broken by a tiny subscription-only magazine called *FACTA*, whose editor Abe Shigeo quit his job at the *Nihon Keizai Shinbun* (Japan's leading financial daily) after being told to withdraw a story on corruption in the securities industry. 'There are no real scoops in Japanese newspapers', he told me (McNeill 2012).

It is not difficult from the above to see two very different dynamics at work. Unlike their foreign counterparts, Japanese reporters for the big

---

23   The documentary's home page is here: <http://docs311.jp/eng.html> accessed 7 June 2013.

media had little to gain from breaking ranks and disregarding government warnings on the dangers of reporting close to the nuclear plant. Moreover, the cartel-like behaviour of the Japanese media companies meant they did not have to fear being scooped by rivals (see Freeman 1996, 2000). To freelance journalist Uesugi Takashi, the herd system of big media, with systematic external constraint and self-imposed internal restraint, is a uniquely Japanese phenomenon that does crippling damage to freedom of the press. In an interview with him that I conducted a few days after the disaster, he described how politicians who wanted to include freelancers and foreign media in their press conferences were forced by the press clubs to hold two separate press conferences in separate rooms (McNeill 2010).

This kind of information cartel was applied to the delicate question of how to describe what was going on at Fukushima No.1 plant. Most of the big newspapers and networks in Japan agreed early on to avoid using the word 'meltdown' (*roshin yōyū* or *merutodaun*), going no further than 'partial melting' (*bubunteki yōyū*), although the decision was made only after much debate. It was also noticeable that very little appeared in the Japanese media about the plutonium fuel in reactor No.3 at the Fukushima No.1 plant.

In particularly dangerous situations, managers of TV networks and newspapers will form agreements (known as *hōdō kyōtei*) in effect to collectively keep their reporters out of harm's way. In an interview with me on 16 September 2011, Jimbo Tetsuo, founder of the pioneering broadcaster Video News Network, explained: 'Once the five or six big firms come to an agreement with their competitors not to do anything, they don't have to worry about being scooped or challenged'. Jimbo said the eruption of Mount Unzen in Kyushu in 1991 and the 2003 invasion of Iraq, both of which led to fatalities among Japanese journalists, copper-fastened these agreements – one reason why so few Japanese reporters can be seen in recent conflict zones such as Burma, Thailand or Afghanistan. *The Times'* Asia Bureau Chief Richard Lloyd Parry, who has reported from all those conflicts, sums up his observations thus: 'Japanese journalists are among the most risk-averse in the world'.[24]

24   Personal interview, 6 October 2011. Those Japanese journalists who do get in harm's way tend to be freelancers or employees of small independent agencies, like Yamamoto

Frustrated by the lack of information from around the plant, in the end Jimbo took his camera and dosimetres into the 20km zone on 2 April 2011 and, like Sakurai, uploaded a report on YouTube that was viewed all over the world.[25] He was the first Japanese reporter to bring television images from Futaba and other abandoned towns, and those images never made it onto broadcast TV in Japan – though images from the zone, shot during government-approved incursions, would later appear on regular TV news. 'For freelance journalists, it's not hard to beat the big companies because you quickly learn where their line is', he said. 'As a journalist I needed to go in and find out what was happening. Any real journalist would want to do that'. He later sold some of his footage to three of the big Japanese TV networks: NHK, NTV and TBS.

Japan's state broadcaster NHK has a network of 54 bureaus throughout Japan, thousands of journalists, 14 helicopters and over 60 mobile broadcasting units. It reaches 50 million households and is among the most trusted news sources in the world. Throughout the disaster, it was striking how it was a key source of information, always flickering on screens in the corner of hotels, restaurants, emergency shelters. 'If you rolled ABC, NBC and CBS News together, you'd have something equivalent to the place of NHK in Japanese media', Ellis Krauss, a professor of Japanese politics and policymaking at the University of California told the *Washington Post* in March (Harlan 2011). With that network, and its exclusive access to disaster information, NHK did an efficient job of relaying information from government and corporate sources but did less well in analysing it, says Jimbo. 'For two months they were showing graphics on TV about what was happening. All they did was quote experts, TEPCO and others from the "nuclear village". So that meant that everything they showed was wrong'.

In the months that followed, NHK broadcast numerous excellent documentaries on the disaster. They, and their private-sector competitors,

---

Mika of the Japan Press, who was killed while reporting the civil war in Syria on 20 August 2012.

25   <http://www.youtube.com/watch?v=yp9iJ3pPuL8> accessed on 7 June, when Jimbo's video had over 1 million hits, against 450,000 for Mayor Sakurai's video.

worked hard to follow the tribulations of the disaster victims. Occasionally there was some excessive sentimentality, but, by and large, a thorough job was done. In the area of slowly developed, considered documentary, the Japanese media did well. But that was after the fear of radiation had subsided, and when there was no longer any immediate risk of further explosions at Fukushima No.1. It was in the white heat of the emergency that big media showed its innate conservatism and risk-aversion, leading to criticism like that by Jimbo Tetsuo.

Conservatism was also apparent in the media coverage of the growing protests against the restart of Japan's remaining nuclear reactors. There were demonstrations throughout the summer of 2011, climaxing with an estimated 60,000 people in Tokyo's Meiji Park on 19 September. Satoh found that 16 demonstrations received a total of 686 words in the nation's most popular (and pro-nuclear) newspaper, the *Yomiuri Shinbun*. Analysts showed that while 'progressive' outlets such as *Mainichi Shinbun* and *Tokyo Shinbun* fared better, Japanese newspapers generally devoted more column inches to anti-nuclear protests in Germany, than in Japan. TV cameras rarely showed up to record the start of the Tokyo summer demos, which often began just outside NHK headquarters in Tokyo's Yoyogi Park (Satoh 2012).

A series of large anti-nuclear demonstrations in front of the National Diet building beginning on 29 March 2012 were also initially ignored by the mainstream Japanese media. Organizers relied on online social media and word of mouth to spread the word. A crowd estimated by organizers at 170,000 people rallied outside the prime minister's official residence on 29 June 2012, probably the largest demonstration in Tokyo since the era of the Vietnam War. The figures were of course disputed by the police, and by many of the journalists who were there. There was, however, one conspicuous absence. 'The *Yomiuri* didn't mention any figures, because it didn't cover it.'[26]

---

26 See Philip Brasor, 'Strength in numbers for protestors, but just how many are there?' *Japan Times*, 22 July 2012. <http://www.japantimes.co.jp/text/fd20120722pb.html> accessed September 13, 2012.

Conclusion

Singling out the foreign media for criticism, as Higashikokubaru, *Newsweek* and Japan's government all did in the weeks after 11 March, set up an unhelpful binary and perpetuated the soft nationalism that was one of the more unfortunate side effects of the disaster. '*We* stayed and did our job. *They* ran away. We can't rely on them'. I have tried in this paper to question that simplistic notion, showing how journalists from all sides were subject to structural constraints that affected their coverage. It makes as little sense to single out the 'foreign' press for particular criticism of poor reporting as it does to blame the entire Japanese media for being complacent, deferential and overly process-orientated. As we have seen, freelance Japanese journalists were also frustrated at many aspects of big media reporting of the crisis, while foreign commentators were deeply critical of the more sensationalist 'parachute' hacks.

I have cited some of the more striking examples of media manipulation, including the effective blackout of taboo words like 'meltdown' and 'plutonium', and the widespread use of government-approved experts to spin the limited information leaking from the Fukushima plant. One of the more striking features of the Japanese media, however, is its remarkable self-regulation. It is puzzling to outsiders to see reporters for the largest companies operating in apparent concert, as they seemed to do inside the 20km zone and in Minami-Sōma, disregarding what many foreign reporters would see as the natural rules of competition.

Though now regularly compared to the Chernobyl disaster of 1986, Fukushima was in at least one important way very different: it took place in a country with an ostensibly free media. Reporters working during the dying days of the old Stalinist system that ran the Soviet-controlled Ukraine were banned from investigating or writing about Chernobyl. Scientists were placed under house arrest or put in prison. There were no such restrictions in Fukushima, making it a unique case for study.[27] We are still digesting the

---

27   Interestingly, however, some Japanese magazines say that while the Soviet government was criminally negligent in its first response to Chernobyl, it later worked

full implications of what happened in the weeks after 11 March 2011 and what it tells us about how our media performed; I have only scratched the surface here. One important consequence is that big media journalists have been forced to acknowledge the anti-nuclear lobby after years of largely snubbing it and underreporting the dangers of building so many reactors in one of the planet's most seismically unstable countries. Some grudgingly turned up to report a 19 September 2011 anti-nuclear demonstration in Tokyo, one of the largest on record, to hear freelance journalist and activist Kamata Satoshi launch an angry tirade against them. 'Those journalists have become too institutionalized', he said, pointing in their direction. 'They cannot openly express their anger or fear because they are under pressure from their bosses not to do so. We are all paying the price'.

References

Arita Eriko (2011). 'Satoshi Kamata: Rebel spirit writ large', *The Japan Times*, 2 October. <http://www.japantimes.co.jp/text/fl20111002x1.html> accessed 7 June 2013.

—— (2012). 'Keeping an Eye on TV News Coverage of the Nuke Crisis', *The Japan Times*, 8 July.

Brasor, Philip (2012). 'Strength in Numbers for Protestors, but Just How Many Are There?' *The Japan Times*, 22 July. <http://www.japantimes.co.jp/text/fd20120722pb.html> accessed 7 June 2013.

DeLange, William (1998). *A History of Japanese Journalism: Japan's Press Club as the Last Obstacle to a Mature Press*. London: Routledge.

Freeman, Laurie Ann (1996). 'Japan's Press Clubs as Information Cartels', *Japan Policy Research Institute, Working Paper* No.18, April 1996. <http://www.jpri.org/publications/workingpapers/wp18.html> accessed 6 September 2012.

—— (2000). *Closing the Shop: Information Cartels and Japan's Mass Media*. Princeton: Princeton University Press.

---

much harder than the Japanese authorities to move children away from the irradiated zone. See for instance *Josei Seven*, 26 May 2011. Available online at <http://www.news-postseven.com/archives/20110518_20367.html> accessed 27 November 2011.

Gamble, Andrew, and Watanabe Takesato (2004). *A Public Betrayed: An Inside Look at Japanese Media Atrocities and their Warnings to the West*. Washington, DC: Regnery Publishing.

Hall, Ivan P. (1997). *Cartels of the Mind: Japan's Intellectual Closed Shop*. New York: W.W. Norton.

Hammer, Joshua (2011). 'Inside the Danger Zone', *The Daily Beast*, 3 April. <http://www.thedailybeast.com/newsweek/2011/04/03/inside-the-danger-zone.html> accessed 7 June 2013.

Harlan, Chico (2011). 'In Japan, Disaster Coverage is Measured, not Breathless', *Washington Post*, 28 March. <http://www.washingtonpost.com/lifestyle/style/in-japan-disaster-coverage-is-measured-not-breathless/2011/03/26/AFMmfxlB_story.html> accessed 7 June 2013.

Hirose Takashi (2011). *Fukushima Meltdown: The World's First Earthquake-Tsunami-Nuclear Disaster*, Kindle edition. (Self-published translation of *Fukushima Genpatsu Merutodaun* (Asahi Shinbunsha, 2011)).

Howden, Daniel (2011). 'Fear and Devastation on the Road to Japan's Nuclear Disaster Zone', *The Independent*, 26 March. <http://www.independent.co.uk/news/world/asia/fear-and-devastation-on-the-road-to-japans-nuclear-disaster-zone-2253509.html> accessed 7 June 2013.

Itō Mamoru (2012). *Terebi wa genpatsu jiko o dō tsutaeta no ka?* (How did television cover the nuclear power plant disaster?) Tokyo: Heibonsha.

Johnston, Eric (2011). *The Tohoku Earthquake and Tsunami, the Fukushima Nuclear Reactor, and How the World's Media Reported Them*. Tokyo: Japan Times.

Kamata Satoshi (2001). *Genpatsu rettō o yuku* (Travelling the nuclear archipelago). Tokyo: Shūeisha.

Koizumi Tetsuo (2011). 'Genpatsu suishin PR sakusen no ichidoku-santan' (A reading of pro-nuclear power PR strategies). In Media Kenkyūjo (ed.) *Daijishin genpatsu jiko to media* (The media and the earthquake/nuclear disaster). Tokyo: Ōtsuki Shoten.

Legewie, Jochen (2010). *Japan's Media: Inside and Outside Powerbrokers*. Tokyo: Communications and Network Consulting Japan.

McJilton, Charles (2013). 'Shien o kobamu hitobito. Hisai shien no shōheki to bunkateki haikei' (People who refuse aid. The cultural background of the barrier against relief aid). In Tom Gill, Brigitte Steger and David Slater (eds): *Higashi-Nihon daishinsai no jinruigaku: Tsunami, genpatsu jiko to hisaishatachi no 'sono go'* (Anthropology of the great earthquake disasters in East Japan: The victims and the 'aftermath' of the tsunami and nuclear accident), pp. 31–62. Kyoto: Jinbun Shoin.

McNeill, David (2010). 'Japanese Journalism is Collapsing', *No.1 Shimbun*, 17 March. <http://www.fccj.or.jp/node/5491> accessed 7 June 2013.

—— (2011a). 'Sensationalist Coverage', *The Irish Times*, 19 March. <http://www.irishtimes.com/newspaper/world/2011/0319/1224292611835.html> accessed 7 June 2013. (Subscription required.)

—— (2011b). 'Pro-Nuclear Professors Accused of Singing Industry's Tune in Japan', *The Chronicle of Higher Education*, 24 July.

—— (2011c). 'A City Left to Fight for Survival After the Fukushima Nuclear Disaster', *The Irish Times*, 9 April.

—— (2011d). 'In the Shadow of Japan's Wounded Nuclear Beast', *The Irish Times*, 28 March. <http://www.irishtimes.com/newspaper/world/2011/0328/1224293221947.html> accessed 7 June 2013. (Subscription required.)

—— (2011e). 'Thousands Flee Tokyo as Experts Try to Calm Radiation Fears', *The Independent*, 16 March. <http://www.independent.co.uk/news/world/asia/thousands-flee-tokyo-as-experts-try-to-calm-contamination-fears-2242992.html> accessed 7 June 2013.

—— (2012). 'Stop the Presses and Hold the Front Page', *The Japan Times*, 8 January. <http://www.japantimes.co.jp/text/fl20120108x1.html> accessed 7 June 2013.

Ōgi Noriyuki (2011). 'Kenshō: Higashi Nippon Daishinsai to media'. (Investigated: The Great Eastern Japan Earthquake and the media). *Galac* 173, October.

Sanchanta, Mariko (2011). 'Japan, Foreign Media Divide', *Wall Street Journal*, 19 March. <http://online.wsj.com/article/SB10001424052748703512404576209043550725356.html?mod=WSJAsia> accessed 7 June 2013.

Satoh, Kei'ichi (2011). 'What Should the Public Know? Japanese Media Coverage on the Antinuclear Movement between March 11 and September 30, 2011'. In *Disaster, Infrastructure and Society: Learning from the 2011 Earthquake in Japan* 2, 35–39. <http://hermes-ir.lib.hit-u.ac.jp/rs/bitstream/10086/23123/1/dis0000200350.pdf> accessed 5 July 2013.

Takeda Tōru (2011). *Genpatsu hōdō to media* (Media and reporting on nuclear power). Tokyo: Kōdansha Gendai Shinsho.

Wakiyama, Maki (2011). '"The Media is a Mouthpiece for TEPCO": Interview with Toyohiro Akiyama'. *No.1 Shimbun*, June. <http://www.fccj.ne.jp/no1/issue/pdf/June_2011.pdf> accessed 20 June 2013.

Wheeler, Virginia (2011). 'Starving Brit Keely: My Life Trapped in City of Ghosts – Tokyo', *The Sun*, 16 March. <http://www.thesun.co.uk/sol/homepage/news/3473142/My-nightmare-trapped-in-post-tsunami-Tokyo-City-of-Ghosts.html> accessed 7 June 2013.

Yokota Takashi and Yamada Toshihiro (2011). 'Sono toki kisha wa nigeta (At that time, the journalists ran away)', *Newsweek Japan*, 5 April. Published in English as 'Foreign Media Create Secondary Disaster', *No.1 Shimbun*, June 2011. <http://www.fccj.ne.jp/no1/issue/pdf/June_2011.pdf> accessed 7 June 2013.

IKEDA YOKO

The Construction of Risk and the Resilience of Fukushima in the Aftermath of the Nuclear Power Plant Accident

The image of the first explosion at the Tokyo Electric Power Company (TEPCO) Fukushima No.1 nuclear power plant was broadcast on Fukushima Central Television (FCT) on 12 March 2011, soon after it happened at 3.36pm that day. It was the day after the massive earthquake and subsequent tsunami had hit Japan. Seeing the image, I immediately thought of Chernobyl. On 13 March, when I regained access to the internet, which had been down due to the earthquake, I looked up the distance between my home city of Kōriyama, and the nuclear power plant. Kōriyama, with a population of around 333,000, is in the centre of Fukushima prefecture, approximately 60 kilometres from the plant, which is located by the seashore on the eastern edge of Fukushima. At Chernobyl, the 30 kilometre radius from the plant became the 'exclusion zone', where no one has been allowed back to live. So, realizing I was 60 kilometres away reassured me for the time being. However, it still felt surreal that a nuclear accident was happening in my prefecture.

I am a US-trained anthropologist who happened to be living back at home in Kōriyama when Fukushima prefecture experienced its quadruple disaster: earthquake(s), tsunami, the nuclear power plant accident and the harmful rumours (*fūhyō higai*) associated with it. A nuclear accident evokes a fear of the unknown, alongside its actual harm. In the face of unknown possibilities and contradicting information, the boundaries between 'safe' and 'unsafe', 'affected' and 'not affected', and 'contaminated' and 'not contaminated' become blurry, arbitrary and even imaginary. In the aftermath of this accident, Fukushima could no longer be just a prefecture known mostly for its agricultural bounty and the beauty of its natural landscape.

The name became conflated with the nuclear power plant accident. There were varying degrees of radiation contamination within Fukushima and various claims as to how it would affect people's health. Except for the evacuation zones, Fukushima remained open for business; life went on as usual. Yet, living in the aftermath meant becoming aware of risks and taking risks without, necessarily, knowing the odds or the possible consequences. Even at the best of times everyday life entails taking risks, but the nuclear accident has brought a new urgency to the question of what 'acceptable risk' is. Mary Douglas and Aaron Wildavsky (1982: 4) point out that 'which kinds of risks are acceptable to what sorts of people' is a political issue, especially in the face of uncertain knowledge and lack of consent. They argue that 'perception of risk' is a product of social processes and that risk is subjective and cultural, shaped by 'shared beliefs and values' (Douglas and Wildavsky 1982: 6, 194). Ulrich Beck (1992) perceives risk as inherent to modernization and depicts society in advanced modernity as a risk society, which operates not only through redistribution of wealth but also through redistribution of risk. In this chapter, I explore the following questions. How is risk perceived and constructed regarding the Fukushima No.1 nuclear power plant accident? And what are the consequences of the current construction of risk? More so than at the time of any other nuclear disaster, the internet and other media are an integral part of the social process today. I will look at the role of the media and internet in contributing to the making of risk-discourse. I argue that in its recovery, Fukushima is being burdened with a stigma of contamination, both literal and imaginary. This paper is based on my experience living in Kōriyama and also on interviews with several people in Kōriyama and Fukushima cities. These sites are outside the evacuation zone, and thus people have continued with life largely as usual. They are, however, still affected by the fallout, navigating through contradictory information regarding radiation, contamination and risk.

Radiation falling on Fukushima

For months following the earthquake and the nuclear power plant accident, everywhere I went – a restaurant, a gym locker room, a beauty salon
– I heard people talking about earthquakes and radiation, sharing stories
of where they were and what happened on 11 March. Earthquakes were a
daily conversation topic, not least because the central and coastal parts of
Fukushima continued to experience daily aftershocks for about half a year.
Previously exotic terms like 'caesium' and 'becquerel' entered the everyday
vocabulary of ordinary people. Local TV and radio gave hourly updates
on environmental radiation levels in different parts of Fukushima. Many
individuals either purchased or borrowed a Geiger counter and measured radiation levels inside and outside the house. Everyone I talked to in
Kōriyama and Fukushima cities knew the environmental radiation level
in their neighbourhood and knew that some areas had higher levels than
others. People knew the numbers, but they differed on how to interpret
and act on them.

When the first hydrogen explosion occurred at the No.1 nuclear power
plant, people I talked to said they learned about it almost right away from
TV or via the internet. Signs of trouble at the power plant had already been
reported the previous day. The subsequent nuclear disaster was of course
reported all over the world. In the two local newspapers – *Fukushima Minpō*
and *Fukushima Minyū* – the accident and its aftermath have remained part
of the daily news ever since. Also, featured on the front page of local newspapers after 3.11 was the rising death toll from the earthquakes and tsunami,
a number which reached 1,603 dead and 241 missing in Fukushima prefecture, mostly in the coastal area, as of 10 September 2011 (NHK news 2011).

In most cities in Fukushima prefecture, including Fukushima city, the
prefectural capital, and Kōriyama, the prefecture's most populous city, there
was no evacuation order. Many evacuees from the coastal areas were housed
in these cities, first in evacuation shelters and later in temporary housing.
Radiation on 16 March, two days after the second hydrogen explosion at
the troubled plant destroyed the outer building of reactor No.3, was 2.94

μSv/h (microsieverts per hour), against a normal reading of 0.04–0.06, in Kōriyama and 14.60 μSv/h (normally 0.04) in Fukushima (RFC-Radio Fukushima 2011b). It slowly but steadily came down, and the reading on 3 September 2011 at noon, five months after the accident, was 0.86 μSv/h in Kōriyama and 1.04 μSv/h in Fukushima (RFC Radio Fukushima 2011a). Radiation levels inside buildings and houses are generally much lower than outside. Just over a year after the accident, the Ministry of Education, Culture, Sports, Science and Technology (MEXT) put environmental radiation monitoring posts in numerous public sites including major parks and schools all over Fukushima, and the data are on display twenty-four hours a day at these sites, as well as on the website.

Understanding the risks associated with the radiation fallout

Ulrich Beck (1987: 156) points out that since nuclear danger cannot be detected or understood through one's senses, 'information equals reality'. In his depiction of Chernobyl, information is centralized, and scientific authority loses its significance in the construction of risk because no one is a real expert when it comes to atomic danger. Beck argues that no one knows exactly the consequences of radiation exposure. In contrast to the late 1980s when Beck wrote about Chernobyl, the construction of risk in the aftermath of TEPCO's accident seems decentralized. Information regarding risk, whether backed by scientific studies or not, is quickly distributed via the internet and other media and is interpreted and debated almost as rapidly. Individuals today not only receive information from the internet, but also disseminate information by writing blogs or twitter entries, and also by retweeting twitter entries.

A wide variety of experts have commented on the aftermath of the accident. Those who argued that the areas outside the evacuation zones faced minimal risks from radiation fallout were sometimes derogatorily referred to as '*goyō gakusha*' ('lapdog scholars' favourable to the government and TEPCO) by those who perceived them as liars for insisting, 'It's safe'. Those who insisted that regardless of government claims, radiation levels were unacceptably high in the whole of Fukushima, people living there almost certainly faced health problems, and local agricultural products should be avoided, were called '*tondemo*' ('What nonsense!') by critics who argued that they lacked real scientific knowledge to back their claims.

Among those criticized as 'lapdog scholars' (regardless of their lack of affiliation with the government) were Nagataki Shigenobu, a professor emeritus at Nagasaki University specializing in thyroid illnesses, and Yamashita Shun'ichi, Dean of the Graduate School of Biomedical Sciences at Nagasaki University, who became the vice president at Fukushima Medical University and the radiation health risk management advisor to Fukushima prefecture. Yamashita was a core member of the Chernobyl Sasakawa Health Medical Co-operation Project, which studied the health impact of radiation in Russia, Ukraine, and Belarus between 1991 and 2001 (see Sasakawa Memorial Health Foundation 2011; Yamashita and Shibata eds 1997). Both Nagataki and Yamashita have been studying the effects of radiation on the survivors of the Nagasaki and Hiroshima atomic bombings. Yamashita and his staff came to Fukushima city soon after the second explosion at the Fukushima No.1 nuclear power plant. He points out that various long-term epidemiological studies on radiation effects on human heath have led to an international consensus that 100 mSv (millisieverts) is the annual dose beyond which cancer risks are known to increase, and that below 100 mSv is a grey zone (Hashimoto 2011). People who believe Fukushima city is in grave danger have criticized him, almost as though his 100 mSv yardstick would actually cause greater radiation exposure. Yamashita supported the initial government-set exposure limit of 20 mSv per year as a scientifically sound criterion for an evacuation zone. The interim objective of keeping people's exposure below 20 mSv/year corresponds to the International Commission on Radiological Protection (ICPR)'s recommendation for the optimization of protection for people living in radiation contaminated areas (ICRP 2009). This level, however, has been condemned by some citizens' groups, which questioned whether it really was a safe level or not.

Yamashita, as well as some other doctors, gave many public speeches and Q & A sessions in Fukushima early on after the accident. While he helped many people to learn about the potential impact of radiation on human health and to put the situation in Fukushima into perspective, Yamashita also attracted severe criticism from those who accused him of making light of the 'grave danger' people in Fukushima were facing by assuring them that the level of radiation and associated risks in most areas in Fukushima were sufficiently low and by making remarks such as 'the (negative) effect of radiation won't reach people who smile and laugh' in one of his public lectures. When I listened to Yamashita speaking on Radio Fukushima in March 2011, I did not give much thought to the 'smile' remark as it reminded me of familiar but inconclusive discussions on the effects of laughter on health (see Martin 2002) and stress on cancer (National Cancer Institute 2008). However, many people found such remarks deeply offensive or ridiculous, and Yamashita lost credibility in their eyes. Some people and organizations, especially those who insisted that the whole of Fukushima was unfit for habitation, even depicted Yamashita as treating people there as his 'guinea pigs' for his research interests and personal career gain (e.g. see Tanaka 2011).

Interestingly, in 2012 a similar accusation of 'treating the people of Fukushima as guinea pigs' was made against Ethos in Fukushima, a small, citizen-led study group whose aim, according to their website, is to learn about radiation and exchange ideas about living in the post-nuclear area. The group received many negative comments on the internet from those who insisted that people should no longer live in Fukushima prefecture.

Robert P. Gale, a doctor who treated patients and conducted research in the aftermath of Chernobyl, specializes in leukaemia and bone marrow cancer. He views risks as well-managed in the aftermath of Fukushima, though he adds that the government may not be adequately explaining the confusing details (*Diamond Online* 2011). In August 2012, the results of a study conducted by Tsubokura Masaharu of the University of Tokyo and his team on the amount of internal radiation exposure among Minami-Sōma's residents were published (JAMA 2012). Minami-Sōma, located 14 miles north of the Fukushima No.1 nuclear power plant, contained both evacuation and non-evacuation zones. Of 9,498 residents voluntarily enrolled in the screening programme, caesium was detected in 3,286 people, but the doses (all 1 mSv or less apart from one at 1.07mSv) were within the common dose-limit recommended for the public (JAMA 2012). David Weinstock MD of Harvard University was quoted as saying that the doses detected in the research represented 'approximately zero risk' (Boytchev 2012). While medical experts appear comfortable in using statistical and epidemiological approaches in their understanding of risk, many lay people desire something more concrete and easier to comprehend. Some studies show that there are gaps between clinical medical concepts of risk based on statistics and epidemiology, and lay or cultural concepts which individuals filter through perceptions based on their own personal experiences, values and knowledge (Hunt, Castañeda and de Voogd 2006; Reventlow, Hvas and Tulinius 2001).

Among those who emphasized the dangers posed to Fukushima by radiation, some gained more attention than others, either through the media or as a result of their internet followers. Kodama Tatsuhiko, a professor and the head of the Radioisotope Centre at the University of Tokyo, testified on 27 July 2011 at the House of Representatives' Health, Labour and Welfare Committee, pointing out the unevenly distributed and widespread nature of the contamination and the possible long-term consequences, including cancer, of internal exposure to the radiation. He criticized the government for relying on radius distance in maintaining the evacuation zone and for not starting decontaminating efforts sooner (House of Representatives 2012). His passionate plea and arguments concerning the dangers of radiation were praised by many, including anti-nuclear power groups.

Scientific and medical research takes time. Meanwhile, blogs and books for mass consumption quickly became available in post-accident Fukushima. For example, Kinoshita Kōta, who became known as a public speaker on the dangers of radiation after 3.11, began making claims that there had been an increase in the greater Tokyo area in the incidence of sore throats, fatigue, tingling feelings, coughing, metallic tastes, and nose bleeding, as well as numerous other illnesses and deaths due to radiation fallout (Kinoshita 2011). His 'evidence' was a collection of stories submitted to his blog by individuals who speculatively ascribed their symptoms and illnesses to radiation fallout. His own blog profile implies that he has done some journalistic work, but makes no mention of any medical or scientific background. Yet, according to his homepage, over 4000 people have attended his 'medical lectures' (*iryō kōen*) (Kinoshita 2012).

Takeda Kunihiko, a professor of engineering at Chubu University, has gained popular credibility as an expert on radiation and its effects on people's health by publishing numerous non-academic books on the topic since the accident in Fukushima. He has also written many blog entries on his own site regarding Fukushima. Although he is a university professor, his blogs are written in non-academic style and lack proper citations. Yet, the strong opinions expressed in his blog, such as 'It should be forbidden to move things from Fukushima to other prefectures', attract many readers and followers (Takeda 2011). Takeda's blog is merely a vehicle for expressing his opinions, and is not subject to academic or scientific scrutiny. Yet, many people, given Takeda's well-known status as a university professor, view the blog as a legitimate, even authoritative source of objective knowledge.

Currently, the debate on the risks of radiation fallout focuses mostly on physical health. Examination of the impact of Chernobyl on health suggests that many people in the affected areas are also suffering from anxiety and stress, as a result of worrying about the risks to their health (IAEA 2005; Yevelson et al. 1997; *The Economist* 1996). Such anxiety is widespread in Fukushima today. Yet there is also resistance to leaving the area. In a survey of Fukushima residents carried out by *Asahi Shinbun* and KFB (Fukushima Broadcasting Corporation) (Kawaguchi 2011), 62 per cent of 942 respondents rejected the idea of moving to a location either outside Fukushima or to an area with lower radiation levels, and 59 per cent responded that they did not want to leave the area where they live and with which they are familiar.

Living in the aftermath with contradictory information

In the summer of 2011, I interviewed several people from Kōriyama and Fukushima city about their views on risks and safety regarding the nuclear accidents and their aftermath. Kayoko, a woman in her thirties who has lived in Kōriyama almost all her life, was at work when the first explosion at the power plant happened. She learned about it when a colleague shouted out as he saw the news on the internet. Her first reaction was 'I knew it!' She was somehow not surprised, but she said it also felt unreal to see the event she feared actually happening. She knew about nuclear power plants in Fukushima before the accident and had thought, 'What if?' Though worried about radiation fallout, she said she walked to work instead of driving in the following days because of the serious gasoline shortage that hit the Tohoku region after the earthquake. Her anger about what happened led her to sign an online petition to demand that Fukushima prefecture should scrap all its nuclear power plants. But except for that, she focused on practical matters, like how to get to work.

John, a foreign doctor who had been living in Fukushima city with his wife and children for five years, initially took a wait-and-see attitude about the accident. Watching the international news, however, gave him a sense of urgency and seriousness. As a precaution, he avoided food and water from Fukushima. Some of his friends left the city or took their children to grandparents living outside the prefecture. He and his family, however, did not leave, though John said he was 'really concerned about the situation', especially for his small children. He never considered abandoning the people in Fukushima with whom he had built close ties: it seemed 'not fair'. Moreover, he said, he did not consider current radiation levels a risk for adults. He was, however, seriously considering the possibility of evacuating his wife and children, partly because he knew children are more susceptible to radiation effects than adults and also because his parents and overseas friends were pressuring him to do so.

Naomi, a piano teacher living with her elderly parents in Kōriyama, got a call from her brother in Tokyo on the day of the first explosion, offering to evacuate them from the city. Due to earthquake damage, major roads and train lines were shut in Tohoku, and getting in and out of Kōriyama required more effort than usual for weeks after the quake. Her father, who has a bad leg, did not want to go, and she decided to stay. She also felt the city was far enough from the accident site. Nonetheless, for at least a month, she took precautions to protect herself against exposure to radiation by wearing a mask, glasses and coat when going outside.[1] She said she avoided vegetables and fruit from Fukushima and did not often go to parks.

Naomi saw a wide range of responses among her piano students and their parents to the radiation scare. To her surprise, some students showed up as usual in the days after the earthquake and nuclear plant accident. Many students, however, cancelled a couple of lessons to go away – which was made easier because the accident happened to coincide with spring break at schools. Some mothers looked so worried and spoke so nervously about radiation that Naomi felt they were encouraging feelings of anxiety in their children. Some of these worried families left the city eventually, only giving notice at the very last minute that they were leaving. In Naomi's words, 'when they left it was if they had just disappeared'. She suspected that they felt a bit uneasy, perhaps even 'guilty' about leaving while others were staying. Neither Naomi nor other people I talked to spoke negatively of people who decided to leave the city. For a while after the accident, the word 'Fukushima' often evoked conversations about risk. Living in Fukushima, like leaving Fukushima, felt like a choice. It was a statement that somehow seemed to require an explanation or justification.

Masao, a doctor who lives in Fukushima city, said he never considered evacuating his family. He was most concerned about radiation right after the explosion, since he did not immediately know what had happened or how much radiation had reached the city. With his medical expertise and

---

1   Wearing a mask is common in Japan, especially during early spring when many people suffer from allergies. So it was difficult to know, in the months of March to May 2011, which people were wearing masks because of radiation and which because of hay fever.

knowledge of the effects of radiation, he felt comfortable with his family staying in the city once he learned the radiation levels in Fukushima. He was especially relieved when it became apparent that radiation levels were steadily coming down from their peak in March. However, he also thought it was in the best interests of his children that he and his wife reduce the amount of radiation in the house and at his children's schools. They tore up and carted away the lawn in their yard, which helped reduce the amount of radiation there. He appreciated efforts by the city and school parents to clean school building surfaces and remove the surface soil from the playground. All schools in the city were to halt outside activities from the start of the school year in April until the decontamination was completed. At Masao's daughter's primary school, which is relatively new and small, parents were given the option of deciding whether or not to permit their children to play outside after the top soil of the schoolyard had been removed in June and drink milk from Fukushima with their school lunch (the government had been testing all food products, including milk, to ensure their safety). Five out of twenty students in the second grade, including his own children, were given parental permission to play outside and drink local milk in the first term. Masao has heard of friction between parents regarding each other's choices about allowing children to play outside, but witnessed nothing like it at his daughter's school. He viewed the current level of environmental radiation as imposing few real risks to residents of Fukushima city. He argued that the health risks from cigarette smoking and passive smoking were more serious than those posed by radiation from the Fukushima plant.

In contrast, Yuki, a graduate student from Fukushima city, felt that Fukushima was no longer a safe place to live. She had previously lived and worked in the United States where a Japanese-American family treated her like one of their own. Yuki said they were so worried about her that they insisted she come to stay with them. She took up their offer and evacuated to the US for a month. She was in Fukushima when we met, but she was planning to leave for the US for good, strongly believing that Fukushima was unsafe. She had also convinced a friend of hers with a baby to leave Fukushima, despite the initial opposition of the friend's husband. Another friend with a baby, though, was so confident that living in Fukushima was safe that Yuki could do nothing to convince her to go.

Leaving Fukushima seems not to depend solely on whether money or a job can provide the wherewithal to do so, though that certainly is an important issue, and I have heard people say there is no way to leave without the guarantee of another job. However, it also depends on the perceived risk of remaining in Fukushima. While the government seems to have offered an implicit guarantee of safety by not designating Kōriyama and Fukushima city as evacuation zones, everyone I talked to appeared to have formed their own opinions and decided on their own terms whether to leave or stay. People approached their decisions seriously, but their choices still required a balancing act and involved contradictions. Yuki, for example, despite her strong emphasis on the danger of living in Fukushima, dined with me at a restaurant without any special precautions such as mask or glasses to protect herself. And while she insisted that she avoided products from Fukushima, she casually ordered from the menu without investigating the provenance of its ingredients. Some of those who said they were comfortable living in Fukushima, on the other hand, mentioned that they were eating less than they used to or were avoiding some Fukushima fruits or vegetables during the summer of 2011. This inner negotiation and compromise was an art rather than a science. Most of my informants mentioned though, that they found it stressful to think about these things. Choices were constantly being made without knowing exactly what they were based upon. Later on, however, more options became available for learning about the levels of radioactive materials in food, including those harvested in one's own garden. A site run by the Fukushima prefectural government ('*Fukushima shin hatsubai*', literally 'Fukushima newly on sale') allows people to look up the levels of radioactive materials in food by area or food item. In addition to the prefectural government, some businesses such as grocery chain stores and co-operatives, municipalities and citizen's groups have also been conducting their own tests. I was able to test boysenberries harvested in my garden at one of the sites in Kōriyama. Radioactive materials were not detected, and I made those berries into delicious jam.

Studying the social and physical consequences of the Chernobyl disaster, Adriana Petryna (1995) tells the story of a 'post-Chernobyl social imaginary' through the eyes of people affected by the event. She compares the 'atrocities' against the Ukrainian body, damaged beyond the individual's will and control, to the brutality of Soviet history towards Ukrainians. She implies that in heavily contaminated areas, science and the state dominate vulnerable people's lives. In contrast, in Fukushima, at least away from the evacuation zones, what is apparent is not the overwhelming control of the state but individuals' self-negotiations to determine where they draw the line between 'safe' and 'unsafe' and between acceptable and unacceptable risks. Far from being dominated by a hegemonic state-authorized scientific narrative, people after the Fukushima nuclear accident have been forced to deal with a series of ambiguous and mutually contradictory statements from both those in authority and those who make themselves heard via the media.

Contamination and prejudice

Mary Douglas (1966: 2) points out that the concepts of pollution, discrimination, purity and danger are social and closely intertwined cultural constructs. The perception of danger and the instinct to avoid it cause people to draw conceptual boundaries separating purity from impurity. In Japan, *hibakusha* (those who were exposed to the atomic bombings of Nagasaki and Hiroshima), as well as their descendants, have long faced discrimination in marriage and employment based on misinformation and fear of birth defects. They have also experienced prejudice due to their appearance or health conditions caused by exposure to high doses of radiation and/or extreme heat in the explosions, or as a result of incorrect perceptions of these conditions as being contagious.

Birth defects and deformity are commonly mentioned concerns on the internet associated with radiation exposure from the Fukushima accident. Past studies have established that any correlation between foetus malformation and radiation exposure occurs only when the exposure was at a very high dose, and when the exposure happened at a specific time period during pregnancy. In long-term studies of the survivors of the atomic bombing, pregnancies between eight and fifteen weeks exposed to doses over 200 mSv were seen to have an elevated chance of foetus malformation (Takahashi 2011). No one has been exposed to such a high dose of radiation as a result of the nuclear accident in Fukushima. Studies examining the occurrence of severe malformations among 65,431 new-born babies in Hiroshima and Nagasaki between 1948 and 1954 show the rate at 0.91 per cent. Similar studies conducted in Tokyo during the same period showed a rate of 0.92 per cent, indicating that exposure to radiation in Nagasaki did not affect the rate of malformations in later years (RERF n.d.).

Studies examining the rate of birth malformation in the aftermath of Chernobyl show inconclusive data. The WHO, jointly with IAEA and UNDP, attributes a slight increase seen in statistics in Belarus to better reporting since the accident (WHO 2005); Kozenko and Chudley (2010) discuss the puzzling irregularity in reported rates of malformations in contaminated areas of former Soviet Union countries – the rate increased from 1.8 per cent in 1985 to 5.0 per cent in 1987, a year after the Chernobyl accident, but subsequently decreased to 0.6 per cent in 1988. They argue that the most noticeable effect of the accident was an increase in abortions in the affected regions of the former Soviet Union as well as in Western Europe. Dancause et al. (2010) argue that exposure to radiation 'might contribute' to the higher rate of malformations reported in more contaminated areas of Ukraine than in less contaminated areas, but they indicate that the higher rate can also be attributed to alcohol consumption and micronutrient deficiencies. People's exposure to radiation in Fukushima has been much lower than that in the affected areas in Hiroshima and Nagasaki after the atomic bombing or in Chernobyl. Yet, the fear that 'radiation = birth deformity' (especially, physical deformity) has been playing a significant role in the social construction of post-accident risk in Fukushima. Anonymous blogs and twitter entries have spread anxiety with posts such as 'I heard it is happening already' or by speculating that 'There will be such an increase'. The risk discourse on birth deformity linked to Fukushima affects the mainstream media as well. For example, the 5 September 2011 issue of *AERA* (Yamane 2011), a Japanese magazine, featured an article entitled 'Can I bear a normal child? Letters from children of Fukushima'. The article itself provided no medical or scientific basis to support the sensational title.

Yuki, who has decided to leave Fukushima, told me that Fukushima was unsafe, especially for children and for women who are or may become pregnant in the future. The biggest reason she felt she needed to leave was because she is a woman and expects to bear children one day. Her brother, who is still single and staying in Fukushima, told her, 'You should go, but I'm OK because I am a man'. Their idea of risk shows that its construction is gendered as well. Yuki's conversation with her brother reflects their assumption that women's reproductive health is more affected by radiation than men's. Yuki's decision to leave Fukushima to ensure her safety and that of her potential future children is a personal choice. So is the decision to remain in Fukushima, as most people have chosen to do.

The internet provides an easy means for people to express their frustration and fear regarding the accident. The idea of Fukushima as contaminated has seemed to make some people feel as if they are justified and entitled to express their fear and anger by making discriminatory comments toward Fukushima and its people. 'I felt goose bumps realizing that we have become an object of discrimination', Emika, a native of Kōriyama in her thirties, told me as she described her feelings about comments she found on online bulletin boards and blogs a month after the accident. They said, 'You are contaminated with radiation; don't spread it to the rest of Japan!' and 'Fukushima people accepted nuclear power plants and benefited from them. So, you deserve this!' (see for example 2 Channel 2011; Kukurogu 2011). Emika has long been concerned about and opposed to nuclear power plants. Now she feels that the accident has taken away her freedom, her care-free enjoyment of open windows and rain and gardening, and exposed her to discrimination.

Not only anonymous people, but even a university professor, Hayakawa Yukio, in the department of education at Gunma University, gained many followers as well as critics on Twitter (43,961 Twitter followers as of August 2012) for repeatedly describing Fukushima as a polluted aggressor, threatening to pollute others. His tweets included comments like 'Are there any parents who would like their child to marry someone who did not escape from the radiation when they could have? ... They chose not to (escape). Would it really be discrimination to take such personal history into account when selecting a spouse?' (18 July 2011); and 'Fukushima has declared war against Japan' (5 November 2011). Of course, there are many who oppose such a conceptualization of Fukushima. I asked the above-mentioned Masao, a doctor in Fukushima, whether he was worried that his children might face such discrimination for staying there. He replied, 'If they meet someone they like, and the person's parents are so stupid as to say such a thing, then I will probably tell my child to reconsider, because parents who discriminate like that lack intelligence'.

How false rumours spread

Some false, exaggerated or misleading reports and rumours on what was happening in Fukushima in the aftermath of the accident heightened people's fear of radiation and influenced their view of Fukushima. For example, there was a widespread rumour that nosebleeds, a relatively common occurrence in everyday life, resulted from radiation fallout from the accident. Such rumours may be tied to social knowledge that bleeding was one of the symptoms that followed the atomic bombings in Hiroshima and Nagasaki. Bleeding is a symptom of acute radiation syndrome caused by exposure to 10 gray[2] of radiation or higher (RERF 2007). No one, except conceivably for the people working on the site of the damaged Fukushima No.1 plant, faced the possibility of being exposed to such high levels of radiation. Yet in numerous tweets and blogs, people either claimed that their children's nosebleed was due to radiation or they 'heard' that nosebleeds had become a major problem among children in Fukushima (or in Tokyo) after the accident. Such rumours spread further and assumed the status of 'reality' in Fukushima when *Tokyo Shinbun* wrote an article with the misleading composite headline: '50 km from the Fukushima nuclear power plant, what is happening now in Kōriyama: unusual changes in

---

2   The gray (Gy) is a unit of absorbed radiation. 1 Gy is equal to 1 Sievert or 1,000 mSv for gamma rays.

children's health – massive nosebleeds, diarrhoea, lack of energy [...] "link to radiation unclear"[3] (Ideta 2011). The article was about people who attended a health-consultation event in Kōriyama offered by an NPO called *Chernobyl e no kakehashi* ('Bridge to Chernobyl'). The article mentions only *one* specific case in which a mother was concerned that her children experienced nose bleeds for three weeks after returning to Kōriyama from another prefecture to which they had evacuated, and even here the article mentions that an ENT specialist had told her that it was probably due to hay fever. The writer failed to mention whether nosebleed concerns were common among other participants in the event, or whether any complained of diarrhoea or lack of energy.

One of the problems with rumours spread on the internet is that even those which have been challenged and dismissed still pop up in search results and can make a comeback. The Japan Medical Association (JMA) was forced to post on its website a denial of claims circulating on the internet that it had been involved in collecting data showing a rapid increase in leukaemia patients, and that such reports were outright fabrication (Haranaka 2011). There is no guarantee, however, that people will see such denials.

What motivates some people to spread rumours on internet? Perhaps, one reason may be for a moral or political cause. For example, there have been some overlaps between those involved in the anti-nuclear power movement and the use of rhetoric emphasizing the potential deadly consequences of the nuclear disaster. While the collecting and scientific analysis of data on the health consequences for Fukushima will take time, perhaps decades, people pay the most attention immediately after the incident, when it is still a hot topic in the news. Speculation and rumour may fill the void during the time when reliable information is still scarce or not yet available. Writing attention-grabbing sensational claims can attract more traffic to a blog site or more followers to one's twitter account. This no doubt motivates some people to keep posting writings of such a nature. Sometimes, too, blog sites ask for financial donations so that they can continue writing the

---

3   '*Genpatsu 50 kiro Fukushima, Kōriyama wa ima, ko ni taichō ihen jiwari, tairyō no hanaji, geri, kentaikan ..., "hōshasen to kankei fumei"*'.

'truth about Fukushima' that 'the media would not report'. There have also been independent journalists publishing on Fukushima nuclear disaster related-topics in what are called 'mail magazines'. These are self-distributed, net-based 'newsletters' to which people can subscribe, often paying a monthly fee. Such 'mail magazines' eagerly seek 'scoops' to keep their readers interested. Rumours spread fast nowadays as all it takes is a click to 'retweet' on Twitter, and not everyone has the habit of taking time to check on sources or investigate the validity of information. The internet is an extremely effective means of spreading information, but it is not easy to withdraw it once it has been posted.

Imagining boundaries

The notion of pre-existing social and geographical boundaries affects people's perception of contaminated areas. Takeda Kunihiko, the professor mentioned earlier, once said on a TV show that eating vegetables and meat from Tohoku 'is harmful to your health, so, please throw them away whenever possible'.[4] Instead of giving a specific reason, he went on to describe the land contaminated with radiation fallout, using the rather strange simile of potassium cyanide spread on fields. The Japanese government has set what it considers to be safe limits for radioactive materials in food products, and the Fukushima prefectural government has been testing its products and announcing the results. All the food on sale is supposed to be safe for consumption. However, people's comfort levels for risk differ. There can be disagreements over whether the government-set guidelines are low enough or the testing sufficiently rigorous. Consumers avoiding or preferring food from certain regions may be viewed as practising self-protection or preference rather than discrimination. Yet the comments like the one

---

4   *Takajin no soko made itte i'inkai*, Yomiuri Telecasting Corporation; broadcast on 4
    September 2011.

made by Takeda and numerous lay people, who have claimed Fukushima agricultural products are 'unsafe', draw an arbitrary line between acceptable and unacceptable risk and an imaginary divide between contaminated and not contaminated. Note that Takeda was condemning food from the whole Tohoku area, not just Fukushima prefecture. He does not hesitate to lump all the Tohoku prefectures together, as if the whole region were so contaminated that all its vegetables were unfit for consumption. His comments drew many criticisms online, which questioned his scientific and medical expertise for justifying such a claim, but many people praised him for speaking out. Some prefectures in the Kanto area, such as Ibaraki and Tochigi, are in fact closer to Fukushima than some areas of northern Tohoku, such as Iwate. Levels of radiation fallout in western parts of Fukushima have been no higher than the levels recorded in some parts of the northern Kanto prefectures (MEXT 2011). Yet Takeda did not describe vegetables harvested in those parts of Kanto as 'unsafe'. Such arbitrariness of imagined boundaries became apparent when Tokyo began accepting debris from the tsunami disaster from Iwate and received nearly 3,000 complaints from its residents who felt their health was at risk – this despite the fact that the debris had been repeatedly tested for radiation and deemed safe (Takeuchi 2011). Such complaints reflect the perception that something from any part of Tohoku is more 'polluted' and 'contaminated' than something from Tokyo. Yet levels of caesium above the set limit were occasionally detected in food harvested far from Fukushima, such as Shiitake mushrooms grown and dried in Yokohama and tea harvested in Shizuoka (see *Asahi Shinbun*, 5 November 2011). Tests on radioactive contamination conducted on imported food from Europe between 2009 and 2010, well before the Fukushima disaster, indicate that such contamination may occasionally be found in food from other countries as well (Kimura et al 2010). At the same time, there are many food products from Fukushima that contain no detectable trace of caesium at all (see the website, '*Fukushima shin hatsubai*'). As the system for testing food for radioactive materials has become better established, consumer confidence in food harvested in Fukushima as well as other parts of Tohoku seems to be returning. The food markets in Kōriyama and nearby cities specializing in freshly harvested local produce seemed to have plenty of customers every time I visited them in the summer of 2012, and Fukushima produce, which at one point was almost entirely absent from grocery stores outside of Fukushima, is now making a comeback.

However, no amount of testing or reassuring results may be enough for some people. The line where contamination begins and ends is a blur. Some people's attempts to demarcate Fukushima, or the whole of Tohoku, as a contaminated space may be a means of gaining a sense of security by drawing imaginary boundaries, which locate themselves outside of the contamination zones. People's sense of risk is relative. Some people's perception of the risk and danger from the nuclear power plant led them to evacuate on their own initiative, and largely at their own expense, without a government order or advisory. Within Fukushima prefecture, some people moved west to the Aizu area, while others felt the whole of Fukushima was unsafe and moved to neighbouring prefectures. Some people in eastern Japan felt they were not safe there and moved to areas in western Japan, like Osaka; and others left for Okinawa or Hokkaido, feeling that the whole of mainland Japan was too contaminated. A few even evacuated overseas. But outside of the evacuation zones, most people stayed where they were and did not think of relocating. People decided for themselves where danger ended and safety began.

Conclusion: Fukushima's resilience

The nuclear power plant accident in Fukushima forced people from some parts of Fukushima near the plant to evacuate and others to evaluate radiation risk on a daily basis, while being bombarded with widely contradictory information and downright misinformation. The TEPCO Fukushima No. 1 nuclear power plant was built in Fukushima to supply electricity to the greater Tokyo area. As Beck's notion of 'risk society' suggests, the location of the nuclear power plant highlights the issue of risk distribution within a society. Obviously, the accident has affected Fukushima to a much greater degree than it has affected Tokyo, both in terms of the amount of radiation fallout received and the stigmatization by association with the disaster. Fukushima, and to a lesser extent Tohoku generally, have been burdened with the image of contamination. In some cases, the fear and image of radiation contamination, rather than the actual contamination itself, caused real problems; for example, Miyagi and Iwate prefectures in Tohoku have had great difficulty finding municipalities in other prefectures to help process and dispose of the colossal amount of debris left by the tsunami. The debris has been tested and shown to have radiation levels no higher or even lower than those in regular incinerated garbage generated in the cities accepting it. Yet when cities announced that they were accepting tsunami debris, they often attracted vocal protesters, notably in Kitakyūshū city in southwest Japan and in Shimada city in Shizuoka prefecture, as well as vehement opposition online by people who do not even live in the area. In post-disaster Fukushima and in Japan overall, separating real contamination from imagined contamination is not as easy as one might think.

Everyone I talked to in Fukushima in the summer of 2011 was feeling some kind of stress in thinking about radiation in their everyday lives. Still, many Fukushima residents have been resilient, balancing concerns over radiation with getting on with daily life. Living in Fukushima, I have witnessed all sorts of efforts to restore economic and social health, and to keep agriculture, tourism and other businesses going despite the severe impact of *fūhyō higai* ('damage by harmful rumours'). I have much hope that Fukushima will bounce back from the disastrous events of 2011, and it is evident now that the process is already well underway.

References

Beck, Ulrich (1987). 'The Anthropological Shock: Chernobyl and the Contours of the Risk Society', *Berkeley Journal of Sociology*, 32, 153–166.
——(1992). *Risk Society: Towards a New Modernity*. London: Sage.

Boytchev, Hristio (2012). 'First Study Reports Very Low Internal Radioactivity after Fukushima Disaster', *The Washington Post*, 14 August. <http://articles.washingtonpost.com/2012-08-14/world/35490898_1_average-radiation-dose-health-risk-internal-radiation> accessed 11 June 2013.

Dancause, Kelsey Needham, Lyubov Yevtushok, Serhiy Lapchenko, Ihor Shumlyansky, Genadiy Shevchenko, Wladimir Wertelecki and Ralph M. Garruto (2010). 'Chronic Radiation Exposure in the Rivne-Polissia Region of Ukraine: Implications for Birth Defects', *American Journal of Human Biology*, 22, 667–674.

Diamond Online (2011). '*Hōshanō osen o meguru Nihonjin no gokai to seifu no setsumei sekinin: Chernobyl no sanjō o shiru hibaku chiryō no ken'i Robāto Gēru hakase ni kiku*' (Japanese people's misunderstandings about radiation contamination and the government's responsibilities to explain: An interview with Dr Robert Gale, an authority on treating radiation-related illnesses, who is familiar with the misery of Chernobyl), 6 April. <http://diamond.jp/articles/-/11772> accessed 11 June 2013.

Douglas, Mary (2002 [1966]). *Purity and Danger: An Analysis of Concepts of Pollution and Taboo*. London: Routledge.

Douglas, Mary, and Aaron Wildavsky (1982). *Risk and Culture: An Essay on the Selection of Technological and Environmental Dangers*. Berkeley: University of California Press.

The Economist (1996). 'Chernobyl, Cancer and Creeping Paranoia', *The Economist*, 338, 81–82.

Fukushima Shinhatsubai (n.d.). *Fukushima shinhatsubai: Nōrinsuisanbutsu monitaringu jōhō* (Fukushima newly on sale: Monitoring information on agriculture, forestry and fisheries) <http://www.new-fukushima.jp/monitoring.php> accessed 13 June 2013.

Haranaka Katsumasa (2011). Netto-jō no kakikomi 'Hakketsubyō kanja kyūzō igakukai de takamaru fuan ni tsuite' (Regarding the internet posting 'Leukaemia patients increasing rapidly, rising anxiety in the medical world). *Japan Medical Association* online, 29 November. <http://www.med.or.jp/people/info/people_info/000614.html> accessed 11 June 2013.

Hashimoto Yoshiko (2011). '"*Fukushima wa shinpai nai*" to ieru riyū wa aru' (I have reason to say, 'There is no need to worry about Fukushima') Interview with Yamashita Shun'ichi for *Kodomo Kenkō Kurabu* (Children's Health Club), 5 July. <http://kodomo-kenkou.com/shinsai/info/show/985> accessed 11 June 2013.

House of Representatives (2011). *Bideo raiburari, 2011-nen 7-gatsu 27-nichi, Kōsei rōdō i'inkai* (Video Library, 27 July 2011, Health, Labour and Welfare Committee) <http://www.shugiintv.go.jp/jp/index.php?ex=VL&deli_id=41163&media_type=> accessed 11 June 2013.

Hunt, Linda M., Heide Castañeda, and Katherine B. de Voogd (2006). 'Do Notions of Risk Inform Patient Choice? Lessons from a Study of Prenatal Genetic Counseling', *Medical Anthropology*, 25, 193–219.

IAEA (International Atomic Energy Agency) (2005). Chernobyl: The True Scale of the Accident. <http://www.iaea.org/newscentre/pressreleases/2005/prn200512.html> accessed 11 June 2013.

ICRP (International Commission on Radiological Protection) (2009). 'ICRP Publication 111, Application of the Commission's Recommendations to the Protection of People Living in Long-term Contaminated Areas after a Nuclear Accident or a Radiation Emergency', *Annals of the ICRP*, 39(3). Amsterdam: Elsevier.

Ideta Ao (2011). 'Genpatsu 50 kiro Fukushima, Kōriyama wa ima, ko ni taichō ihen jiwari, tairyō no hanaji, geri, kentaikan …, "hōshasen to kankei fumei"'. (50 km from the Fukushima nuclear power plant, what is happening now in Kōriyama: unusual changes in children's health – massive nosebleeds, diarrhoea, lack of energy … 'link to radiation unclear'), *Tōkyō Shinbun*, 16 June.

JAMA (The Journal of the American Medical Association) (2012). 'Studies Examine Health Consequences of Meltdown, Damage to Fukushima Nuclear Power Plants in Japan', *For the Media*, 14 August. <http://media.jamanetwork.com/news-item/studies-examine-health-consequences-meltdown-damage-fukushima-nuclear-power-plants-japan/> accessed 16 September 2012.

'*Kansō shiitake kara kijun-goe seshiumu, Yokohama-shi no kōen de kakō*' (Over-the-limit caesium from dried shiitake mushroom, processed in a park in Yokohama city) (2011). *Asahi Shinbun*, 5 November.

Kawaguchi Atsuko (2011). 'Hōshanō fuan 9-wari-goe: yoron chōsa kosodate katei kencho' (Over 90 per cent are worrying about radiation: More so for families raising children, a public opinion poll), *Asahi Shinbun*, 10 September, Fukushima Edition, 31.

Kimura Keisuke, Fujimura Kenji, Kayashima Masashi, Ozawa Hideki, and Ushiyama Hirofumi (2010). 'Yunyū shokuhin-chū no hōshanō nōdo' (Heisei 21-nendo) ('Radioactive contamination in imported food, April 2009 to March 2010), *Tōkyō-to kenkō anzen kenkyū sentā kenkyū nenpō (Annual Report, Tokyo Metropolitan Institute of Public Health)* (61) 249–254. <http://www.tokyo-eiken.go.jp/assets/issue/journal/2010/pdf/01–29.pdf> accessed 15 March 2013.

Kinoshita Kōta (2011). 'Keikoku: Tōkyō nado shutoken de teisenryō hibaku no shōjō ga kodomotachi ni okite iru to iu jōhō' ('Warning: information suggests symptoms due to exposure to low-level radiation are occurring among children in Tokyo and neighbouring areas). Blog entry, 29 May. <http://blog.goo.ne.jp/nagaikenji20070927/e/945898fc22160543b404a9ca949cefe5> accessed 5 July 2013.

Kukurogu (2011). 'Daremo iwanai node yūki o dashite ore ga iō, "Fukushima-kenjin wa genpatsu jiko jinsai no kagaisha da"'. (Since nobody else will say it, I will be courageous enough to say, 'Fukushima people are culprits in this nuclear power plant man-made disaster'). Blog entry, 10 May. <http://blog.2os.net/?p=225> accessed 11 June 2013.

Martin, Rod A. (2002). 'Is Laughter the Best Medicine? Humor, Laughter, and Physical Health', *Current Directions in Psychological Science*, 11(6), 216–220.

MEXT (Ministry of Education, Culture, Sports, Science & Technology in Japan) (2011). 'Hōshasenryō bunpu mappu' (A map of the distribution of radiation levels). <http://ramap.jaea.go.jp/map/map.html> accessed 6 November 2011.

National Cancer Institute (2008). 'Fact sheet: Psychological Stress and Cancer: Questions and Answers'. 29 April. <http://www.cancer.gov/cancertopics/factsheet/Risk/stress> accessed 11 June 2013.

NHK News (2011). 'Shinsai no shisha, fumeisha 20,000-nin jaku' (Dead and missing from the earthquake/tsunami just under 20,000), 10 September.

Petryna, Adriana (1995). 'Sarcophagus: Chernobyl in Historical Light', *Cultural Anthropology*, 10(2), 196–220.

RERF (Radiation Effects Research Foundation) (2007). 'Acute Radiation Syndrome'. <http://www.rerf.or.jp/radefx/early_e/acute.html> accessed 11 June 2013.

RERF (n.d.). 'Shusseiji shōgai (1948–1954-nen no chōsa)' (Malformations at the time of birth: 1948–1954 survey) <http://www.rerf.or.jp/radefx/genetics/birthdef.html> accessed 11 June 2013.

Reventlow, Susanne, Anne Charlotte Hvas, and Charlotte Tulinius (2001). '"In Really Great Danger?" The Concept of Risk in General Practice', *Scandinavian Journal of Primary Health Care*, 19(2), 71–75.

RFC Radio Fukushima (2011a). *Fukushima kennai kaku-chihō kankyō hōshanō sokuteichi (zanteichi) dai 4123 hō* (Environmental radiation measurements for all regions of Fukushima (provisional) No. 4123). 3 September at 12pm. <http://www.rfc.co.jp/files/f011197120110903.pdf> accessed 3 September 2011.

——(2011b). *Fukushima kennai kakuchihō kankyō hōshanō sokuteichi (zanteichi)* (Environmental radiation measurements for all regions of Fukushima (provisional)). 16 March at 18:00. <http://www.rfc.co.jp/files/f012920110316.pdf> accessed 11 Jun 2013.

Sasakawa Memorial Health Foundation (2011). 'Activities – Chernobyl Sasakawa Health and Medical Cooperation Project'.<http://www.smhf.or.jp/e/activities/chernobyl.html> accessed 16 September 2012.

Takahashi Mariko (2011). 'Hōshasen no eikyō: Hiroshima, Nagasaki no chōki chōsa kara wakatta koto' (Effects of radiation: Things learned from long-term research in Hiroshima and Nagasaki), *Asahi Shinbun*, 7 April. <http://www.asahi.com/special/10005/TKY201104070102.html> accessed 11 June 2013.

Takeda Kunihiko (2011). 'Fukushima no mono o idō shite wa ikenai no?' Dokusha kara no shitsumon' (Should it be forbidden to remove things from Fukushima? A question from a reader). Blog entry, September 27. <http://takedanet. com/2011/09/post_7848.html> accessed 11 June 2013.

Takeuchi Ryō (2011). 'Higashi-Nihon daishinsai: gareki uke'ire kujō Ishihara chiji ga hihan' (The great disaster of Eastern Japan: Governor Ishihara criticizes complaints against accepting debris), *Mainichi Shinbun*, 4 November. <http:// mainichi.jp/select/weathernews/news/20111105k0000m040048000c.html> accessed 4 November 2011.

Tanaka Ryūsaku (2011). 'Mr 100mSv' Yamashita kyōju no kainin motomeru Fukushima kenmin shōmei' (Petition signed by the people of Fukushima demanding the dismissal of 'Mr. 100mSv' professor Yamashita), *Tanaka Ryūsaku Jānaru* (Tanaka Ryūsaku Journal), 21 June. <http://tanakaryusaku.jp/2011/06/0002531> accessed 11 June 2013.

WHO (World Health Organization) (2005). 'Chernobyl: The true scale of the accident: 20 years later a UN report provides definitive answers and ways to repair lives', 5 September. <http://www.who.int/mediacentre/news/releases/2005/ pr38/en/index.html> accessed 11 June 2013.

Yamane Yūsaku (2011). 'Futsū no kodomo umemasu ka: Fukushima no kodomotachi kara no tegami' (Can I bear a normal child? Letters from children of Fukushima), *AERA* 20 (40). 5 September. 10–15.

Yamashita Shun'ichi and Shibata Yoshisada (eds) (1997). *Chernobyl: A Decade: Proceedings of the Fifth Chernobyl Sasakawa Medical Cooperation Symposium, Kiev, Ukraine, 14–15 October 1996*. Amsterdam: Elsevier

Yevelson, Ilya I., Anna Abdelgani, Julie Cwikel, and Igor S. Yevelson (1997). 'Bridging the Gap in Mental Health Approaches between East and West: The Psychosocial Consequences of Radiation Exposure', *Environmental Health Perspective Supplements*, Supplement 6, 105, 1–11.

2 Channel (2011). 'Shutoken o teiden saseru, hōshanō o makichirasu, osen sareta shokuhin o shukka suru, Fukushima kenmin wa gomikuzu no atsumari' (Causing blackouts in the Greater Tokyo area, spreading radiation, shipping out contaminated food, Fukushima people are a bunch of trash), 16 April. <http://2chnull. info/r/news/1302957783/> accessed 11 June 2013.

MORIOKA RIKA[1]

Mother Courage: Women as Activists between a Passive Populace and a Paralyzed Government

The Ayumi daycare centre[2] is located in the rural south of Miyagi prefecture, bordering Fukushima, about 60 kilometres north of the stricken Fukushima No.1 nuclear power plant. In May 2011, parents, especially mothers, were concerned that radiation from the Fukushima No.1 nuclear power plant might have contaminated the school grounds where their children play. The mothers asked the daycare principal, a town employee, for information on the radiation level of the grounds. They wanted assurance that it was safe for their children to play in the sandbox or swim in the pool. The principal said she did not know. Two months after the hydrogen explosions at the Fukushima plant, the government had not even begun to measure the level of radiation at ground level. All they had was data from several pre-existing monitoring posts at locations on higher ground. The principal first resorted to this information available on the internet and posted on the front door a daily report of the radiation level at the nearest site. But pressed by the mothers for more information, she began contacting township authorities requesting an assessment of accumulated radiation in the school grounds. The town hall, however, possessed only a few Geiger

---

1 The author wishes to thanks all her informants in Tohoku and Tokyo who kindly shared their experiences and concerns during this very difficult time. She would also like to thank those who read and commented on earlier drafts of the paper, especially Scott North of Osaka University.

2 *Hoikusho* has been translated as 'daycare', and *yōchien* as 'nursery school'. The former are open long hours and cater mainly to children of working mothers, while the latter operate only four or five hours a day and have slightly more emphasis on education. I use 'preschool' as a general term to refer to both. All individuals and schools in this paper are referred to by pseudonyms to protect their identities.

counters, which obliged officials to visit schools and other public facilities one by one to measure the levels of radiation. Ayumi daycare received at most only a brief, weekly stop during their rounds. The mothers were not satisfied. They wanted daily measurements of the radiation level, which changed according to the direction of the wind and other factors. When the mothers started to question the adequacy of measurements taken at a certain height from the ground, and the safety of the soil that came into the building on children's shoes, the principal had no choice but to ask the town office to obtain a Geiger counter for the daycare centre. The prefectural government finally decided to provide counters to local city and town offices after receiving formal requests. The local offices in turn handed one instrument to each school and preschool. It took three months following the disaster for the government to act, but when the Geiger counters finally arrived, they were visible progress for the mothers who demanded more accurate information and governmental action. Without their push, the government would not have made the counters available. By the end of June, Ayumi daycare was checking the level of radiation every day on potentially hazardous grasses, mud, and water puddles on the school grounds. The teachers found that the level of radiation was around 0.08μSv/h (microsieverts per hour) in mid-July, far below the maximum limit of 3.8 μSv/h set by the government.[3] However, at another daycare centre in the same town, teachers found a level of 0.2 μSv/h, and requested the government to clean up the soil, although it was below the revised government-set figure.

In the wake of the Tohoku disasters, women, particularly mothers, pushed local governments to act to mitigate the possible health hazards of radiation on children. Endowed with the powerful state-sanctioned and culturally validated status of motherhood, they managed to compel the government to respond to their demands. This paper examines three actors in the Tohoku disaster: the passive populace, overburdened local governments, and concerned mothers. It illustrates the gap between people's passive expectation for governmental assistance and the reality of local governments plagued by

---

3   The Japanese government increased the radiation exposure limit from 0.19 μSv/h to 3.8 μSv/h (1 mSv/y to 20 mSv/y) after the Fukushima disaster. The increase has been criticized by many including the Canadian Medical Association Journal (21 December 2011), which condemned the change as 'unconscionable'.

a lack of resources in responding to the disaster. Against this background, the paper further points out the often unnoticed contributions of mothers and housewives to social change in Japan. I argue that the contributions of these women, who dare to speak up in the midst of a passive populace, represent an important element in social movements that have the potential to trigger changes in Japan. They raise awareness and give courage to others who want to voice similar concerns, at times resulting in local and nationwide activism. Moreover, the consequences of women's activism are not always minor; they can compel government to act and sometimes to change laws.

When the magnitude 9.0 earthquake shook north-eastern Japan on 11 March 2011, I was in the US, sleeplessly glued to the images of the massive tsunami swallowing up cities, and the terrifying explosions at the wrecked nuclear power plant in Fukushima. The world media quickly took note of the stoic suffering of the Japanese victims patiently waiting in line for food and other critical supplies. I had mixed feelings of pride and scepticism about these depictions of my fellow citizens as model disaster victims who possessed extreme discipline. Unable to just watch any longer, in mid-April I flew to Sendai, Miyagi prefecture, where I worked as an emergency relief worker for an international agency for five months. The work entailed assisting preschools in affected areas in Miyagi with reopening and maintaining the facilities so that small children would have safe places to go to. As I visited preschools and local governments, I met with teachers, mothers, and city/town officials, who often chatted with me about their experience of the disasters. The observations presented here are based primarily on these conversations.

Miyagi prefecture had over 11,500 people dead or missing, the highest number of casualties among the affected prefectures (National Police Agency 2011). However, when I arrived, I was stunned to see people in Sendai acting as if nothing had happened. Banners in arcades *did* read '*Ganbarō Tōhoku*' (Come on, Tohoku!) and buildings with cracks were being repaired and reinforced against the daily aftershocks that kept coming for months after the initial quake. But I felt slightly silly for being so upset over what I had seen on the computer screen when I found people in Sendai behaving so calmly. The physical damage from the earthquakes may have been small in the city, but the threat from the Fukushima plant was real. In retrospect, however, I realize that they were dealing with it in the way they knew best – trying to ignore things they could not change. It is not uncommon to hear Japanese people say '*shikata ga nai*' (nothing can be done) and accept difficulties as they are. The society as a whole sometimes seems to overlook serious problems until there is a great build-up of concern. When resistance does occur, it is often spearheaded by women, politically marginalized mothers and housewives, who do not possess formal power or status (LeBlanc 1999). The response to the threat of radiation from the Fukushima No.1 plant was one such case.

Passive populace as the social context for mothers' protest

Mothers who were concerned with radiation found their neighbours silent on the issue. People in Tohoku often mentioned perseverance (*gaman*) as a characteristic of Tohoku culture in the face of difficulties. They did not shout, complain, or demand; instead, they waited and endured passively. In regard to the radiation, most people sensed that the government in Tokyo was not telling the whole truth, and that it could be much worse than the authorities would like people to believe. Yet, people in Miyagi were inclined to keep their mouths shut. '*Mina, amari iimasen ne*' (people just don't talk about it much) was a typical response when asked about radiation. 'We are concerned, but there is nothing we can do', said one teacher. She told me that people around her felt it was useless to talk about the radiation. The mother of a ten-year-old, originally from Iwate prefecture, explained the complexity of the people's thoughts:

> They couldn't express their worries ... If they were sure that it was not safe, they would have evacuated. But for many reasons, they had to stay. Some couldn't leave their work behind, some didn't have anyone to rely on, and some had to take care of animals and so on. They didn't want to disparage (*hitei suru*) the place where they had to stay. They couldn't discuss whether it was safe – that this may be dangerous or that may be bad. So they behaved as usual on the surface: it was like a wish that things would remain the same ... They just didn't speak about it ... It must be in the character of Tohoku people. They couldn't bear to make matters worse (*koto o aradaterarenai*) by saying 'I am worried' when everyone else was eating the same vegetables and things.

Uncertainty about the health effects of radiation produced by the contradictory information from the government and the media created space for denial. Details of the accident and nuclear meltdowns were gradually becoming clear to people, even in the selective coverage of mainstream media, indicating that things were not as safe as they thought. If the health threats were clear, it would have been easier for them to decide on what actions to take. But most people chose to live with wishful optimism and fatalism, and suppressed their fear with silence.

Their silence may also be related to the decades of state-sponsored nuclear energy policy that supported the local economy and promoted acceptance of nuclear-energy. Miyagi prefecture also has a nuclear power plant, at Onagawa,[4] 160 kilometres up the coast from Fukushima No.1 and adjacent to the city of Ishinomaki. A man in the fishery business in Ishinomaki, who was actively opposing the nuclear-power plant, commented on the silence of the people.

> Before the earthquake it was even harder to talk about it ... If you speak up, the power company will come and question you. The cost of raising a voice in protest is high. So people just bear with it (*jitto gaman shite iru*) ... People in general are mostly ignorant of the issue. If the government says it is OK, people end up believing everything is fine. People are concerned that others would be annoyed if you question, protest, or stick out ... There are people who are concerned, but the local people cannot dissent because the nuclear power company is still there.

This man said that Tohoku Power Company, the owner of the Onagawa plant, used to come to public schools in the area and lecture children on the benefits and safety of nuclear energy. Material benefits were handed out to local residents, including cash, and many people grew to rely on income sources related to the plant. He was one of the very few who voiced concerns openly. He told me that the power company contacted him and tried to dissuade him from opposing them. Decades of nuclear energy promotion

---

4   The Onagawa plant has three reactors, opened in 1984, 1995 and 2002 respectively. They survived the tsunami, despite being twice as close to the epicentre as Fukushima No.1. The Onagawa plant had a seawall 14 metres high, whereas that at Fukushima No.1 was only 5.7 metres.

had created a local environment in which people did not feel free to voice their fears of radiation from Fukushima, even after the disaster occurred.

People I met in Miyagi showed a perplexing mix of cynicism, resignation and dependence towards government. Onodera-san, a forty-one-year-old driver from Iwanuma (85 kilometres north of Fukushima No.1), chatted during a long trip to an affected coastal area. Despite losing his job he had decided not to move away from his town after the disaster because he was living with his elderly mother.

> We are all thinking about it in our minds, but nobody talks about it. It is useless to talk to anyone (*dare ni itte mo shikata ga nai*). The government is supposed to know what they should do without us telling them. I personally gave up ... They may give you some money, but they won't do anything to protect you from radiation ... Would they (the authorities) listen to us if we said anything? Some people can't complain because they don't want to leave the shelter ... You can eat free meals. You can't complain ... People in Tohoku are always on the defensive. It must be our culture. We are slow to go out and fight ... When I was a child, I often heard older people say '*itte mo dame-dappe*' (It's useless to complain). It is a phrase I hear quite often these days.

With the slow responses of central and local government to the triple disasters, people in Tohoku were increasingly frustrated and cynical about what the government could do for them. Beneath their quietude, there was a smouldering resentment towards the unresponsive government. At the same time, there was also an attitude of resignation and passivity. Onodera-san expected the government to know what should be done, and was ready to give up even before speaking up. He also saw that some people were too dependent on the government to complain as they continued to rely on the government for shelter, food, and long term recovery.

Is this attitude unique to Tohoku? Many people I talked to attributed it to '*Tōhoku no kishitsu*' (the Tohoku character). Onodera-san even referred to the history of Tohoku during the Boshin War in 1868, which led to the demise of the Aizu and Sendai fiefs, to illustrate their tendency to be 'slow' to change and to actively fight for a cause. But the regional differences may be a matter of degree. His account of conservative Tohoku culture bears interesting similarities to culturalist narratives of Japanese culture as a whole, which is often described as having a high degree of political cynicism and a sense of powerlessness (Richardson and Flanagan 1984; Martin and Stronach 1992). An editorial in the *Asahi Shinbun* (14 August 2011) commented on the causes of the Fukushima crisis and the mistakes of the Pacific War made over seventy years ago. The common denominator, the article pointed out, was 'the closed specialist system' (*heisateki senmonka shisutemu*) and 'the apathy of the majority of the citizens'. It went on to say:

> ... the citizens left it up to bureaucrats and specialists, even in matters concerning their own lives and wealth, sometimes just looking on and at other times fanatically joining in (*kyōhon shita*). This irresponsible attitude that leaves important matters to others is at the bottom of the repeated mistakes that the Japanese made.

The majority of people I met in Miyagi spoke little of the radiation risk and passively waited for the government to do something about it without telling them what they wanted. Even though they did not really trust the authorities, they still clearly expected them to take care of the problem somehow.

Limitations of government

On the one hand, Miyagi possessed a frustrated but resigned populace depending upon local governments to restore normality. On the other hand, city and town officials, themselves disaster victims, were so overburdened with the massive responsibilities of providing relief after the tsunami that dealing with the invisible and uncertain threat of radiation often seemed to be a secondary concern. Even their responses to the tsunami were close to paralysis in some areas, and this led to mounting frustration.

Despite the cynicism and passivity, people's underlying expectation that the government would help them was particularly strong in cities and towns afflicted by the tsunami. They expected the authorities to provide housing and distribute food, household necessities and cash in a fair manner to all victims. A woman in Ishinomaki complained that local government did not distribute goods fairly to those who moved into private-sector apartments (although the city did pay their rent), compared to those who moved into temporary public housing built especially for the victims. She had received some donations in the form of cash and electric appliances, but did not receive any other public support.

> My house was washed away on 11 March by the tsunami, and I lost everything. Fortunately, my family was safe, so initially I was grateful for that fact alone. But after five months, I can't help but notice the gap in the way we receive support. Initially, our family went to stay with my son who lived in Sendai, but later, in May, we rented an apartment to be independent ... For people who similarly lost their homes completely, the city is providing a complete set of household goods for four, even when there are only two people, but for people like me who tried to be independent as soon as possible, the city doesn't provide the same support. It is not fair ... I feel resentful when I see the numerous boxes of goods at the shelters. Those are all paid for by our taxes, aren't they? Some people can repair their homes, some can still use their own futon, furniture, and clothing. Even so, they are receiving one million yen so long as their houses were completely destroyed (*zenkai*). I don't think this is right ... Can't they at least give me the same futon and household goods as those in the temporary housing? ... I hear that some food, such as *o-bentō* (lunch boxes) and rice-balls, is being discarded in the shelters. Why is there no support or psychological care for those who live in subsidized apartments?

The local governments operated under the *Hisaisha seikatsu saiken shien-hō* (Victims' Life Reconstruction Support Law), a law created after the Kobe earthquake in 1995 that regulates the provision of public support to natural disaster victims. Even if they felt that the distribution of funds and materials was slow and inefficient, people still relied on local governments to provide necessities, and expected the governments to not only function for them, but provide fair, high quality assistance to thousands of households.

Local officials, though generally dedicated and hardworking, were too overburdened to meet the expectations of the victims. Although they received crucial emergency assistance from the Self-Defence Forces, the police force, and other prefectural governments in their disaster relief efforts, local governments lacked the human resources and innovative thinking needed to deal with this unprecedented disaster. For example, Ishinomaki, a city of 160,000, had over 100,000 evacuees at the peak of the disaster, and even five months later it was still providing daily meals to over 10,000 people living in 3,000 households, as well as about 3,500 people in 174 shelters (*Kahoku Shinpō*, 4 August 2011). The lack of human resources hampered their efforts to distribute much-needed goods and money to the victims. As a result, local governments in the three affected prefectures were criticized for not distributing donated cash of 95 billion yen. The prefectures explained that the reason was due to lack of manpower needed to check against possible fraud and administer the funds properly (*Asahi Shinbun*, 14 August 2011).[5]

Local governments also seemed to have difficulty discarding the usual rules of good practice in an emergency. Their actions tended to be bureaucratic and slow, responding to an extraordinary situation with ordinary procedures, a strategy bound to create frustrations. For the first few months after the earthquake, local governments were kept busy issuing '*hisai shōmei*', the official proof of disaster damage, to the survivors waiting in long queues at town and city halls. They were also tasked to issue another document, '*risai shōmei*', needed to sort and label people according to the level of damage incurred, so that the local governments could provide the guaranteed assistance stipulated in the law in a fair manner. For this, they additionally had to manage *juminhyō* (residence certificates) to keep track of people moving in and out. Considering that the National Policy Agency reported over 357,000 homes damaged in Miyagi prefecture, it is no wonder that local governments were slow to respond. More problematically, the officials sometimes displayed inflexibility concerning pre-disaster rules and laws. Susanna Hoffman, writing in her co-edited book *The Angry Earth* (Oliver-Smith and Hoffman 1999), found that people generally tend to develop more 'traditional' roles and behaviour after a disaster, rather than exploring new ways of doing things. Steger (in this volume) shows how that applied to gender roles in daily life in shelters. I would add that it applied just as strongly to the working practices of public officials. A telling example of this was an incident during a meeting with city officials

---

5   This task required intimate local knowledge and could not be done by those bureaucrats from other prefectures sent to Tohoku for support.

discussing concerns over inadequate nutrition in school lunches. The lunch only included bread and milk, but a city official expressed his hesitation in changing the menu. 'I really want to let the children eat. But there are lots of rules and regulations concerning school lunches'. He did not want to increase the variety of food in the menu because he thought that the available food and facilities in the disaster areas might not meet the standards set by pre-disaster regulations.

Many local public officials were continuing to work, despite being victims of the earthquake and tsunami themselves, and having lost family members or seen their homes destroyed. Yet self-conscious about their own position as public workers, they tried to make their official duties their first priority.

> For the first month, we slept in the city hall and worked around the clock, taking naps on the floor. We didn't go home. But we couldn't eat the food delivered (for the disaster victims), as we were city employees. We also lost homes and families, but we couldn't eat like other victims as we were public officials.
>
> (A section chief in Ishinomaki city hall)

The level of personal sacrifice was remarkable, but it was driven by fear of criticism from the citizens as much as by a sense of duty. The accepted social norm was that being a public employee took precedence over being a victim of the disaster. A city employee of Kesennuma, Kawase Yōko, lost her home to the tsunami, and was forced to commute to the city hall from a shelter in a nearby school gym where she lived with her family. When her number finally came up in the lottery for temporary housing, she could not bring herself to accept the housing offered. She felt she could not move in before other people in the city, and was afraid that she might be criticized by those who had not yet been successful in the lottery. In the end, she gave up the housing and continued to live in the shelter. She was just one of the employees who tried to serve the city in this condition, constrained by social norms that took precedence over her personal needs.

While their dedication seemed to go unrecognized and taken for granted, many workers were overburdened to the point of collapse. The *Asahi Shinbun* reported on 23 July 2011, that 88 of 1,450 city employees in Ishinomaki suffered from stress disorders extreme enough to require psychological care. The number was 'more than expected', according to a faculty member from Tohoku University who conducted the survey. Many had lost their family members and homes, and required counselling. But the city was just beginning to realize the need 'to learn how to identify workers who require care and help'. Providing material support to city and town hall employees was neglected, let alone psychological care. In this condition, local governments naturally relied on what they knew best in trying to respond to the disaster, and despite the expectations of the public, they were often inflexible in their mind-set, unable to act innovatively and swiftly in times of crisis.

The slow response of the government increased frustration for residents who desperately needed the normality of pre-disaster life to return. A nursery school teacher wrote a letter to an international agency appealing for assistance almost five months after the disaster. The school had been washed away, but their reconstruction plan had been suspended for months by the city. She made a personal decision to write without telling her principal because it became clear to her that with 'the current condition in which people just wait for the state, the prefecture, or the city to do something', it was 'impossible to rebuild' (*saiken nante muri*).

> We have been asked by many parents to rebuild the nursery. But we were told (by the government) that the original site is likely to become an industrial zone, and that we may not be able to use the site. Yet, the city planning itself has been too slow and unclear, and we are stuck unable to take any action ... We wrote a letter to the city with our local representatives. As expected, we received no response, nor were we shown a direction for the future.
>
> (A nursery school employee in Ishinomaki, 29 July 2011)

They were thwarted by the indecision of the city government, which could not provide a definitive city-plan. In her words, the city itself had been 'victimized' (*hisai shite iru jōtai*) and 'everything was in chaos' (*nanimo kamo ga konran*) even five months after the disaster. The agency she contacted could not respond to her appeal, as the availability of land on which to rebuild the facility was a prerequisite for their assistance.

Mothers' concerns and actions

What happens when the passivity of a populace meets the paralysis of government? In the case of the disaster in Japan, amid the general silence, I found some women stepping up to demand change in how governments deal with the crisis. They were mothers concerned about the health hazards to their small children of toxic material, especially radiation. Conflicting reports of radiation measures and governmental inaction confused and worried the mothers. *The New York Times*, for example, was reporting that radiation levels a quarter of a mile from the Fukushima nuclear power plant had at one point reached 0.1 rem (1 millisieverts) per hour, a level considered to increase the overall risk of cancer after less than four days of exposure (Grady 2011). Yet, scientists representing opinions of the government were insisting on the safety of the leaked radiation. Faced with uncertainty, the mothers managed to organize themselves and make the prefectural government distribute Geiger counters to local offices, some of which in turn provided the instruments to schools. They also forced local governments to measure the level of radiation at public facilities, make the information public and clean radioactive soil from schools and playgrounds.

Most mothers first asked for information on the level of radiation and preventive measures being taken in public services that they directly had contact with in their daily lives. Suzuki Kanako, the mother of a two-year-old child in the town of Yamamoto (65 kilometres north of the Fukushima No.1 power plant) had been worried about the effects of radiation on the child. When she visited a *hokensho* (public clinic) for her child's regular health check-up, she asked questions about the danger of the radiation for children. But the nurse she talked to did not know much more than she did. 'What are you thinking and doing about it as a nurse working for the town?' she demanded. The nurse had little to say, as there were no policies or strategies in place at the time (May 2011) regarding health effects of the radiation from Fukushima. This incident and similar questions by others prompted the Yamamoto town authorities to invite an 'expert' from the University of Occupational and Environmental Health in Kyushu and organize an information meeting in early July 2011. Interestingly, many people who attended the meeting, including school teachers and parents, did not feel the information provided was necessarily trustworthy. A teacher explained that it was because it came from a person who was not 'anti-nuclear-power' (*han-genpatsu*).

For the mothers of school children, public schools and preschools were often the first place they went for information. The principal of a daycare centre in Yamamoto town explained:

> We began gathering information about the radiation level in the area from the internet. We need to know because mothers come and ask us about it. They ask us if it is safe to bring their children here, and what precautions we are taking. We can't just say we don't know. So we have to learn and think about what we can do.

Some mothers found preschool teachers their best allies and source of information, as most teachers sincerely tried to respond to parents' concerns. The mother of a five-year-old in Sendai city expressed her appreciation for the principal of her daughter's nursery school.

> In the letter from the principal in May, she expressed her views (on radiation), included newspaper clips, and information on vegetables and milk. She also told us that if we were worried about school lunches, we could let our children bring their own packed lunch. They even let us use the school lunch box (so that nobody would notice that their children were bringing their own lunch). I am thankful. ... I really appreciate the teachers who are trying to find solutions in the midst of the uncertainty, and when there are many parents with different opinions.

This mother took up the option of making lunch for her own child and concealing the fact by putting it in a nursery school lunch box. At lunchtime some children would be eating different food from their friends, and trying to hide the fact. But of course the moment the food emerges from the box it is obvious which kind of food it is, so children were obliged to turn their backs on their friends and eat furtively. This was an equally obvious way of revealing the truth – that their mothers considered the food that many of their friends were eating to be potentially impure and unsafe. Similarly, some schools and preschools offered parents the option of whether or not their children should be allowed to play outdoors. This led to a situation where some of the children would be stuck indoors, looking through the windows at their friends playing outside. Were mothers of the indoor children being over-protective? Or were mothers of the outdoor ones being reckless with their own children's lives? Thus the muted, ambiguous response to radiation often presented others with an impossible choice, while generating a difficult atmosphere and souring friendships in many classrooms around Tohoku.

To an extent, these impossible choices were foisted upon mothers by well-intentioned preschool teachers who were compelled to take every precaution they could think of and to keep the worried parents informed, even when they themselves were not sure about what was dangerous and what actions were effective. They had to do something to satisfy mothers' concerns while also recognizing that those concerns were not universally shared and not always based on scientific evidence. They came up with some elaborate compromises. A mother in Sendai city, 100 kilometres north of the No.1 plant, described the efforts made at her son's daycare.

> There was a parents' meeting on 25 May at the daycare centre my son attends. Till the end of April, they only opened the daycare in the morning and didn't let children play outside. But they started regular hours in early May, allowing outdoor play for a limited time. They provided explanations for this in the meeting. They had removed all the weeds from the playground, put the sandbox off-limits, and allowed children to play outside only for thirty minutes a day, twice a week. They let children wear face masks if parents provided them, and after the outside play, they would carefully wash the children's hands and faces … The teachers are trying to deal with the uncertainty every day, but they are not sure how careful they have to be. They said it's been hard on them. I appreciate their thoughtfulness, but I am still full of worries.

The daycare centre provided lunch twice a week, and told the parents that they were purchasing food from vendors as far away as possible. Many protective parents asked them not to give the children milk, and to supply bottled water to avoid drinking tap water. As described above, some had their children eat home-cooked food out of the same lunch boxes that preschools provided. In such ways, concerned mothers carved out a little space for subtle resistance against the government that insisted on the harmlessness of radiation and the acquiescent public, dominated by men, which wanted to accept the government assurances in hopes of a quiet life.

The mothers' questions and concerns also obliged local officials to respond. As a result of requests made through teachers of public preschools, the town of Watari (75 kilometres north of the Fukushima No.1 plant) increased the frequency of radiation checks around publicly owned schools and playgrounds, as well as expanding the number of locations monitored. Teachers in preschools found that the officials were becoming a little more responsive.

> They used to measure (radiation) only in the middle of the ground, but now they do it at a few more places, including the back of the building where radiation may easily accumulate. Because we asked, they now measure closer to the ground also. They come more frequently too. Things are improving.
> (An employee of a public daycare centre in Watari)

The impacts of these mothers' demands and actions were felt at the prefectural level as well. Some concerned mothers in Sendai organized themselves into the 'Group for Children to Grow Up Healthy after Five Years, Ten Years' (Gonengo jūnengo kodomotachi ga sukoyaka ni sodatsu kai). They submitted an official letter of request, demanding more information and governmental action on radiation. Their specific requests included 1) the measurement of radiation levels in the atmosphere and release of detailed information; 2) the measurement of radiation levels in school lunches; 3) provision of Geiger counters to schools and preschools; and 4) prohibition of the use of swimming pools until radiation levels were being systematically measured (*Kahoku Shinbun*, 10 June 2011). The Miyagi prefectural government accepted their requests for the most part, distributing Geiger counters to all cities and townships. They began releasing measurements collected at public schools and preschools on their homepage in July 2011.

The officials did not necessarily like the mothers' meddling, but were compelled to respond. It sometimes appeared that their measures to deal with radiation were prompted more by their obligation to respond to the local mothers' inquiries than by genuine concern for children's health. A section chief in the Miyagi prefectural office could not hide his annoyance when he told me that 'a self-appointed group of mothers (*nin'i no okāsangata*) had submitted a formal letter of request'. 'Some of them have inaccurate knowledge. We need to provide workshops and educate them', he said. But the problem was that any discussion of radiation from Fukushima contained uncertainties. What could be considered 'accurate' was open to debate. As mentioned earlier, the women who participated in one of these workshops organized by the government clearly knew this uncertainty, and did not blindly accept the government version of what was accurate.

It is important to mention that not all women were empowered enough to confront the government from the beginning. Women who organized themselves or even asked questions to authorities were the minority of mothers in Miyagi. They often found themselves worrying alone at first and being confused as their concerns put them at odds with those around them. One woman, the mother of a first-grader at an elementary school in Sendai, was angry and confounded at the same time because her son's public school was not taking enough precautions against radiation exposure and was acting as if nothing had happened.

> They told me that there would be 'mud play' (*doro asobi*) as part of the school curriculum. Under normal circumstances, this would have been a nice experience in nature, but at this time? ... The teachers must be assuming that it will be OK, without giving much thought to it (the health hazards of radiation). People around me continue to live life as usual. Do they think it will become OK if we don't worry about it? I've learned that even 0.16 microsieverts an hour caused damage in Chernobyl. I am getting confused.

She was dismayed to see the seeming indifference (*mukanshin*) of other people around her towards the danger of radiation, discrepant with her own feelings. To reiterate, people in general did not speak about the issue of radiation, and many mothers found themselves unable to voice their concerns. Some people were also in denial: it was too much to deal with radiation after the earthquake and tsunami. A daycare teacher in Watari remarked: 'I don't think they want to think about it. It has been horrible just to deal with the earthquake and tsunami, and on top of that, it would be too much to think about radiation'. The denial and silence of so many people confused some mothers who felt alarmed and wanted to know more about it.

Even when a mother tried asking about it, it was often difficult to voice her concern in the midst of the silence. The mother of a middle school student was concerned about contaminated food and tried to let her son bring his own bottle of tea to drink at break-time so that he could avoid drinking tap water provided by the school. She felt she should ask the school for permission to do so, but her request was ignored by the school and the local education committee (*kyō'iku i'inkai*). 'I didn't ask again, since talking to the unsympathetic teachers once more wouldn't be good for my mental health. It is too bad that I have no way but to take the path of silence, since those who don't worry about radiation just brush me aside as *shinkeishitsu* (nervous, over-sensitive)'. Compared with daycare centre employees, public school teachers had a more distant relationship with parents and so tended to be less sympathetic to mothers' concerns. One teacher confided that when some mothers called and asked about radiation, teachers would treat them with a 'cold attitude' (*tsumetai taido*) and hang up the phone. The mother who was concerned about drinking water in school was effectively banned from giving her child a drink she considered safe and forced to allow him to carry on drinking tap water that she viewed as possibly dangerous. Her plight was shared by many other mothers; when they asked questions about the effects of radiation, they had their concerns dismissed by school teachers as the irrational fears of nervous, fussy women.

Unsympathetic husbands

Worried mothers often found that even their husbands did not share their concern, and brushed them aside saying, *daijōbu ja naika* ('it will probably be OK'). Some mothers seriously thought of evacuating their children to safer locations, but found it hard to convince their husbands. The mother of a pre-schooler who was active in a child health-protection group said, 'Somehow what I say does not stick in my husband's head … It is hard for a mother to keep trying (to protect children from radiation) alone in the household. The father needs to understand it too … Recently I really feel that. I think there are lots of families like this'. The fathers' silence on the matter has been noted by others as well. Alarmed by the state-sanctioned feeding of possibly contaminated foods to children, Professor Takeda Kunihiko from Chubu University in his blog urged fathers to stand up and join mothers' protests. 'Strangely, fathers are not interested in children's health', he wrote. 'They [the government, producers, distributers, and the media] have shouted down mothers who search for radiation-free foods ... Again, I want to appeal to fathers. Please return to the frontline (of the protest)' (Takeda 2011). His call, however, was not heeded by many fathers. Although some fathers were concerned and a few, particularly those in jobs with flexible hours, participated in protests, those protests were clearly led by women.

An illustrative example occurred on 27 October 2011. A group called 'Fukushima Women who do not Need Nuclear Power' and their supporters had been staging a ten-day sit-in in front of the Ministry of Economy, Trade and Industry in Tokyo. During the course of the sit-in protest, they were finally admitted to the ministry offices and granted a meeting. Facing seven male officials in a conference room, representatives of the women demanded the evacuation of children from areas with high radiation levels, along with other demands including the permanent shutdown of nuclear reactors (USTREAM, 27 October 2011). The thirty protestors were almost all women. The scene was a striking image of impassioned women pleading with exaggeratedly impassive men in suits, whose main strategy was to say nothing and wait for the women to finally shut up.

The optimism of some fathers on the safety of nuclear energy may have to do with the government's conscious efforts at turning fathers into nuclear energy supporters. Recently discovered guidelines on nuclear public relations issued by the former Ministry of Science and Technology in 1991 revealed that the ministry specified fathers as a target group for 'legal manipulation of public opinion' as they can expect 'the effects to be large when fathers of the current generation become opinion leaders'. Ironically, the guidelines described women as an irrelevant population since they thought housewives would see the issue as 'someone else's problem unless there is a power plant next to them' (*Nishi-Nihon Shinbun*, 20 July 2011).

Robin LeBlanc's (2010) analysis on masculinity as a constraint on men's participation in politics in Japan provides another clue to the enigma of the fathers' indifference. Most non-elite men, LeBlanc asserts, are excluded from actively participating in local politics just as women are, because of gender expectations about men's work outside the home as household breadwinners. Expectations about men devoting themselves to paid work 'constrain men's life choices to the extent that men must fight employers and social norms in order to fully participate in some aspects of life that seem a natural right such as fatherhood', she points out (LeBlanc 2010: 43). In the same way in which Japanese men are excluded from local politics, I argue, they are also barred from participating in civil society. Most fathers did not actively participate in the efforts to guard their children from harmful radiation, because protecting children's health was not within the realm of their masculine role. State-sanctioned gender expectations about what it means to be a good father, namely to be a good worker, powerfully dictate what constitutes masculinity in Japan and may even prevent men from fulfilling the most fundamental responsibility of fatherhood – protecting the lives of their children.

In contrast to men, for women, being a mother in the affected areas provided sufficient grounds to organize and reason to believe that they could do what the government could not do to protect children. One of the leaders in a mothers' group said, 'I painfully realized how so many people are horrified of the radiation, quietly enduring the stress born of it ... First we have to speak out, raise our concerns ... Then we can protect our children better than the government'. Mothers' confidence grew, particularly after finding others with similar concerns through schools, community groups and the internet. They realized that the government was not as reliable as they thought, and that they had to take matters into their own hands.

> With this earthquake, I realized that what the government can do is limited ... They don't even measure radiation for us. At the places like preschools, we started to do it ourselves. Once we started, we saw that some spots, like under the slide in the playground, contained a great deal of radiation. We began to realize that there are things we can actually do.
> (Ōtsuki Keiko, mother of a three-year-old nursery school pupil)

Through speaking up and taking action, these women were encouraged to find that there were others willing to join in. 'There will be a measurement of radiation level at my son's nursery. I will go and observe it ... I am beginning to realize that there are other parents who are interested', a mother said. 'So I have requested the nursery to put up a poster about the talk by Tanaka Yu[6] organized by the Co-op (on nuclear power plant disasters and radiation issues)'. The subtitle of the lecture was 'towards a society that does not rely on nuclear power'. The act of simply asking for a poster to be put up may be an insignificant gesture in any other setting. But it required lots of courage for her to do so in the midst of a silent populace. It was a radical act for a young Japanese mother to provoke thoughts on nuclear energy that differed from those of the state, and to ask people to take even such a small action as attending a lecture.

Conclusion: The empowering and constraining influence of feminine stereotypes

Women, especially Japanese women, are often depicted as apolitical. With the exception of a few outstanding works (Pharr 1981; Bernstein 1991; Uno 1993; LeBlanc 1999), Japanese women's role in social and political change has tended to be seen as secondary, overshadowed by male actors in the frontline. Women are generally seen as uninterested in politics, and participation in social protest is considered unnatural for women. Even in the Western context, women's contributions have been, in West and Blumberg's words (1990), 'ignored, misrepresented, or erased from history in a patriarchal world' despite the historical reality of resistance by women. They point out that we are likely to overlook women's involvement in social movements and protests as long as political actions are defined narrowly as participation in formal 'power from above'. LeBlanc (1999), who examined the relationship between politics and the daily lives of non-elite Japanese homemakers, found that ordinary Japanese women do in fact engage in political activities based on their status as housewives. In local politics and

6   Tanaka Yu is a social/environmental activist in great demand since the disasters.

community activities, she argues that 'housewife' is a public identity that provides a common ground and legitimacy to unite. Mothers are at the centre of these local activities. The actions of mothers who are responding to the Fukushima disaster represent Japanese women's 'power from below' – grassroots action with the potential for long-term impacts.

The political power of Japanese women has its moral justification in their state-sanctioned status of being mothers and wives. Despite women's increasing labour force participation in postwar years, the realm of responsibilities for Japanese women still centres on domestic matters: running the household, ensuring the health of family members, and educating children. Andrew Gordon (1997) persuasively argues that the state and corporations actively constructed gender roles to ensure that the household was run efficiently by women, so that men could provide labour power and devote themselves to economic activities. Gordon argues that through social campaigns like 'The New Life Movement' in the 1950s and 1960s, the state naturalized a model of gender relations in which women of all social strata managed the home, while men managed the workplace. Throughout its modern history, the voices of women's associations have been incorporated by the state to produce unified efforts to advance the interests of the nation-state. Campaigns such as encouraging ordinary women to be frugal and rational homemakers were actively co-opted by the state to promote saving (Garon 2000). But Japanese women have not been passive tools of state policies either. Throughout the postwar period, women themselves have interpreted and reinterpreted the ideal of *ryōsai kenbo* (good wife, wise mother) to make sense of and justify women's activities outside the home (Uno 1993).

The Japanese state's strategy of constructing gendered roles, putting the responsibility of household management solely on women's shoulders, has largely succeeded; Japan is probably more sharply gender-differentiated than any other industrialized society in the world. However, I would argue that the strategy has also produced an unintended consequence: women have become the leading voice against corporate abuse and state irresponsibility over the health of workers and children. Despite the images of Japanese women as apolitical and subservient, housewives and mothers have been a hidden and sometimes not-so-hidden driving force for social activism in Japan (McKeen 1981). For example, the lawsuits against Chisso, the chemical company responsible for Minamata disease in the 1960s, would not have been possible without litigant women being willing to challenge the corporation and the authorities, which were essentially on the corporation's side. Their legal victory compelled the government to establish the Environmental Agency in the Office of the Prime Minister in 1971, and institute severe penalties for polluters. Recent examples also include anti-*karōshi* movements that made the term *karōshi* (death by overwork) a household word. Over the last three decades, female plaintiffs, mothers and wives of *karōshi* victims have led prolonged efforts to challenge the state and corporate authorities, forcing the government to change labour-related regulations and workers' compensation laws (Morioka 2008). Motherhood, empowered by the moral imperative to protect children, gives women a license to trust their feelings and challenge other prevalent cultural norms of obedience to governmental and corporate authorities. Unlike during World War II, when the state asked mothers to abandon their protective role and sacrifice their sons to the war effort, no counter-ideology challenges the legitimacy of maternal protectiveness in contemporary Japan. Women in social protests have drawn, consciously or unconsciously, on the prevalent cultural assumption that deem women in general, and mothers in particular, to be selfless nurturers with natural protective instincts.

There is, however, a significant limitation to the women's influence. Their voices are heard precisely because they hold the subordinated status of housewives and mothers whose realm of influence is confined to domestic matters. As a result, they are only able to speak effectively on issues traditionally related to female roles, such as the health and safety of workers and children. The women in Tohoku, for example, would probably not be taken seriously if they complained about the deplorable lack of political representation of Japanese women in their localities. This is the other side of the coin from which they draw their moral legitimacy and cultural power as housewives and mothers. Ironically, the same feminine/maternal role that gives their voices a degree of authority also obliges them to limit their sphere of political participation to family related issues.

All things considered, however, the presence of mothers who dare to speak up provides a degree of hope for democratic social change in Japan.

The mothers' willingness to protest denotes resistance against the government and powerful corporations, whose overwhelming power largely determines cultural norms and assumptions in Japan. In Miyagi, the majority of the populace was in denial about radiation, and passively dependent on the government for recovery. The struggling local government was too overburdened with urgent work and hamstrung by inflexible bureaucratic procedures to proactively address radiation concerns. The central government acted as if the disasters were localized problems. Without the women who first voiced their concerns and dissatisfactions in their localities, we might not have seen many of the demands and protests made against the local government after the disaster. The series of antinuclear protests after 3.11 were partly the results of activism led by mothers joining forces with existing antinuclear activists and younger generations of protesters. They included the largest antinuclear demonstration ever held in postwar Japan, in Tokyo on 19 September 2011, the ten-day sit-in protest by Women Who do not Need Nuclear Power in November 2011 which led to the establishment of 'Tent-Square' as an on-going protest hub in front of the Ministry of Economy, Trade and Industry, and the weekly protests in front of the prime ministers' official residence that drew tens of thousands of people in June and July 2012. The actions taken by the mothers in Tohoku exemplify the courage of women demanding accountability from the government and corporations in Japan. Such actions have seldom been needed more.

References

Bernstein, Gail L. (ed.) (1991). *Recreating Japanese Women, 1600–1945*. Berkeley: University of California Press.

Garon, Sheldon (2003). 'From Meiji to Heisei: The State and Civil Society in Japan'. In Frank. J. Schwartz and Susan. J. Pharr (eds), *The State of Civil Society in Japan*, pp. 42–62. Cambridge: Cambridge University Press.

Gordon, Andrew (1997). 'Managing the Japanese Household: The New Life Movement in Postwar Japan', *Social Politics*, 4(2), 245–283.

Grady, Denise (2011). 'Radiation Is Everywhere, but How to Rate Harm?' *The New York Times*, 4 April. http://www.nytimes.com/2011/04/05/health/05radiation.html?pagewanted=all&_r=1&> accessed 7 June 2013.

LeBlanc, Robin (1999). *Bicycle Citizens: The Political World of the Japanese Housewife*. Berkeley: University of California Press.

—— (2010). *The Art of the Gut: Manhood, Power, and Ethics in Japanese Politics*. Berkeley: University of California Press.

McKean, Margaret (1981). *Environmental Protest and Citizen Politics in Japan*. Berkeley: University of California Press.

Morioka Rika (2008). *Anti-Karōshi Activism in a Corporate-Centered Society: Medical, Legal, and Housewife Activist Collaborations in Constructing Death from Overwork in Japan*. PhD Dissertation, Department of Sociology, University of California, San Diego.

National Police Agency (2011). 'Hisai jōkyō to keisatsu sochi' (Post-disaster conditions and police measures). <http://www.npa.go.jp/archive/keibi/biki/higaijokyo.pdf> accessed 23 September 2011.

Oliver-Smith, Andrew, and Susanna Hoffman (eds) (1999). *The Angry Earth: Disaster in Anthropological Perspective*. New York: Routledge.

Pharr, Susan J. (1981). *Political Women in Japan: The Search for a Place in Political Life*. Berkeley: University of California Press.

Richardson, Gardley and Scott C. Flanagan (1984). *Politics in Japan*. Boston: Little Brown.

Takeda Kunihiko (2011). 'Rinri no ōgonritsu to gyūnyū, kona miruku' (The golden rule of ethics and fresh and powdered milk). <http://takedanet.com/2011/10/post_d5f2.html> accessed 11 June 2013.

Uno, Kathleen (1993). 'The Death of the "Good Wife, Wise Mother"?' In Andrew Gordon (ed.), *Postwar Japan as History*, pp. 293–322. Berkeley: University of California Press.

USTREAM (2011). 'Genpatsu iranai Fukushima no onnatachi' Keisanshō kōshō' (Fukushima women who do not need nuclear energy in negotiations at the Ministry of Economy Trade and Industry. <http://www.ustream.tv/recorded/18140229#utm_campaign=synclickback&source=http://blog.livedoor.jp/amenohimoharenohimo/archives/65772087.html&medium=18140229> accessed 11 June 2013.

West, Guida, and Rhoda Lois Blumberg. (eds) (1990). *Women and Social Protest*. Oxford: Oxford University Press.

TOM GILL

This Spoiled Soil: Place, People and Community in an Irradiated Village in Fukushima Prefecture[1]

What constitutes a community? At the simplest level, a community is a group of people who live in the same place. In rural Japan, the link between people and place, between the soil and the people who work it, retains an overwhelming ideological significance – a significance encapsulated in the word '*furusato*'. It is translated as 'hometown' or 'native place'. Yearning for the *furusato* is expressed in countless sentimental ballads, many of which praise the mountains, valleys, woods and rivers of a particular *furusato*. One particular song, simply entitled *Furusato*, has been sung by all children attending state schools in Japan since 1914.[2] As Jennifer Robertson correctly observes, 'the ubiquity of *furusato* as a signifier of a wide range of cultural productions effectively imbues those productions with unifying – and ultimately nativist and national – political meaning and value' (Robertson 1988: 494). Love for one's home community is an emotion endorsed by the national culture in a similar way to love for one's mother.

Yet there is an irony here. The cultural emphasis on the *furusato* has persisted despite the fact that most Japanese long since ceased to live in the prototypical rural village. Nowadays 90 per cent of Japanese people live in urban areas, and the rural/urban imbalance in population is more acute

---

1   I wish to thank all the people of Nagadoro hamlet for their willingness to put up with my visits during all the trials and tribulations. In this paper, there are no pseudonyms. I asked each informant if they were preferred to be anonymous; only one did. Most said they were happy for the world to learn their names.

2   Toivonen in this volume (p. 247) mentions how this song would reduce evacuees to tears.

than in any other major industrialized society.[3] Thus the gap between the *furusato* as an actual place and as an idealized symbol of primordial native identity has widened into a chasm. Moreover, intense urbanization has happened recently enough for many families to still have elderly relatives living in the countryside. They will endure the ordeal of tremendous traffic jams and intensely overcrowded trains to return to their rural origins in the midsummer and new-year holiday seasons, in part to expiate feelings of guilt for having abandoned their homeland and ancestral family house (*jikka*). There is also an element of comfort in the idealized *furusato*. It is an anchor for the heart – a thing much needed at a time of crisis and uncertainty. Meanwhile, for those who *do* still live in ancestral villages, the concept of maintaining the *furusato* has taken on ever deeper significance, for there comes a point where the ageing and dwindling of the community reaches the point where it is no longer viable: it becomes a 'marginal settlement' (*genkai shūraku*; see Ōno 2008) and then may disappear altogether – as thousands already have.

The disasters of 3.11 pose an intellectual and practical challenge to *furusato* ideology. They impacted a largely rural, thinly populated part of Japan, with many communities that do resemble the ideology of the *furusato*. Some of these communities were instantaneously destroyed by the tsunami; others were forced to evacuate to escape radiation, not knowing if or when they might be able to return. The link between people and place has been abruptly severed, and close-knit communities scattered. The idea that people should be enabled to 'go home' has an obvious appeal.[4] But some of those communities are now officially uninhabitable, while others may or may not be inhabitable according to how people read and interpret radiation readings. Tens of thousands of rural people are now temporarily

---

3   The *United Nations Demographic Yearbook* (2011) says that only 12 million Japanese live in rural areas, in a total population of 128 million – roughly 10 per cent. That compares, for example, with 18 per cent for South Korea, 19 per cent for the United States, and 33 per cent for the Netherlands.

4   Recognizing this, the Liberal Democratic Party headlined its December 2012 election manifesto with the slogan 'First, recovery. Bring back the hometown' (*Mazu, fukkō. Furusato o, torimodosu*). The party won a landslide victory.

living in cities. It has been very disruptive, often heart-breaking. On the other hand, many of the evacuees have discovered that it is actually rather convenient to live in cities. It is difficult to say so openly, however, because love of the *furusato* is a national ideology, albeit one more honoured in the breach than the observance. When told that their irradiated home community is going to be decontaminated, at tremendous expense, so that they can return to their isolated life in the mountains and valleys, the people are supposed to be happy.

This chapter focuses on Iitate, a village in Fukushima prefecture that was totally evacuated because of radiation from the Fukushima No.1 nuclear power plant. After the initial trauma, a range of complex issues has developed around this and other disrupted communities. Who will return, and when? Who will leave the village permanently, and where will they live instead? And who is going to pay for it all? The disasters have forced the victims to confront issues that normally are never raised. Is the ideology of the communal rural lifestyle a simple expression of what is in people's hearts, or is there a disjuncture between popular discourse and the way people really feel? And is the essence of the beloved hometown a particular location, or the people who live there?

In Iitate, things are further complicated by a deep ambiguity over the physical and social consequences of ionizing radiation. The Fukushima meltdowns contaminated the village physically, leaving radioactive iodine and caesium in the air, soil, water, flora and fauna. But how serious was the contamination? Experts do not agree. It is somewhere in the grey zone between the village being inhabitable in the fairly near future, and not. Moreover, the degree of contamination varies widely from one part of the village to another, with widely differing social and economic implications for hamlets just a few miles apart.

Separate from that is the issue of conceptual contamination: damage to reputation that may have only the loosest connection to actual pollution of the environment. The name of Iitate and its constituent hamlets may well remain stigmatized long after the radiation has faded from the land.

Each inhabitant has been forced to assess the radiation risk and drastically rethink their future lives. The local and national governments have also been confronting these issues, in an elaborate three-sided game with

hundreds of billions of yen at stake in compensation payments and reconstruction funding. This chapter will trace the contours of the tense and
unpredictable negotiation that has circled around the question of how to
respond when the *furusato* is grossly violated by human error.

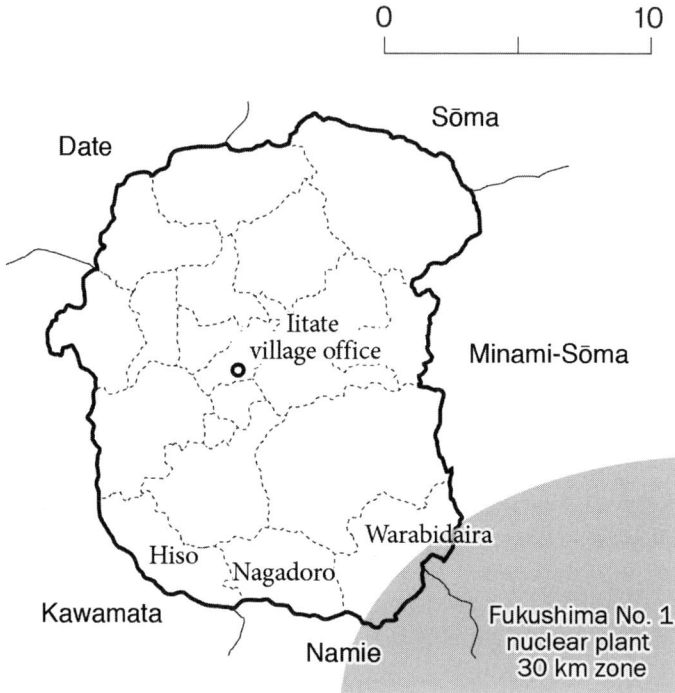

Map of Iitate village, displaying the three southern hamlets of Hiso, Nagadoro
and Warabidaira, and neighboring townships. Unit: kilometres. Reprinted
and translated from Gill et al., *Higashi Nihon daishinsai no Jinruigaku*
(Jinbun Shoin, 2013), p. 202.

A discovery in the woods

Iitate village is located just outside the 30 km evacuation zone, north-west of the Fukushima No.1 nuclear power plant. Unfortunately, the winds were blowing Iitate's way when a series of hydrogen explosions at the plant sent radioactive material into the atmosphere, and untimely snow then deposited much of it on Iitate, giving the village higher levels of radioactivity than some districts much closer to the plant. For several weeks the national government refused to acknowledge that reality. The evacuation zones were determined simply by distance from the nuclear plant, resulting in a neat semi-circle of radius 30 kilometres. For forty days the government refused to accept that the pattern of radiation did not match its neat semi-circle on the map, and so Iitate was not evacuated.

I first parked my car outside the village office in central Iitate on 22 April 2011, the day before the government finally redrew its radiation map. Deeply ignorant and curious, I had got there by taking the name off the newspaper and keying it into my car's satellite navigation system. The word 'village' (*mura*) suggests a homely cluster of cottages, but the area around the village office, on a windswept hilltop, felt more like a moon base. The village office was a smart, modern, grey building, as were the nearby clinic, junior high school, old people's home, and village-run bookshop. But there were only a couple of dozen houses to be seen, and I wondered where the population of 6,000 could be. The bookshop[5] turned out to be open, and a young woman working there explained that Iitate consists of twenty hamlets (*buraku*), scattered over 230 square kilometres (90 square miles) of mountainous, forested terrain. Iitate itself is an artificial unit, created by bureaucratic fiat, most recently through the 1956 merger between the villages of Ōdate and Iiso, which roughly correspond to the north and south of Iitate. Ōdate and Iiso were in turn the product of a series of earlier mergers, dating back to the nineteenth century. Even some of the hamlets

---

5   This bookshop, called *Hon no Mori* (Forest of Books) was run by the village. Its story is told in manga form by Ishizuka (2013).

had double-barrelled names, reflecting mergers of smaller hamlets. The hamlets had an average population of 300; and within some of them there was a yet smaller unit, the *aza*, or sub-hamlet.[6]

Knowing this makes the issue of community survival more complex. When people talk about *furusato*, they might be referring to village, hamlet, or sub-hamlet. Moreover, I now learned that the radiation in the three southernmost hamlets was so much higher than in central Iitate that some of their inhabitants had evacuated to other parts of the village. Clearly, not everyone in Iitate would have the same prospect of returning home. I reprogrammed my satnav and drove ten kilometres south to Nagadoro.

I drove through the hamlet in twilight – a few little clusters of houses off a narrow road running through forested mountains. I saw not a soul, and I assumed everyone had long since left. On the verge of driving away, I spotted a stone Shinto gate. Beyond, a crumbling staircase led up the mountain to a small shrine. Curious, I ascended through the pine trees. At the top of the steps there was light shining from the shrine. Then I heard voices, and laughter. A middle-aged man slid open the paper door, peered at me, and invited me in. Five men were drinking saké and eating cheap sushi and octopus legs. Four were from the hamlet. The fifth was a producer from the national TV network, NHK, who'd already been researching the place for a month.[7] The men were celebrating the completion of three days' hard work repairing earthquake damage to the shrine, making it fit to allow the return of the hamlet's tutelary deities (*ujigami*). Instead of the gods, however, it was I, a portly Englishman, who walked through the door.

6   The very important distinction between village and hamlet, or *mura* and *buraku*, was pointed out long ago by John Embree in his classic pre-war study of Suye village in Kumamoto prefecture (Embree 1939). Embree discusses the political tensions between the two social units and argues that the political integration of Suye village had been achieved at the expense of the social life of its 17 constituent hamlets (Kuwayama 2012).

7   He had permission to work in the radiation zone from his employer, NHK. This was in sharp contrast to the *Mainichi Shinbun* reporter mentioned later in this paper, and to the practice of the mainstream Japanese media described by McNeill elsewhere in this volume. Even within the same news organization, safety practices would vary from one section to another – from hard news to documentaries, in this case.

Everyone was surprised. I had assumed the hamlet was deserted. Instead, the trouble they had taken to repair the shrine and welcome back the gods seemed to indicate that they thought the worst was over. One of the men was hamlet headman Shigihara Yoshitomo. He told me that out of 71 households in Nagadoro, only nine were currently evacuated. A few more had sent their children away, but he estimated that 80–90 per cent of the hamlet's population of about 250 were still there, including more than half of the 40 children. About 40 households *had* evacuated, towards the end of March. It had been a 'voluntary evacuation' (*jishu hinan*) – most had gone to stay with relatives, a few to a gymnasium some 200 miles away, an option arranged by the village authorities. However, most had come back within a couple of weeks.

Why? The physical discomfort of life in a gym, and the awkwardness of imposing on in-laws were acknowledged. But the main reason was that they thought things were gradually returning to normal back in Nagadoro. An eminent radiation expert, Professor Takamura Noboru of Nagasaki University, had stated, at a public meeting in Iitate on 25 March 2011, that the level of radiation would halve in about ten days; and that it was safe to continue living in Iitate so long as one took basic precautions like washing hands and wearing a facemask when outdoors.[8]

One of the isotopes that fell on Iitate was iodine-131, which has a half-life of eight days. But the radiation in Iitate also contained large quantities of caesium-134 (half-life: two years) and caesium-137 (30 years). The radiation level in Nagadoro was 27μSv/hr on the day of that meeting. It was still at 14.5 over six months later, on 10 October. Predictably enough, there was a fairly rapid decline while the short-lived iodine faded away, slowing to a virtual halt once the iodine was gone and only the longer-lived caesium remained.

8   See Iitate village newsletter special edition No.1, 30 March 2011. <http://www. vill.iitate.fukushima.jp/folder.2011-03-30.9092271369/osiraseban_gougai01.pdf> accessed 18 August 2013. All the newsletters may be viewed (in Japanese) at the award-winning village website: <http://www.vill.iitate.fukushima.jp/saigai/>.

The headman described the clinching reason why most of the people in Nagadoro were still there 40 days after the disaster thus: 'It's all very well saying "get the hell out of here", but what are we supposed to do after that? Where are the jobs? How are we supposed to make a living? At least while we're here, we can eat our own rice and vegetables'.

Since the villagers had only been invited to 'voluntarily evacuate', there was no financial compensation on offer, and they would have to do it mostly at their own expense. With almost no financial help and no inkling as to where or how to make a living after abandoning their houses, it made perfect sense to hunker down in the village – unless you thought you were in immediate danger of seriously damaging your health. On that point the villagers heard many conflicting opinions from 'experts' and mostly preferred to believe the more optimistic ones. Various official announcements encouraged their optimism. On 1 April, for example, the ban on drinking tap water was lifted.[9]

Ironically, however, the very day I arrived in Iitate, Friday 22 April 2011, the national government ordered the evacuation of the whole village by the end of May. The return of the gods would shortly be followed by the departure of the people.

Alternative rural life

Like many Japanese towns and villages, Iitate has its own song. Entitled *Yume ōraka ni* ('Let your dreams be big and generous'), its lyrics read in part:

> *The mountains are beautiful, the water is pure*
> *Its name is Iitate, our* furusato ...
> *Aah, now is the time for us firmly to join hands,*
> *And make our village prosper, make our village prosper.*[10]

9   Village newsletter special edition No.2, 1 April 2011. <http://www.vill.iitate.fukushima. jp/folder.2011-03-30.9092271369/osiraseban_gougai01.pdf> accessed 18 August 2013.
10   Japanese original at <http://www.tokyo-sports.co.jp/blogwriter-watanabe/39/> accessed 18 August 2013.

There is a distinct urgency in the call for solidarity and the repetition of the final phrase. It has not been easy for Iitate to prosper in the face of urbaniza-tion, agricultural trade liberalization, and many other threats to the rural economy. The village population dwindled from 9,385 in 1970 to 6,211 in 2010; rather than lacking children, the village was losing people in the 20 to 40 age range,[11] for want of employment opportunities. Those who did remain in the village after reaching adulthood mostly commuted to waged work outside the village and would patch together an income through that and part-time agriculture. Household income was low, but offset by eating home-grown produce and drinking free water from the village wells.

Despite these substantial challenges, Iitate was a viable community before 11 March 2011. As of 2006 mean household size was 3.84 people, the birth-rate was 2.02, and 15.1 per cent of the population was aged under 16 (Madei 2011). Those figures were above average for Fukushima prefec-ture and for Japan as a whole. In a population of 6,000, only 110 people were over 65 and living alone. Most people were living in two- or three-generation households.

Some of the credit for maintaining this vitality belongs to Iitate's dynamic mayor, Kanno Norio. First elected in 1996, Kanno has sought to define a viable rural lifestyle in contemporary Japan. He is associated with the 'slow life' movement: Iitate's slogan is '*madei* life', *madei* being a Tohoku dialect term that signifies a slow, thorough way of doing things. For 15 years Kanno encouraged organic farming and healthy lifestyles. He took a progressive approach to gender issues, organizing trips to Europe for housewives, and issuing 'fathering handbooks' to encourage men to spend more time with their children. He shared out rural development grants among the 20 hamlets, encouraging them to find creative ways of strengthening the local economy (Madei 2011). From decorative flowers to frozen radishes, the hamlets branched out from their traditional main-stays of rice farming and livestock. In Nagadoro, the money was used to develop a new crop – *yacon* – an Andean tuber starting to get known in Japan as a health food.

11   This demographic data, derived from government censuses, is easily accessible at the Japanese-language version of Iitate village's Wikipedia page.

After the nuclear disaster, mayor Kanno's determination to defend the physical territory of the *furusato* would have far-reaching consequences for the villagers, as we shall see.

11 March and after

At the crossroads in the centre of Nagadoro, I found a notice board covered with radiation reports. Attached to the top of it by bureaucratic red tape was a plastic box. I prised it open. It contained three Geiger counters. A hand-written note said they were the property of the Ministry of Education, Sport, Science and Technology (MEXT). Every morning someone from the ministry came and updated a chart on the notice board. On 22 April 2011 the reading displayed on the noticeboard was 13.5μSv/h (microsieverts per hour).

Pre-disaster atmospheric radiation in Japan was roughly 0.05μSv/h.[12] On 22 April 2011 Tokyo registered about 0.07μSv/h; Fukushima city about 2μSv/hour (40 times normal); the Iitate village office 4.3μSv (86 times normal); and here at the Nagadoro crossroads the reading was about 270 times normal. It was also three times higher than the level published for Iitate village, which was published every day by the *Japan Times* as the 'maximum level' for the whole of Fukushima prefecture. That obviously untrue statement was sourced to MEXT – which also recorded the much higher levels at Nagadoro. The ministry dutifully published those frightening levels on-line, while blandly ignoring them in its more widely read statements about prefectural radiation levels – an intriguing case of ministerial doublethink.

---

12   There is of course much regional variation. For instance, prior to 3.11, government data gave the normal range for Tokyo as 0.028–0.079μSv/h, and for Fukushima prefecture as 0.037 to 0.046. See the government information site at <http://radioactivity.nsr.go.jp/ja/> accessed 19 June 2013.

For two years MEXT published new radiation data every day. On 1 April 2013, the job was handed over to the Nuclear Regulation Authority (NRA; Genshiryoku Kisei I'inkai), which still publishes the data in English[13] and Japanese. The national data gives a figure for 'Fukushima prefecture', at a single location in Fukushima city, about 80km away from the nuclear plant, which by 2013 had crept down to around 0.8μSv/h. The Fukushima prefectural data includes many much higher figures. Results from a different set of monitoring posts are displayed at the Fukushima prefecture home page.[14] They are often strikingly different from the national figures.[15]

The first reading recorded on the Nagadoro notice board was for 16 March 2011 – 7. 5μSv/h. The following day, it had jumped to a terrifying 95.1μSv/h: about 2,000 times higher than normal. After that it had rapidly declined, dipping below 10μSv/h on 19 April 2011. But the following day it snowed and the reading jumped to 16.3μSv/h. For months after, it hovered in the mid-teens. Until 11 March, the Japanese government had set 1mSv/year (millisievert a year) as the maximum safe dose for citizens of Japan; after the Fukushima meltdowns it raised it to 20mSv/year, amid bitter criticism. The levels of radiation in Nagadoro in March and April were roughly equivalent to 150mSv/year.[16] Cumulative radiation had already exceeded 20 millisieverts by the end of May 2011, when the evacuation was finally enforced, 80 days after the disaster.

Bombarded with conflicting information, the people's response could seem admirably calm, or frighteningly slow. Most of the people were still living in their houses, waiting for the authorities to tell them what to do. Headman Yoshitomo kindly invited me to his house the day after I arrived. That evening a dozen villagers dropped by and a party developed. A young

13   <http://radioactivity.nsr.go.jp/en/> accessed 18 August 2013.

14   <http://fukushima-radioactivity.jp/> accessed 18 August 2013.

15   The prefecture collected its own data until March 2012, when the work was transferred to MEXT, which in turn handed over to the NRA a year later. Data is periodically moved or removed, but I have preserved some samples at my home page: <http://www.meijigakuin.ac.jp/~gill/englishv/Shinsai.html>.

16   1 mSv = 1,000μSv/h. 1mSv/year. 1μSv/hour = 8.76 mSv/year.

journalist from the *Mainichi Shinbun* was there. He was shocked that so many people were still living in Nagadoro. He repeatedly asked why they had not evacuated immediately. The headman explained that power cuts had blacked out the TV news for about three days.

'Didn't you listen to the radio?'

A pause. 'We don't listen to the radio very much in these parts'. Another long silence.

As this incident showed, the headman's attitude to the radiation threat was passive. He waited for instructions from above and it did not occur to him to switch on a radio and act independently – though he had sent his wife, children and grandchildren to the less irradiated north of the village to be on the safe side. As for the journalist, he was shocked that the villagers had not evacuated, but he himself had broken his own employer's rules by entering Nagadoro.[17] He admitted he would have to pretend that he obtained his Nagadoro quotes by telephone. True, he was not spending as much time in the highly irradiated zone as the Nagadoro headman, but he was younger and therefore in a more at-risk age bracket. It seemed that most people's decisions on whether to stay or to leave had more to do with personality and purpose than with scientific risk assessment. The same was true of myself – many friends thought I was crazy to go to the irradiated zone, but it did not bother me. I instinctively felt that if so many people were willing to carry on living in the zone, it would probably be OK for me to drop in occasionally.

I visited Shōji Masahiko, a Nagadoro farmer, heart-broken because his carefully nurtured shiitake mushrooms would now be unsalable. He had a glasshouse with racks of mushrooms growing out of brown bricks of fertilized soil, and now he was removing them one by one with nail scissors (very *madei*), when in truth he might as well have thrown the whole lot away. He gave me five kilograms to take home. This gesture showed he did not really believe the mushrooms were dangerous. He could not sell them, because they had been deemed dangerous. But he would eat them himself, and give them to other people to eat. Refusing to accept the mushrooms

---

17   For more on the Japanese media's staff safety policy, see McNeill in this volume.

would be hurtful to him – perhaps implying that I thought his village was defiled. In contrast, accepting the mushrooms would be a gesture of solidarity with Nagadoro. So I took them back to my home in Yokohama.

I intended to eat them, but that night the TV news said that radiation 14 times higher than the government-approved level had been found in shiitake mushrooms from Iitate. I carried my five kilos to a nearby patch of wasteland, and sorrowfully cast them into the long grass. It was a year later that I finally found the courage to admit to Shoji-san that I had thrown them away. I think he forgave me.

Purification and farewell

On 4 May 2011 I returned to Nagadoro, arriving just in time to attend the 10am purification ceremony (*oharai*) at Shiratori Shrine. The physical work of restoring the damaged shrine had been completed; now ritual purification was necessary to restore its spiritually auspicious status and allow the gods of the hamlet to return. But in the meantime the evacuation order had been announced and now everybody knew the hamlet would shortly be evacuated. Hence the ritual took on a deeper significance. Some 60 people, about a quarter of the hamlet's population, were crowded into the single room of the Shiratori shrine, and the mood was sombre. This was a rite of spiritual cleansing[18] that had been planned to mark the rebirth of the community, but instead was heralding its dissolution.

18   The Shinto ritual of *oharai* (also pronounced *oharae*) is a very literal cleansing ritual in which a Shinto priest waves a wand called an *ōnusa* or *haraigushi*, virtually identical in appearance to a household duster, over the heads of the participants. However, it is not to be confused with *moral* cleansing. The Roman Catholic sacrament of confession is designed to cleanse the believer of guilt for his/her bad deeds; *oharai* is designed to cleanse people, places or things of bad luck. Hence it is used to bless sports teams, newly acquired cars etc. This particular *oharai* ritual signified that the people of Nagadoro had been unlucky, not that they had been bad. A failure to

The service was unusually political – led by a passionate young monk who called upon the gods to protect the local people from the evil wrought by TEPCO and its cursed nuclear plant. At 11 we adjourned to the Nagadoro community centre, for what was essentially a farewell party, though no-one would use that term. Evacuation plans were well advanced. Out of 250 people living in Nagadoro, about 40 would be moving to a newly built Ministry of Finance dormitory in Yoshikura, central Fukushima city. Seventy more would evacuate to a hotel at Iisaka hot spring, on the western outskirts of Fukushima city, while waiting for the prefecture to finish building temporary housing units (*kasetsu jūtaku*) for them. (That happened in mid-August 2011 and the hot-spring evacuees moved to a colony of grey pre-fabricated boxes on a disused industrial estate on the southern fringe of Fukushima city.) The remaining 140 would mostly be moving into private residences with the rent paid by the prefecture. The intense aversion to being in someone else's debt, and the strain of having to worry about making trouble for others,[19] plus the sheer difficulty of getting two large families into a house designed for one, meant that very few would be living with relatives.

The 60 people at the party were addressed by two youngish TEPCO employees, who apologized with foreheads touching the ground, and then explained how to obtain the 'provisional payment' (*kari-barai*) that TEPCO was offering to evacuees: 1 million yen per household. There was a little heckling, mostly by an older man who objected to the term 'provisional payment', demanding a clearer admission of guilt and remorse, but generally the TEPCO men got off lightly. Someone remarked that the company had been clever to send these junior employees: 'It's hard to hate them – they obviously aren't the people responsible'.

There were also speeches by the headman and the monk, who broke down in tears. Everyone admired his sincerity. By noon the saké was flowing freely. Most of the conversation was good-natured, but there was

---

differentiate these two different concepts is at the root of social discrimination in Japan and many other places around the world.

19   Men tend not to have close relationships with in-laws who live outside the village.

some criticism of the townships of Ōkuma and Futaba, which had jointly accepted TEPCO's siting proposal fifty years before. One man lamented that the crippled power plant had been named Fukushima No.1. He correctly pointed out that virtually all the other nuclear power plants in Japan were named after the host township. By calling it the Fukushima plant, rather than the Ōkuma-Futaba plant, TEPCO had tainted the entire prefecture by association with its own folly. He made a crucial point. Actual physical pollution was limited to a fairly small area around the plant, but the simple choice of the facility's name had polluted the entire prefecture in people's minds, probably exposing Fukushima people to discrimination for decades to come.

He also said that he envied the tsunami-ravaged communities of Miyagi and Iwate. 'At least they know who's been killed, and whose houses have been destroyed. We have no idea what's going to happen to us. That's the thing with radiation'. He admitted to feeling ashamed to say that, and preferred to remain anonymous. But he may well have put into words what many others had in their hearts.

The party ended on a sour note. Masahiko wanted to get out the karaoke machine, but was physically restrained by the treasurer, who considered it inappropriate to have a sing-song on the eve of evacuation. A shouting match ensued, with the headman finally restoring order. The karaoke machine was left unused; the party broke up quietly.

Last days in Nagadoro

I returned to Nagadoro on the last weekend in May 2011. Most people had already left. The problem of the cattle had been resolved by holding a special auction at a nearby town. Many cows were bought, at quite a reasonable price, by farmers from Miyazaki prefecture. (It was a case of favours returned – some farmers from Fukushima had sent cattle when the Miyazaki herds were afflicted by foot-and-mouth disease a year before.) Meat from the Iitate cows was probably ultimately sold to consumers in Kyushu who did not know they were originally from Fukushima. The Nagadoro farmers argued that the radiation would disappear in six months, through excretions and natural decay, after which the cow could be safely slaughtered and eaten.

On the afternoon of 29 May 2011, I was sitting on my own on the bench in front of Nagadoro's only shop (which had been permanently shuttered a year before the disaster). It was raining steadily and the cross-roads was deserted. A man came along in a white truck and got out to greet me. This was Kanno Kōhei, a burly man with a ready smile and the only person I'd met to admit he had worked for TEPCO. When he noticed I had a Geiger counter he advised me to hold it by a nearby rain gutter. It beeped hysterically, registering 243μSv/h[20] – radiation from the entire roof had gathered in a narrow pipe, driving up the reading by about 1,000 per cent. Kōhei laughed at my consternation. It was a lesson in how easy it is to manipulate radiation readings. And yet this reading was neither untrue nor meaningless. Any attempt to repopulate the village would have to take account of rainy days as well as sunny days, and children would have to be warned against playing near rain gutters.

Meanwhile, former headman Takahashi Masato had arrived in another white truck and was sowing seeds in the field by the crossroads, which belonged to a different villager, Kanno Toshio. He said he was planting sunflowers to make a brave show for when people visited Nagadoro (which would be permitted under the evacuation plan).[21] He'd had a few drinks and lectured me about the bucket chains they used to put out fires in Iitate. He wished they could get a bucket chain together to put out the 'fire' at the Fukushima nuclear plant. I took it as a satirical commentary on the dangers of modern technology not held in check by the traditional social cohesion represented by the bucket chain.[22] His was a view that mixed sadness with sardonic humour.

---

20   I videoed the moment: <http://www.youtube.com/watch?v=OmgdKi0QdgM> accessed 18 August 2013.

21   See my video at <http://www.youtube.com/watch?v=rPp9BBG-48E> accessed 18 August 2013.

22   <http://www.youtube.com/watch?v=FUP3Tti-ShI> accessed 18 August 2013.

I later noticed that the *Fukushima Minyū* newspaper had that very morning carried a front-page photograph of Iitate mayor Kanno Norio and the Minister of Agriculture, bent double and sowing sunflower seeds elsewhere in Iitate. Sunflowers had been found effective to a limited degree at absorbing radioactivity at Chernobyl, and this was an experiment at 'natural' decontamination. I realized that Masato must have seen that article and decided to do some decontaminating of his own.[23]

Life after evacuation

By mid-July 2011 only one person was still living in Nagadoro: Shiga Takamitsu, then 63. After decades away, he had returned to his native Nagadoro just six weeks before the disaster, with his golden retriever, Ray. Takamitsu ran a small business distributing dried seaweed, mostly to sushi restaurants. He stayed on in Nagadoro for a whole year after everyone else had left. He had studied radiation, and decided it was safe for a man of his age, working mostly indoors, to stay. He insisted that his customers knew about his unusual circumstances and were not deterred from buying his seaweed. After all, it did not come from the sea off Fukushima – he had it delivered from all over Japan, and it only spent a few moments exposed to the air in Nagadoro, while he chopped it up and re-bagged it in his out-house. Like the people in Kyushu who probably ate beef from the Nagadoro cattle, the people who ate Takamitsu's seaweed had no idea the food had been in the radiation zone. And in view of the very small quantities of radiation involved, it is almost certainly fair to say that what they did not know would not hurt them. I personally enjoyed the dried seaweed that Takamitsu gave me.

---

23   Government agencies and NPOs did various experiments with sunflowers and rapeseed to absorb radiation from soil. But on 14 September 2011, the Ministry of Agriculture announced that its sunflower experiment had reduced soil radiation by only 0.05 per cent (*Asahi Shinbun*, 19 September 2011).

Less sanguine about radiation was Takamitsu's daughter. Though living 250 kilometres away in Tokyo, with radiation less than a hundredth of Nagadoro's level, she was so concerned about the health risk to her children that she finally emigrated to New Zealand with the whole family – a striking gap in perception of risk within a single family.

Mayor Kanno feared that disaster might spell the end of the village. Determined to prevent that, he embarked on a series of policies designed to maintain the link between people and place. His critics – of which there were many – accused him of delaying the evacuation out of reluctance to break up his beloved community, thereby endangering lives. Once evacuation became inevitable, he negotiated to organize temporary housing that was no more than a one-hour drive from Iitate. He successfully lobbied to keep nine factories open for business in the evacuation zone. The village, apparently, was too dangerous to live in, but safe to work in – so long as one stayed indoors. Most controversially, mayor Kanno obtained government permission to keep the old people's home open – thereby enabling 110[24] very old people to live on in an area officially condemned as unfit for human habitation. The mayor's critics accused him of abandoning the old – and their carers. In an interview with me on 16 July 2011, mayor Kanno defended his position, pointing out that since 11 March many old people had died from the stress of evacuation, whereas no-one, as yet, had been killed by radiation. He consistently argued that the evident risks of stress, tiredness, loneliness, poverty and unemployment outweighed the more nebulous risk of radiation-related illness (Kanno 2011: 150–154).

Mayor Kanno also created the *mimamori-tai* (self-protection patrols) – in which villagers drive around their hamlets to check radiation levels and guard vacated houses from burglars, wild animals etc. There are three shifts: 6am–2pm, 2pm–10pm, and 10pm–6am. This project, still running well into 2014, created jobs for about 360 villagers who had lost their jobs after the disaster. Wages (7,000 yen per shift plus travel expenses) came from the government's special disaster countermeasures budget. Added

---

24   Materials distributed at public meeting at Matsukawa temporary housing project, 2 November 2011.

to the compensation payments of 100,000 yen per person per month for 'psychological damage' (*seishinteki songai*) from TEPCO, this was a living wage – just about.

The wide differentials in radioactive contamination within Iitate were a challenge. In the central and northern districts, the patrols worked four shifts a week, but in the heavily contaminated southern districts, only two shifts were allowed. This left the Nagadoro people with a much lower income. They wanted to swap shifts with less contaminated hamlets, but the latter refused. Village solidarity did not extend to the point of hamlets sharing each other's radiation.

Nagadoro people suffered some discrimination. Yoshitomo the headman worked part-time at a factory in Minami-Sōma, making stainless steel kitchen draining boards, and became used to his co-workers saying 'uh-oh, here comes the radiation' when he arrived for work. At break times he would deliberately sit separately, sparing them the embarrassment of having to avoid him.

The schools in Iitate were closed down and most of the children went to school in the neighboring town of Kawamata. The Iitate elementary school children were taught in a disused block of a Kawamata junior high school, so they seldom encountered the older Kawamata children. The Kawamata children wore coloured glass badges that would darken if radiation accumulated. The Iitate children, though taught on the same premises, got no glass badges. The village education committee, following the mayor's line, had decided that the stress of being constantly reminded about radiation would do more harm than good – although some parents complained. 'Why', one mother asked me, 'is it necessary to measure the radiation dose of Kawamata children but not Iitate children?' (fieldnotes, 2 November 2011). The truth was that 'necessity' was assessed in subjective, political terms. The Kawamata authorities, not faced with evacuation, wanted to express their extreme vigilance. The Iitate authorities wanted to avoid anything that might cause panic and make evacuated villagers flee still further. Keeping the two sets of children apart helped to avoid discord over these strikingly different approaches. Finally, personal dosimetres were distributed to the

Iitate children on 24 January 2012 – over ten months after the disaster.[25] Importantly, whereas the badges were permanently visible, the dosimeters could be kept in one's pocket, reducing the risk of discrimination.

The village authorities encouraged local districts to hold reunions during the mid-August Obon period, again trying to preserve the link between people and place. I attended a party at the Nagadoro community centre on 14 August 2011, prior to which many families cleaned up their ancestral grave sites and prayed for the dead. This time only about 25 people showed up, but they were remarkably good humoured. The party was limited to two hours, the maximum time considered safe in Nagadoro. Speeches dwelt upon mayor Kanno's pledge to enable the people to return to Iitate within two years – a figure which the mayor had himself admitted to having 'no particular scientific basis' (Kanno 2011: 12, 176).

Though the evacuation was not compulsory, by 1 October 2011, outside the old people's home only 13 people were still living in Iitate,[26] including Shiga Takamitsu in Nagadoro.

Masato cuts the grass

On 10 October 2011, Takahashi Masato arrived in Nagadoro and persuaded a younger villager to cut the unseemly long grass in Kanno Toshio's field by the crossroads. Overnight, MEXT's officially published radiation level for Nagadoro dropped about 25 per cent, from 14.6 μSv/h to 11.2 μSv/h. By having the irradiated grass removed, Masato had created a tiny zone of lower radiation at the precise spot where it was being measured. It was no coincidence that he had sowed the sunflower seeds in exactly the same place.

25   From Magazine 9: <http://www.magazine9.jp/oshidori/110914/index.php> accessed
      16 June 2013.
26   Same source as footnote 24 above.

Once people realized what had happened, many were furious. Masato's irresponsible action had distorted the radiation readings, creating an entirely false impression that things were getting better. He received a severe scolding from the headman and had to make a formal apology to the village authorities. When I asked Masato during my visit on 2 November 2011 why he did it, at first he said he simply hoped to hasten the date when everyone could return to his beloved Nagadoro. That sounded like wishful thinking. However, he then came up with a more compelling defence.

He pointed out that the MEXT measuring spot was at the edge of the road, next to an open field. In the middle of the road, the reading was about half the level at the official measuring spot. What criteria made the higher reading correct?

I retorted that every time it rains, radioactive material would be flushed off the hard asphalt surface of the road, making that level unnaturally low compared with the fields, where it would be absorbed in the soil. So would not the field reading be more significant than the road reading? He countered that the area of the field by the side of the road would have an artificially *high* reading because of radiation washed off the road and into the edge of the field. He added that in other places the MEXT Geiger counters *were* located in the middle of the road, so why did the same logic not apply to all measuring sites?

Then he mentioned the other measuring spot in Nagadoro, outside the community centre, on a gravelly surface in an elevated location. That machine – installed and monitored by the prefecture rather than the national government – had been showing 7 or 8μSv/h for months. Why did the Ministry not publish *that* as the representative figure for Nagadoro? Moreover, if people were still living in Nagadoro, they would be keeping the grass neatly cut, not letting it grow shoulder high. In sum, what he had been doing was not *distorting* the data but *correcting* it.

Masato had a point. High ground versus low ground; soil versus concrete or asphalt; these things massively influence radiation readings. Which reading is more relevant? For cultivating crops, the level of radiation in the fields matters. But for dwelling in Nagadoro, the community centre reading would arguably be more relevant since most of the houses in Nagadoro are on higher, gravelly ground. How carefully had the MEXT men chosen their spot?

On 4 November 2011, I made a tour of Iitate and environs, starting at Nagadoro (MEXT monitoring post no. 33) and visiting three more, in the neighbouring town of Namie: no. 31 (Tsushima Nakaoki), no. 32 (Ako'ugi Teshichirō), and no. 81 (Ako'ugi Ishikoya). All three points were on elevated mountain roads. Each had a cross made of MEXT red tape clearly marked on the road. Two of them, no. 32 and no. 81, were located in the middle of the road. My own Geiger counter showed that in every case, the reading was higher by the side of the road than in the middle of the road. So the siting was inconsistent.

That evening I told Yoshitomo, the headman, about Masato's defence and my own observations which seemed to support it. What did he think?

Yoshitomo was not persuaded. He too was deeply attached to Nagadoro. He hung on until 21 June, three weeks after the government evacuation deadline, to sell his last cow. But later he realized that Nagadoro was too irradiated for people to live there for many, many years to come. They had to swiftly accept the grim reality, and concentrate on getting the government to buy up the land so that the evacuees could buy land and housing elsewhere. It suited the government and TEPCO to downplay radiation levels so that they could hold out the possibility of an early return and thereby delay or reduce compensation payments.

Hence the headman's anger with Takahashi Masato: not for distorting the radiation reading, but for moving it in a politically inexpedient direction. Where Masato felt the high readings were unrepresentative and sullied the reputation of the hamlet, the headman felt the high readings were a necessary stimulant for government action. Thus the response to radiation in Nagadoro was neither simple nor uniform. These two men both recognized the crucial divide between radiation and the representation of radiation. They attempted to use that divide to further their opposed political agendas – agendas reflecting conflicting interpretations of the *furusato*. Where Masato dreamed of restoring the people to their ancestral land, Yoshitomo had largely abandoned hope of that and was concerned rather to protect the welfare of the people.

The complexity of representing radiation is also apparent at the government level. The government website (formerly run by MEXT, now by the NRA) carries abundant data, which at first glance looks like an impressive exercise in open government. Yet it may have been selected for political ends and accidentally or deliberately distorted. Some government data is conflicting; for example, three MEXT documents all dated 15 July 2011 give the level at the Nagadoro crossroads as 7.1μSv/h, 14.7μSv/h and 18.0μSv/h.[27] I do not think any of these statements is actually *untrue* (they were taken at different times or with different machines): but there is no attempt to explain how such different values can coexist or which should be taken as meaningful. And which data is taken as 'representative' can influence evacuation plans, compensation programmes, and ultimately, the fate of communities.

Decontamination versus resettlement

On 28 September 2011, Iitate mayor Kanno released a plan for decontaminating the whole village over the next two years. It was budgeted at 322.4 billion yen (Iitate-mura 2011: 8), roughly 200 million yen for every household in Iitate. Yoshitomo saw no point in spending colossal sums of money on a decontamination programme that would probably not bring the inhabitants back anyway. That winter, he broke ranks and took a move very radical for the headman of a small hamlet – he instructed a group of lawyers to prepare a formal legal demand (*mōshitate*) for compensation from TEPCO for the people of Nagadoro. The amount of compensation claimed was over 100 million yen ($1 million) per household. The mayor thoroughly disapproved, and none of the other 19 hamlets in Iitate were taking legal action. It took guts for Yoshitomo to take the plunge. Like the mayor, he sought to defend the community. But for him, the community was the hamlet rather than the village, and the human community was to

27   These pages have been removed from the MEXT website, but are displayed at my home page (see footnote 15 above): 'Ambiguous MEXT Fukushima radiation data published on 15 July 2011'.

be defended by demanding enough money to start a new life elsewhere, assuming that the contaminated ancestral dwelling place would not be inhabitable for many years to come. Roughly 60 of the 71 households in Nagadoro joined the class action. On 13 July 2012, the demand was submitted to the Nuclear Power Dispute Resolution Centre.[28] If a settlement could not be agreed, the next step would be legal action in the courts.

On 11 March 2012, I attended a mass rally at a baseball stadium in Kōriyama city on the first anniversary of the disaster.[29] Among the speakers was Kanno Hiroshi, a farmer representing the group *Makenēdo Iitate* (No Surrender Iitate). In a powerful speech,[30] he bemoaned the demise of agriculture in his beloved village. I fully expected him to demand rapid decontamination. But to my surprise, he clearly opposed mayor Kanno's line and called upon the government to provide a new village in a safe location elsewhere.

His opinion is shared by many villagers, including another activist group called *Shintenchi o motomeru kai* (Group to demand a new world). They say that decontaminating the village would merely line the pockets of the civil engineering firms that would do the work – many of which had already profited from building the nuclear power plant. Meanwhile, villagers who declined to return to the village would not benefit. The money would be better spent providing a safe environment elsewhere, creating a 'New Iitate' (Shintenchi 2012a). Essentially this was the theme of the Nagadoro demand, expanded to the whole village.

28   *Genshiryoku songai baishō funsō kaiketsu sentā*. This is an arbitration unit set up by MEXT specifically to resolve disputes over compensation claims relating to the nuclear disaster. As of 10 June 2013, 6,705 claims had been submitted to it, of which 2,969 had been settled, 551 withdrawn and one rejected. That left 2,711 cases still being negotiated and 473 where arbitration had failed. <http://www.mext.go.jp/a_menu/genshi_baisho/jiko_baisho/detail/1329118.htm> accessed 16 June 2013.

29   It was the biggest anti-nuclear rally ever held in Fukushima prefecture. Organizers estimated that 16,000 attended. But like so many similar events, it was barely mentioned in the Japanese media.

30   Viewable here: <http://www.youtube.com/watch?v=poiTaoqs81s> accessed 16 June 2013.

On 5 June 2012, Shintenchi (2012b) published an attitudinal survey of 576 Iitate householders in which 283 (49 per cent) said they had no intention of returning to the village, against 116 (20 per cent) saying they would return right away or if the government declared it safe. The rest of the respondents said they would return once radiation was below a certain level. On 22 June the village office released its own survey (Iitate-mura 2012) of 1,788 villagers, of whom 33.1 per cent said they had no intention of returning, against 12.0 per cent saying they wanted to return once the village was decontaminated. In between, 45.5 per cent said they did not plan to return to the village any time soon, though they would like to return 'someday' (*izure*).

The village office added 45.5 to 12.0 and stated '57.5 per cent want to return to the village' (Iitate-mura 2012: 63). This was politically motivated optimism: unless it seems that a substantial proportion of the villagers plan to return, the critics of the expensive decontamination project might appear vindicated. In fact, even in the village's own survey, only 10.7 per cent said they believed the village could be properly decontaminated, against 44.1 per cent who had little or no hope (ibid. 58). As for whether people wanted to move the whole village or their hamlet to a new location – the question was not asked. The entire survey was founded on the assumption that the end goal was to resume village life in the same physical location as before.

Yet as the months turned into years, the mayor's idealism steadily lost its plausibility. Most of the families were now living in cities. People, especially children, were making new friendships and enjoying a lifestyle far more varied and convenient than Iitate could offer. The notion of putting up with a bit of radiation to go and live in a remote mountain hamlet had little appeal. No-one would put it that way, but a lot of the evacuees were falling out of love with the *furusato*. They would still applaud the idea; but only a minority, of mainly elderly people, fancied the reality.

A village divided

In between the publication of these rival surveys, on 15 June 2012, the national government announced a major rezoning of the evacuated districts of Iitate. They were divided into three types: type 1 (atmospheric radiation under 20 mSv/year); type 2 (20 to 50 mSv/year); and type 3 (exceeding 50 mSv/year). The government announced plans to reopen type 1 zones within two years and type 2 zones in two to five years. But type 3 zones were to be barricaded up as no-go zones for at least five years.

In Iitate, six hamlets in the north of the village were classified as type 1; 13 in the central and southern districts as type 2; and only Nagadoro as type 3.[31] The new rules came into force at midnight on 17 July 2012. In a solemn little ceremony aired on national TV news, government officials closed and padlocked the gates on six roads leading into Nagadoro. The 'barricades' (*barikēdo*) are in fact simple green metal gates. Anyone can walk around them – they only obstruct vehicles. During the day there is a guard at the gate, dressed in a full-body white radiation suit. The one I talked to said he felt incongruous because all the Nagadoro people would come and go in their ordinary clothes. He also confessed he was sweating like a pig.

No-one from Nagadoro was quite sure what the barricades were for. Some said they were to stop radiation escaping on vehicles or clothing. Others thought they were to deter burglars; yet others reckoned they were there to protect outsiders from unwittingly drifting into this high-risk zone. Oddly, though, the people of the hamlet were free to come and go, having been told the four-digit number of the combination lock to allow after-hours access. Why was it too dangerous for passing travellers, but not for the hamlet people? Why did *they* not have to wear a radiation suit? Did it mean they were 'expendable'? No-one really believed that, but they joked about it, slightly uneasily.

---

31   Shiga Takamitsu finally evacuated to Fukushima city at the end of May 2012, know-
      ing the barricades were coming.

Shōji Masahiko probably had the best explanation. 'They serve no practical purpose', he said, 'but they are a concrete symbol to make the people of Nagadoro understand that they really can't go back and live there anytime soon'.

On the day the gates were locked, Nagadoro headman Shigihara Yoshitomo commented: 'When we evacuated we were all in it together, but now it seems just Nagadoro has been left behind. All this has happened through no fault of ours, and it's extremely distressing'.[32] Where the tsunami had brought a sense of togetherness to some communities (see Steger in this volume), the protracted battle over the radiation was slowly breaking up Iitate, and many other affected communities.

The headman of neighbouring Warabidaira hamlet, Shiga Mitsuo, was also distressed, but for the opposite reason – because his hamlet was *not* declared a five-year no-go zone, despite having petitioned the village to be so designated. Being put in the most contaminated category may be stigmatizing, but it does help in the battle for compensation. TEPCO's lawyers cannily announced that the compensation payments of 100,000 yen per person per month would continue, but that since Nagadoro was definitely off-limits for five years, they would pay its residents five years' worth of compensation up-front. A family of five would get 30 million yen – big money for low-income villagers. In September 2012, Warabidaira announced plans to file a legal demand for compensation similar to the Nagadoro one.[33] Mayor Kanno's book (2011) was entitled 'Radiation fell on a beautiful village'. In a sense that was true: but the heaviest radiation had fallen on the two beautiful hamlets of Nagadoro and Warabidaira. Their decision to take legal action shows that in this case at least, the hamlet is the real hometown of the heart.

On 2 September 2012 I visited Nagadoro along with some 15 reporters and cameramen. Showing unexpected media savvy, headman Yoshitomo had won government approval to admit the media to the 'no-go zone' twice a month. He met the press at the Nagadoro Community Centre, which has

32   Quoted in *Yomiuri Shinbun*, 17 July 2012. <http://www.yomiuri.co.jp/national/ news/20120717-OYT1T00252.htm> accessed 16 June 2013.

33   Some 50 households of Warabidaira duly filed the demand in January 2013.

a large, fixed Geiger counter in the car-park. On 2 September 2012 there were several dump trucks there from Taisei Construction. They had just finished removing several tons of topsoil, in a MEXT experimental decontamination project. The reading on the Geiger counter – the representative reading for Nagadoro at the Fukushima prefecture website – had just tumbled from 4.7μSv/hr to 1.2μSv/hr.[34] To a casual observer accessing the website, there appeared to have been a sudden drastic decline in radiation in Nagadoro. Ironically, MEXT had done exactly the same thing Takahashi Masato did a year before – decontaminating one small part of Nagadoro and creating a false impression of improvement.

Decision time

The autumn of 2012 brought a series of major developments. On 24 September, mayor Kanno formally notified the national government that the village had decided on a schedule for the return to Iitate. Counting from 11 March 2011, Nagadoro would be reopened to habitation in six years; Warabidaira, Hiso and Maeta-Yawaki in five; and the other 16 hamlets in four. The next day, the national government suddenly announced it would commence full-scale decontamination of Iitate village immediately, decontaminating the western half of the village by 31 March 2013, and the eastern half by 31 March 2014. This exactly matched the schedule proposed by mayor Kanno a year earlier, though the one-year delay left the government with a wholly implausible six months to decontaminate the western half.

---

34   This is the same Geiger counter as mentioned earlier by Masato as having a lower reading than the one at the crossroads. See <http://fukushima-radioactivity.jp/environ-mapdetail.php?category_cd=1&genre_cd1=-1&point_no=96> accessed 16 June 2013. Screenshots from late October 2012 are displayed at my home page (see footnote 15 above).

On 2 October 2012, the national government told the village it would accept the mayor's repatriation schedule except that the 16 less-contaminated hamlets would be reopened a year earlier – in March 2014 rather than March 2015.[35] Clearly the timing was designed to dovetail with the decontamination schedule announced the previous week.

On 11 October 2012, the period for filing candidacy in the Iitate mayoral election came to an end. The incumbent, Kanno Norio, was the only candidate, so the vote was cancelled and his re-election became a certainty. None of his numerous critics even managed to field a candidate. He promised to enable all the villagers to return before the end of his fifth four-year term – despite the fact that one of the 20 hamlets had just been declared off-limits for the next five years. Here the word he used for 'return' (*kison*) is important. It literally means 'return to the village'. The people of Nagadoro might be able to go and live in another part of Iitate, but whether they would consider that 'returning home' is another matter.

On 19 October 2012, the village assembly formally accepted the government schedule, thus becoming the first authority in Fukushima prefecture to set a date for ending evacuation. It was also agreed that TEPCO compensation payments would be calculated on the basis of this schedule.[36] Accepting the government's one year earlier return date meant that people in the 16 low-radiation hamlets effectively lost 1.2 million yen a head (12 months of psychological damage payments of 100,000 yen a month), saving the government about 6 billion yen.

On 21 October mayor Kanno's re-election was officially confirmed. Two days later, he was out harvesting rice from an experimental decontaminated paddy-field in central Iitate, a symbol of agricultural normality.

But despite these impressive shows of progress, almost no-one believes the village really can be decontaminated. It is a scientific fact that radiation cannot be destroyed. 'Decontamination' means moving it somewhere else. The question of 'where to?' is the biggest NIMBY problem in history.

35 *Fukushima Minpō*, 3 October 2012. < http://www.minpo.jp/news/detail/20121003 4016> accessed 10 October 2012.
36 *Fukushima Minyū*, 20 October 2012, p. 1.

While the huge issue of a final resting place floats in political limbo, local governments are being asked to create 'intermediate storage locations' (*chūkan chozō-chi*). In Iitate, local opposition to building one in a government-owned forest has forced mayor Kanno to establish 'temporary dump-sites' (*kari-okiba*) for each hamlet. They too are bitterly opposed. In September 2012 he asked Nagadoro and Warabidaira to let some land be used as 'temporary-temporary dump-sites' (*kari-kari-okiba*), for rent of 90,000 yen per hectare per month. The choice of the two most contaminated hamlets as dump sites was seen by the villagers as a tacit admission that it would be politically impossible to expect villagers to return to hamlets with radioactive waste dumps on their territory. The ever receding prospect of a final solution chimes strangely with the government's new-found confidence that it can start reopening the village in a year or so. Nonetheless, the announcements of October 2012 effectively dashed any prospects of 'New Iitate' materializing. Despite the deep scepticism of the villagers shown in survey results, the big-money decontamination programme was on.

Conclusion: On community and locality

It is a tragic irony that Mayor Kanno's policies, designed to maintain the link between people and place, will probably speed the dissolution of Iitate as a sphere of human relationships: most of the population will be permanently dispersed.

Why? Firstly, there are enormous practical challenges to decontaminating a mountainous rural community. In January 2013 a series of media reports on 'sloppy decontamination' (*tenuki josen*) exposed shocking negligence by the construction companies that had won the big-money decontamination contracts, and heavy winter snow and frost soon made a mockery of the government's blithe announcement of autumn 2012 that half the village would be decontaminated by spring 2013. The Ministry of

Environment's official website finally announced that as of 31 March 2013, decontamination had *started* in just two of the eleven western hamlets, covering 1 per cent of residential land and 4 per cent of forestland.[37] As usual, there was no explanation or apology offered.

Secondly, since most villagers understandably no longer trust the government on the radiation issue, they would not believe assurances of safety even if they happened to be true.

Thirdly, even if they themselves believed it were safe, they would not want other people to associate them with the stigmatized names of Iitate village and its hamlets.

Fourthly, these concerns will be greatly magnified for anyone with children, since it is now well known that the dangers of radiation are greater for growing children than for mature adults.

The October 2012 announcements on the return dates caused far more consternation in the 16 low-radiation hamlets with early return dates than in Nagadoro. If Nagadoro people were seriously thinking of returning, then the prospect of having to wait another four-and-a-half years would be devastating. But apart from Masato, Takamitsu, and a few other elderly people, they have no intention of returning home – probably not ever. So they were relatively happy to learn they would get six years' worth of compensation rather than three.[38] Since most of the people in the other hamlets are not intending to return to them either, the early return date was bad news because it meant less compensation, just as it was bad news for Warabidaira when their hamlet was not turned into a barricaded no-go zone.

The villagers have not been consulted on what constitutes a safe level of radiation. The government is aiming for 20mSv/year, which is still 20 times higher than the pre-disaster 'safe' level. Moreover, the decontamination programme only applies to the land around houses and roads. The fields are

---

37   <http://josen.env.go.jp/area/details/iitate.html> accessed 16 June 2013.

38   On 24 May 2013, the Dispute Resolution Centre proposed a settlement of 500,000 yen per adult, and 1 million yen for children and pregnant women, for 'distress' (*fuan*) caused by exposure to radiation. TEPCO rejected the settlement and the case was still deadlocked by January 2014. So the 6 million yen payment to each person of Nagadoro for five years' displacement from home took on even greater significance.

supposed to take another five years, and some doubt it is even possible to decontaminate the densely forested mountains that cover three-quarters of the land in Iitate. But if the mountains are not decontaminated, radiation will be washed down into the inhabited valleys every time it rains. Many villagers are naturally unwilling to live in homes with radiation levels far higher than were deemed safe before 3.11, with fields that cannot be cultivated, amid even more irradiated forests and mountains. Even if their 'psychological damage' is officially over and their compensation payments stopped, families with children will almost certainly not return. Iitate village will be reduced to a small fraction of its pre-disaster population, with a very high proportion of retirees and almost no children.

And yet, nearly all my informants showed a genuine love for their *furusato* – often defined as hamlet rather than village. It is the community they know. Could not the community have been preserved in another place, as so many argued? Did it have to be these particular mountains, these particular forests, this particular patch of spoiled soil? The idea of giving the community a chance to continue in a different location was much discussed by the villagers, but – unlike in the case of Chernobyl – never countenanced by the authorities. Tragically, the commitment to maintaining the link between people and place will likely finish the job started by the nuclear disaster, destroying the community once known as Iitate village, leaving only a nostalgic yearning for a lost way of life. Before our very eyes, the welfare of the people is being sacrificed for a fetishized ideal of a place.

References

Embree, John F. (1939). *Suye Mura: A Portrait of a Japanese Village.* Chicago: Chicago University Press.

Iitate-mura (2011). *Iitate-mura josen kikaku-sho* (A plan for decontaminating Iitate village). Iitate village.

——(2012). *Iitate-mura no nanmin seikatsu jittai oyobi kison ikō nado ni kan-suru ankēto chōsa hōkoku-sho* (Report of a survey on the circumstances of refugee life, attitudes to returning to the village, etc.)

Ishizuka Yumemi (2013). *3.11: Ano hi o wasurenai (1) Iitate-mura, hon no mori de matte iru* (3.11: Never forget that day. Vol. 1: Waiting in the Forest of Books, Iitate village). Tokyo: Akita Shoten.

Kanno Norio (2011). *Utsukushii mura ni hōshanō ga futta* (Radiation fell on a beautiful village). Tokyo: Wani Books.

Kuwayama Takami (2012). 'Dai-2-ji sekai taisen zengo no Amerika-jin kenkyūsha ni yoru Nihon sonraku no kenkyū' (Research on Japanese rural communities by American researchers before and after World War II), *Minpaku Tsūshin* (Bulletin of the National Museum of Ethnology), 139, 10–11.

Madei Tokubetsu Hensei Chiimu (2011). *Madei no chikara* (The power of prudence). Fukushima: Saga Design Seeds.

Ōno Akira (2008). *Genkai shūraku to chiiki saisei* (Marginal settlements and regional revitalization). Nagano: Shinano Mainichi Shinbunsha.

Robertson, Jennifer (1988). 'Furusato Japan: The Culture and Politics of Nostalgia', *International Journal of Politics, Culture and Society*, 1(4), 494–518.

Shintenchi o motomeru kai (2012a). 'Yōbōsho' (Petition). <http://www.mocweb.co.jp/iitate/youbousho.html> accessed 16 June 2013.

——(2012b). 'Iitate-mura sonmin ankēto shūkei kekka' (Results of a questionnaire survey of Iitate villagers). < http://www.seikeitohoku.com/img/201206_iitate_3.pdf> accessed 20 June 2013.

PART 3

Insider/Outsider Encounters

TUUKKA TOIVONEN

Youth for 3.11 and the Challenge of Dispatching Young Urban Volunteers to North-eastern Japan

> Regardless of the fact that there has been a severe shortage of volunteers following the Great East Japan Earthquake, we have witnessed a situation where many interested students have been unable to partake in volunteering. Youth for 3.11 believes that students – the supporters of tomorrow's Japan – have an important role to play in the solution of social problems. This is why it is our aim to realise, through the provision of accessible volunteering opportunities, both a swift recovery as well as a society where students can take part in the solving of social problems.
>
> — Mission Statement, Youth for 3.11 (Youth for 3.11, 2012)

As amply documented in this volume, the aftermath of 3.11 has thrown up a plethora of vexing puzzles of great anthropological and sociological significance. At the micro-level, diverse volunteers have found themselves colliding with the tricky moral dimensions of giving and receiving aid (see Slater in this volume). At the mezzo-level, many domestic and international aid organizations have experienced considerable frustration as their offers of assistance have been turned down by local government officials and other gate-keepers (see McJilton 2013). By shifting the focus from 'adult' volunteers and established aid organizations onto Japanese young people in their late teens and early twenties, in the present chapter I expose yet another important conundrum: why is it that urban youth have found it so difficult to engage in volunteering in the disaster-struck areas of north-eastern Japan despite the evident need for assistance? In particular, what may have inhibited direct volunteer participation by Japan's university students – a demographic group famous for having plenty of spare time and a high interest in 'contributing to society' (see Furuichi 2011)?[1]

The following account addresses these queries by examining the story of Youth for 3.11, a student-led organization that suddenly emerged via social media in the immediate aftermath of Japan's triple disaster and went on to grow into the largest student-run volunteer aid organization in Japan. As of 23 September 2012, the group reported it had successfully dispatched a total of 1,921 individual student volunteers and facilitated over 12,000 individual volunteering trips (a figure which includes repeaters), mainly to the Tohoku area.[2] Key activities there have included cleaning up of wreckage and mud; building playgrounds for children; cooking and serving food to evacuees; collecting lost photographs and passing them on to survivors; and organizing small festivals and socializing opportunities for the inhabitants of temporary housing units. The group has 9,018 registered members from across Japan, and many have done volunteer work nearer to home, for instance by dying hand-made *yukata* (cotton kimono) with Kyoto-based craftsmen, for children living in temporary housing, as documented in a programme by a Yomiuri TV crew that followed participating students in both Kansai and Rikuzen-Takata (Kansai Jōhō Netto TEN, 20 September 2012).

This chapter offers an overview of how volunteer tours proceed, how Youth for 3.11 itself was born, why students choose to volunteer, and how they describe their experiences in the field. It also looks at the many barriers that have constrained the dispatching of young volunteers since 3.11. My recent exchanges with Youth for 3.11 confirm that there have been few

1   In 2012, Japan had nearly 2.9 million students enrolled in four-year institutions (MEXT 2012: see below sections for further discussion on numbers). In the absence of reliable statistics, I estimate that less than one per cent of this demographic – fewer than 29,000 individuals – directly participated in volunteer activities in the tsunami-ravaged areas between mid-March 2011 and September 2012. Official estimates from the volunteer centres in the prefectures of Iwate, Miyagi and Fukushima show that these areas had received altogether 1.1 million registered volunteers by September 2012, but unfortunately these estimates do not distinguish between specific age-groups and count repeaters each time they come (Zenshakyō 2012).

2   From summer 2012 onwards, students have also been dispatched to provide support to flood victims in Kyushu, Shikoku and Kansai.

changes in this respect since my initial ethnographic fieldwork in July 2011,[3] except that a gradual decline in the number of interested student volunteers and the dwindling of (already limited) funding flows from donors now present further challenges for the group (interview with the new Youth for 3.11 representative Shimada Yūji and two other staff members, 28 August 2012). Seen through the lens of Youth for 3.11, universities, labour markets and parents are among the most relevant institutions and actors to be grappled with, though by mid-2012 the organization's leaders had also become increasingly aware of the ways in which the very image of 'a volunteer' (*borantia*) – i.e. the dominant social construction of this category – seems to act as another serious deterrent for many students who might potentially wish to contribute to recovery efforts. In closing, I consider whether the tactics, models and ambitions of Youth for 3.11 reflect the emergence of a new 'socially entrepreneurial' style of civic activity, or whether they by and large fall within the pervasively government-shaped strategy of 'facilitating spontaneity' set out by Simon Avenell (2010) in his excellent account of independent volunteerism in Japan since 1945.

Two caveats are called for. While most other chapters in this volume focus on micro-level interactions in the disaster zone, my focus is more on the organizational logic of Youth for 3.11, viewing its leaders and the role of their group as an interface or mediator between urban youth, volunteering opportunities in Tohoku and 'mainstream Japan'. The process by which intermediaries turn prospective youth volunteers into actual youth volunteers is as fertile an area for investigation as the interrelationship between, say, the aid-giver and the aid-receiver or 'insider' and 'outsider' groups of volunteers.

3   I was 31 years old at the time of participant observation, a process which started with me signing up online for a Youth for 3.11 programme, exactly as Japanese students and graduate students would do. I took part in a project in Tome City, Miyagi prefecture, in early July following an orientation session in Tokyo. I also attended a long 'reflection meeting' (*hansei-kai*) two weeks later. The chance to observe several Youth for 3.11 events on four consecutive days in Tokyo in July 2011 – including an emotional two-hour discussion by a group that had just returned from a volunteer project in Kesennuma – generated vital data. Four further meetings with the leaders of this organization (November and December 2011, June and August 2012) as well as continued discussions with the group's Kansai representative since May 2012 have helped me prepare this paper for publication.

The second caveat is that, while the activities of Youth for 3.11 and similar groups potentially open up a vast range of fascinating new research puzzles, I am consciously limiting my focus in this article to the obstacles that, from the perspective of Youth for 3.11, make the dispatch of young urban volunteers a formidable challenge. Therefore I do not attempt to review all the factors that may, from a more generic viewpoint, plausibly suppress youth participation in volunteering. Additionally, while I do make an effort below to shed light on the nature of the volunteering experience itself, it is also beyond the scope of this particular account to investigate systematically how joining Youth for 3.11 may have 'changed' the participating university students in the long term, e.g. by affecting their career choices.

Joining a volunteer tour

At 8am on Saturday 1 July 2011, I found myself boarding a chartered bus from Iidabashi in central Tokyo with a group of about twenty volunteers, all except one of whom were Japanese. Our driver set course for Tome City, Miyagi Prefecture, where we would be providing support to people who had lost their houses – and currently lived in evacuation shelters – due to the massive tsunami that had hit their hometown of Minami Sanriku on 11 March. Most of the participants were in their fifties or sixties, and several were already experienced volunteers. They included an ex-school teacher and environmental activist, representatives of a Buddhist religious organization, and a staff member of the TVAC in her 30s – the only female member of our crew.

The logistics of the trip, from the seven-hour bus ride to shared accommodation to the identification of specific volunteering sites, were handled by the Tokyo Disaster Volunteer Network (TDVN; Tōkyō Saigai Borantia Nettowāku or 'Tōsaibo' for short).[4] This organization operated under the Tokyo Voluntary Action Centre (Tōkyō Borantia Shimin Katsudō

---

4   See <http://www.tosaibo.net> for details.

Sentā; TVAC[5]), itself a branch of the Tokyo Council of Social Welfare (TCSV; Tōkyō Shakai Fukushi Kyōgikai or Tōshakyō[6]). TCSV is one of the old-style NPOs that existed before the passing of the NPO Law (Law to Promote Specified Non-profit Activities that has since 1998 enabled small voluntary groups to achieve NPO status). Though technically non-governmental, the TCSV was set up at government initiative and receives substantial government funding. Tōsaibo therefore in some ways represented 'old' strands of volunteering and state-guided civic activity in Japan (see, e.g. Pekkanen 2006; Avenell 2010). It was not surprising, then, that many of the participants in our volunteer programme were elderly.

But sitting next to me on the backseat of the only mildly air-conditioned, sweaty bus were three members of a much younger generation whom I shall call Shige, Tomo and Yūta. They were aged 25, 23 and 18, respectively. I had initially met them two days prior to our departure at an orientation session held in Nakano, Tokyo, by Youth for 3.11. All of us had signed up for our volunteering programme through this student-led entity, so we were somewhat surprised to discover that students were in fact a small minority as we set out.[7] In any case, Shige, Tomo and Yūta, like many of the 500 or so others who had volunteered through Youth for 3.11 by this time, were students at relatively high-ranking universities, and they were simply bursting with energy. At our orientation session we had decided, based on a longish discussion as well as some input from student facilitators, to make it our small team's policy to face our volunteering work with a smile (*sumairu*), to honestly air our sentiments and grievances (*hakidashi o suru koto*) during regular meetings, and to be as considerate as possible when talking to tsunami victims. The first rule was intended to help us connect smoothly with victims; the second to protect ourselves from psychological stress; and the third to avoid hurting the feelings of evacuees

5   TVAC was founded in 1963 as Tokyo Volunteer Bureau, renamed Tokyo Volunteer Centre in 1981 and given its present name in 1998.

6   Founded in 1951 under article 110 of the Social Welfare Law, an occupation era innovation. <http://www.tcsw.tvac.or.jp/>.

7   Youth for 3.11 generally collaborates with other NPOs and volunteer organizations (which leads to mixed teams), though it does also sometimes send all-youth teams of its own.

through indiscreet remarks or questions (e.g. 'how is your family?'), which, we were told, had caused some trouble in the immediate past. Although our numbers were rather small compared to previous cohorts and groups dispatched to other locations (partly because early July was still term-time at most Japanese universities, most of which were less than keen to promote wide-scale student volunteering; see below), I felt rather glad about my choice to sign up through Youth for 3.11. It appeared that I was about to enter a novel, still largely undocumented world of student activism that was already having a significant impact in disaster-hit areas while also striving to build a socially entrepreneurial movement that might one day contribute to broader social change across Japan.

The founding of Youth for 3.11, its vision and strategy

The founding story of Youth for 3.11 has all the elements of a present-day myth. On the fateful March 11 afternoon that a powerful earthquake struck Tokyo, four of the founders-to-be were working as volunteers for the NPO Learning for All, which dispatches elite students to deprived schools. Subways and trains having stopped, the emerging team, led by Watari Kentaro (Stanford University) and Funato Yoshiaki (Tokyo University), decided to remain in the office they had been using that day in Shibuya. Realizing the potential magnitude of the crisis through watching the initial media reports, the four launched a brain-storming session to consider what they could do to address the plight of the tsunami-hit regions.

The leaders-to-be were already keenly aware that, despite an initial influx of about 1.3 million volunteers to the city of Kobe after the Great Hanshin-Awaji Earthquake of 17 January 1995 (which killed 6,430 people; see Schwartz 2003), the number of volunteers had dropped sharply only three months later. They wished to develop ways to help avert a similar decline in the months following the tsunami's destructive arrival in north-eastern Japan.

At this initial spontaneous crisis meeting, a whiteboard was used to visually sketch out a process called 'the volunteer flow', i.e. the flow of individual volunteers via various institutions (mainly non-profits, or NPOs) to the disaster areas to conduct effective relief and reconstruction work (see Figure 1). Puzzling over how they could join this process, as a new group with few resources and no record of past activities, the four friends decided to specialize in the recruitment and dispatch of university students to locations requiring volunteers. Being students themselves, they saw their peers as an obvious group to target. As for logistics and material resources on the ground, the group decided they had to rely on the cooperation of more established NPOs and governmental associations who possessed the necessary 'hardware'.

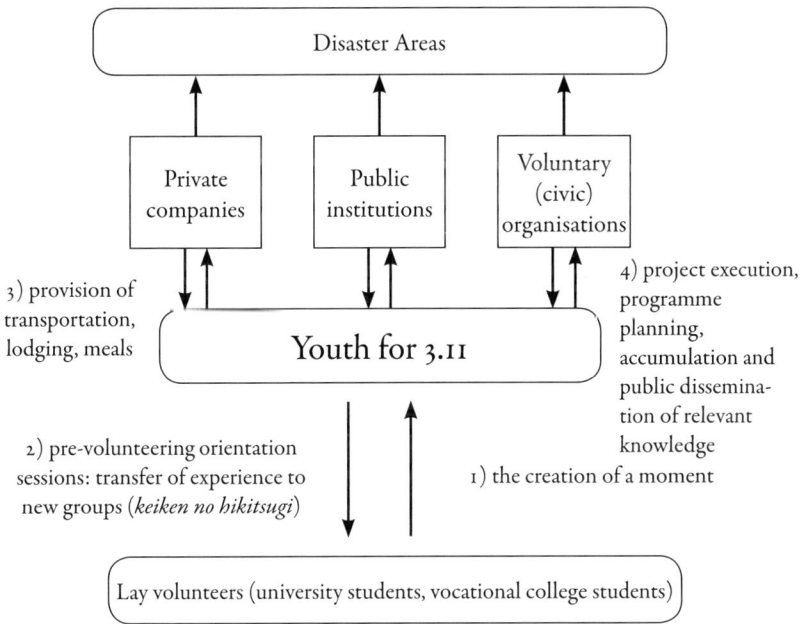

Figure 1 The intended role of Youth for 3.11 within the 'volunteer flow'. Source: Youth for 3.11 website (translated word-for-word by the author).

Neither student recruitment nor the solicitation of cooperation from established institutions would turn out to be easy, but leveraging social media was the first way in which Youth for 3.11 began to make some progress towards its goals at a time when it had no formal links to any universities or other organizations. Via Twitter, some 500 students were persuaded to register as supporters (though not necessarily as participants) in the week that followed 11 March. Besides the extraordinary circumstances per se, the leaders were helped by their pre-existing elite status, entrepreneurial experience and IT competence. One of them, the above-mentioned Funato Yoshiaki, was, at the time, a Tokyo University masters student who had recently published an original science textbook (in April 2012, he became an employee of DeNA, a highly regarded software company in Tokyo).

But when Youth for 3.11 tried to reach out to volunteering entities (such as institutionalized volunteer centres, or VCs) with access to key resources, the standard response was that these organizations could not see what 'mere students' could do. In Japan the social category of university student (*daigakusei*) connotes an inexperienced, dependent youngster with little capacity for responsible action (though with slight variation according to university rank, so that students at elite universities are seen as more capable than others). The lack of prior recognized achievements (*jisseki*) – an all-important qualifier for support and cooperation across Japan's organizational universe – further meant that funding was hard to come by.

Eventually however, a number of entities agreed to join forces with Youth for 3.11, seeing the benefits of reaching out to prospective student volunteers through their peers. The first to come on board were the Tokyo Disaster Volunteer Network, and three NPOs called Nicco,[8] 'On the Road,'[9] and Nihon Bōken Asobiba-Zukuri Kyōkai (Japan Association for Creating Places for Adventure and Play).[10] It is not easy to explain why

---

8   Based in Kyoto; launched in 1979, initially to support Cambodian refugees. <http://www.kyoto-nicco.org/>.

9   Based in Tokyo; launched in 2008; started with projects in India and Jamaica. <https://otr.or.jp/>.

10 Based in Tokyo; launched in 2003, with a mission to give Japanese children more chances to play outdoors. < http://www.ipa-japan.org/asobiba/>.

these particular groups chose to collaborate with Youth for 3.11, but the latter's leaders stressed in interviews that existing organizations almost completely lacked the ability to mobilize young student volunteers and thus found it useful to cooperate with an entity specializing in such mobilization. An initial five million yen (about $65,000 at November 2011 exchange rates) was raised from individual donors as well as the Nippon Foundation[11] and the Central Community Chest of Japan[12] two of the few foundations that extended funding to relief organizations without previous experience or a base in Tohoku.[13]. Subsequently, Youth for 3.11 also received a degree of financial support from donors in the US, including many Japanese-Americans.

The volunteer dispatch program of Youth for 3.11 finally kicked off on 2 April 2011 with a six-member team. In this initial month, the group sent a total of 65 students to disaster-struck areas to remove wreckage (*gareki*) and clean up plots of land covered by destroyed buildings. May saw a total of 135 students join in, followed by a steady rise and a peak of 210 and 232, respectively, in August and September when more volunteering programmes were introduced (August and September are also the summer holiday months for university students in Japan). As of early November, 1,115 students had volunteered through Youth for 3.11, approaching 2000 in September 2012 as stated earlier.

Youth for 3.11's strategy goes beyond the mere dispatching of students and provision of relief, however. Its leading members articulated their vision somewhat enigmatically by employing the English term 'movement' (*mūbumento*).[14] The leaders were clearly not using this word in the conven-

---

11   Formerly the Sasakawa Foundation. <http://www.nippon-foundation.or.jp/>.

12   The CCCJ is called Akai Hane, literally 'Red Feather' in Japanese, after the red feather badges it gives to donors. It is another occupation-era legacy, founded in 1947. <http://www.akaihane.or.jp/english/index.html>.

13   Interview with Youth for 3.11 director (*jimukyoku-chō*) Takahashi Kei and PR representative Uchiyama Takehiro, 14 November 2011.

14   The use of this term by Youth for 3.11 is very similar to Learning for All (now called Teach for Japan; see <http://teachforjapan.org/our-mission/>, at which four of the leaders had previously volunteered. The latter organization wishes to build up 'a social

tional political sense, implying explicitly politicized activism reminiscent
of the student movements (*gakusei undō*) of the 1960s and 1970s, which
now carry deeply negative connotations of violence and militant protest
in mainstream Japan. What the leaders emphasized, rather, was the necessity to produce sufficient momentum to ensure that student volunteering
would continue beyond the initial three-month rush, and that volunteer
participation would come to promote student participation in the solving of social problems more generally (see Mission Statement at the top
of this chapter). They wished to generate many second-timers (*ripītā*) and
long-term volunteers (*chōki*); wide-ranging student-led PR activities by
alumni at universities across Japan; and several parallel volunteer groups.
The group is not itself based at any particular university, but by July 2011
had spawned affiliated groups at the universities of Tsukuba and Keio.
This strategy to enhance impact (*inpakuto*) – another English buzzword
adopted by the leaders – by inspiring others to copy the group's activities
and talk about their experiences to peers, reflects the social-entrepreneurial
sensibilities of Youth for 3.11.

If the above mainly reflect the internal discourses of Youth for 3.11,
in its various publications the organization has consistently stressed that
lowering the hurdle to student volunteer participation (*hādoru no sagatta
borantia kikai o gakusei ni teikyō*) is one of its primary goals. The main strategy for achieving this goal has been the near-elimination of direct costs
through the provision of a complete 'volunteering package', including free
transportation from Tokyo or Kansai to work sites in north-eastern Japan,
lodging and meals. Youth for 3.11 has also appealed to collaborators and
local authorities in Tohoku by emphasizing that it supplies 'young power'
(*wakai chikara*) to the disaster-hit areas, implying that youth have the positive energy and mental dexterity that is sorely needed in those areas and
that other types of volunteers may lack.

movement to solve various educational problems' that extends beyond its immediate
activities, which involve dispatching student teachers to help out at deprived schools.

Volunteer activities and reflection meetings

What kind of work do Youth for 3.11 volunteers do? In the months after the disaster, the focus of volunteering activities kept shifting according to perceived need, from simple but physically taxing clean-up tasks (April–May 2011) to cooking and support for evacuees at shelters (June–July 2011) to helping with rebuilding houses and supporting residents of temporary housing units (August–September 2011). In 2012, socializing with temporary housing inhabitants, organizing small festivals and other cheerful events, as well as providing tutoring to young students, became salient activities.

The main activity I participated in personally in July 2011 was cooking for evacuees from Minami-Sanriku in and about Tome City, which gave some opportunities for direct interaction. Through these interactions I learnt of the frustrations, now widely acknowledged, of many evacuees who at this point were staying in evacuation shelters – in one case, a large gym where metre-high cardboard partitions were used to create about two dozen 'rooms' for families and individuals – for almost four months. Nevertheless, most people I met were relatively calm and seemed to enjoy the social aspects of living together with others who had become their friends. My approach to interaction was to quietly listen to the evacuees, to answer questions about Finland (my home country) and inquire about the local dialect. At a small evacuation shelter, I was asked to play the guitar to help the evacuees and fellow volunteers sing songs such as *Ue o muite arukō* ('I Shall Walk Looking Up', a classic pop song[15] that re-emerged following the triple disaster) and *Furusato* ('Hometown')[16], which we correctly predicted would cause some evacuees to cry.

15   Somewhat randomly entitled the Sukiyaki Song and sung by Sakamoto Kyū, in 1963 it became the first and so far only Japanese song ever to make No. 1 in the US hit parade. The song's lyrics ('I walk looking up so that my tears won't fall') are all about bravely bearing sadness and thus had much resonance after the disaster.

16   Initially published in a song book for elementary schools in 1914, this has become Japan's representative sentimental ballad of longing for an idealized rural community. See also Gill in this volume.

The other three Youth for 3.11 members in my group, Shige, Tomo and Yūta, had varied experiences during the week and sometimes felt they did not have quite enough work to do, though at other times they were able to connect with adults and children at schools (which served as evacuation shelters in Minami-Sanriku) or make themselves useful by helping to distribute supplies and exhibit lost photographs (so that survivors could come and recover some of them). We met in the evenings with the entire group as well as separately from the more senior participants. These meetings highlighted sharp generational differences. The inclination of the experienced volunteer leaders and older volunteers recruited by TDVN was to deliver short and relatively superficial 'daily reports' of activities that had taken place on a given day. However, the Youth for 3.11 team members wished to carry out far more searching, open-ended collective reflection sessions. They were keen to locate solutions to apparent problems, including the relative lack of work for them to do at the schools they visited, and they wanted to make it possible to address such issues head-on with more senior volunteers and other organizers. Later into our volunteering week however, our team came to accept, after discussions with older volunteer leaders, that rash attempts to improve work practices or settings would not always be welcomed, and that a certain subtlety was required for successful volunteering.

Perhaps surprisingly, certain educational activities – conducted in urban centres far from Tohoku – are another central part of Youth for 3.11's programme. During fieldwork, I was struck by the dedication of Youth for 3.11 to carrying out long, in-depth discussions before, during and after volunteering activities. These discussions are generally called 'reflection meetings' (*rifurekushon-kai*), and are distinctly different from the more customary debriefings known to everyone in Japan as *hansei-kai*. Although *hansei-kai* literally means 'reflection meeting' many are little more than a convenient pretext for having a drinking party. Youth for 3.11's reflection meetings were much more sober, conducted in a focused fashion in meeting rooms, and the organizers strove to adopt a constructive, positive tone. Students who had volunteered with Youth for 3.11 were invited to talk about such topics as:

- Episodes during volunteering that were memorable to you (*kokoro ni nokotta episōdo*).
- Feelings experienced during volunteering (*katsudō o tōshite kanjita koto*).
- Messages you want to convey to other students (who have not yet volunteered) (*hoka no gakusei ni tsutaetai messēji*).
- How to continue participating in the reconstruction process from now on (*korekara shinsai fukkō ni kakawaritai hōhō*).

These queries clearly steer students' thinking towards engagement in follow-up activities. Reflection meetings seem to be as central to the volunteering experience of Youth for 3.11 participants as volunteering activities themselves, perhaps because they extract maximum meaning and emotional currency out of relatively modest daily achievements on the ground.[17]

Participants' motivations and the volunteer experience

> Why did I want to participate? Well, I noticed that awareness of the damage done by the tsunami and the earthquake was already weakening in the Osaka area and felt very uneasy about this. Also, I thought that if I'd experience something important first-hand (in Tohoku), I could personally convey this to my peers, perhaps inspiring them to join too. I strongly felt that politicians were not seriously tackling the problems in the damaged areas so I wanted to take action myself. My parents didn't resist my participation; they just told me to take good care.
> — FINAL-YEAR MALE STUDENT (21) studying French at Kwansei Gakuin University in Kobe, who volunteered with Youth for 3.11 in July 2011.

17 This style of conducting group discussions appears to be influenced by practices in the US as well as within international NGOs and is relatively rare in Japanese volunteering circles, especially among the middle-aged generation. The style is dramatically more egalitarian than meetings at most companies.

> There are several volunteer organizations out there, including groups like
> Peace Boat that dispatch about 200 volunteers at a time. By contrast,
> Youth for 3.11 has small-scale programmes with 20 or so members. I'd
> heard that, in the unreal (*higenjitsuteki*) conditions prevailing in Tohoku
> now, many people get very depressed, but I thought that with a small
> group it should be possible to make friends easily. Our group turned out
> like a family at the end.
> — FINAL-YEAR MALE STUDENT (21) studying tourism and market-
>   ing at Ritsumeikan University's Kusatsu campus in Shiga Prefecture
>   who volunteered with Youth for 3.11 in July 2011)

Nearly 2,000 individual students had made the decision to volunteer with
Youth for 3.11 by September 2012 despite facing considerable constraints
that I will discuss in the next section. In terms of personal motivations, all
the students I talked to expressed a strong desire to transcend media representations of the triple disaster and engage with the reality of the calamity.
Both of the above quotes from students I interviewed in the Kansai area
reflect this urge to 'experience something (socially and historically) important first-hand' in a suitably secure context and with other young people.
The desire to help the victims of the tsunami was quite often also framed in
terms of 'helping other Japanese people who are just like me', reflecting an
ethnically grounded, or ethnically justified, sense of empathy. In any case, it
is important to stress that many participants were deeply sceptical regarding
the media as well as political decision-makers and government bureaucrats
who were 'not seriously tackling the problems in the damaged areas'.

The student in the second excerpt had recently secured a post-gradu-
ation job position as a reporter with NHK (Japan's national broadcaster).
He viewed it almost as a personal obligation to get out to the 'frontlines'
(*genba*) to witness, and thereby better understand, the extraordinary situation – something he thought most journalists had failed to do. A member
of my own group, Tomo, had felt (prior to participating) that 'one could
not know the true needs' of the disaster-hit areas through the media, which
tended to distort these needs by amplifying a few individual cases, without
spending enough time in the disaster area. For him, engaging in volunteering was a necessary step towards understanding how one could best be of

help in the recovery process. In this sense, volunteer participation was not a one-off contribution but a first step in a longer process of possibly multi-faceted support activities.

The male student in the first quote above had joined Youth for 3.11 in late May when he was a fourth-year student majoring in French, and had been in France when the catastrophe struck. There he had actively contributed to fund-raising activities with other Japanese and local students but nevertheless continued to feel 'uneasy' (*hagayui*) about 'helping from a distance'. Hence, upon returning to his university in Japan, he sought more direct forms of engagement. He discovered the website of Youth for 3.11 and was impressed to find there was such a group of students who bravely took direct action to address the Tohoku crisis (*konna-ni ganbatteiru gakusei mo irun' da to omotta!*) in a context where the vast majority appeared to idly stand by. Once in the disaster area and helping to clear up the wreckage, he was surprised again when he found that most other volunteers around him (i.e. those not arriving via Youth for 3.11) were either foreigners or elderly people. Disappointed, he decided to begin recruiting more Japanese students at his home institution in Kobe to rectify what he saw as a pathetic state of affairs. He had some success, for he began to dispatch volunteers to Tohoku from his home university without the mediation of other organizations in August 2011. This particular student had made a conscious choice to not engage in the established process of job-seeking (*shūshoku katsudō*) that Japanese university students are expected to launch in their third year, the reason being he 'disliked doing things that were generally expected' and wanted to choose his own path. Such critical attitudes to Japan's increasingly dysfunctional job-seeking conventions (see Toivonen 2013) were by no means rare among the student volunteers I spoke to: two female students at the meeting of returning students I observed in late August were passionately interested in social entrepreneurship and wished to enter this field immediately after graduation.

Notwithstanding a strong motivation to engage directly with the crisis and possibly inspire others, most participants hold deep doubts regarding their volunteer participation, asking themselves whether they can really be effective and whether they are simply being hypocritical (*gizen*) by attempting to do 'good' things with too light a commitment (*karui kimochi de sanka suru*).

They typically wonder whether it would not be best to leave relief efforts to 'professionals' (*senmonka*) without the ineffective interference of 'powerless' (*muryoku*) young people such as themselves. Many also harbour serious qualms about 'relying on others to do volunteer work', perhaps reflecting the considerable influence of neoliberal discourses in Japan that have consistently been used, especially since the early 2000s, to emphasize the importance of 'self-reliance' or 'independence'. As we saw, many are concerned that they may indeed not be qualified to become volunteers, though it is precisely this worry that most participants seem to ultimately overcome through engaging in Youth for 3.11's programmes.

In addition to meeting many volunteer participants who had lived abroad in the past, I also encountered several students who had returned to Japan from overseas study programs to participate in volunteering activities during their university holidays. One member of my own Youth for 3.11 team in Tome had extensive experience of traveling outside Japan, while another was contemplating a master's degree in linguistics in either the UK or North America (though he began to think he should stay in Japan and pursue his dream – music – after he witnessed the frailty of life during volunteering in Tohoku). Youth for 3.11 staff believe that for many of their members international experience was an important element in the decision to volunteer.

However, an even more important factor, and one that is easily verifiable, is the predominance among volunteers of those enrolled at relatively elite universities within Japan. From April to November 2011, the ten universities with the highest numbers of Youth for 3.11 programme participants were, from the top, Waseda, Ritsumeikan, Keio, Chuo, ICU, Tokyo, Hitotsubashi, Aoyama Gakuin, Tsukuba and Doshisha.[18] Together, students from these institutions accounted for 411 volunteer participants, compared with 688 from 245 other (Japanese and overseas) universities. When talking to and observing Youth for 3.11 staff members, it was common to hear that most participants were perceived to belong to a strata of Japanese students with a 'high awareness' (*ishiki ga takai*) and it was admitted that

18   This passage is based on Youth for 3.11 statistics that were passed on to me by staff.

this tended to mean those studying at the most competitive educational institutions and those active on various social media.

What about the volunteering experience itself? Something that most of the students appreciated about Youth for 3.11 was that it allowed them to start concrete volunteer activities immediately upon arrival at the designated site – whereas many groups took several days to prepare before any actual work could be carried out (though at least a few other groups also allowed speedy participation, including SET and Tokyo University's UT AID, both of which are smaller in scope compared to Youth for 3.11). Students I met were also impressed by three other things. First, they enjoyed the subtle but powerful bits of feedback they received from the people they were helping. In one student's words, the locals seemed happy and encouraged by the arrival of so many students from faraway locations, as this signalled that they 'had not been forgotten'. These motivating, often emotionally powerful, episodes were shared and amplified at daily evening meetings and final reflection meetings. The short personal reports by student volunteers available for public viewing on Youth for 3.11's website (http://youthfor311.com/) consistently reflect these same themes, as exemplified by the words of Fukazawa Seiko (fourth year student at International Christian University, who worked in Minami-Sanriku 27 July to 30 July 2012; translation by the author):

> Just from seeing that they (temporary housing unit residents) had been happy we'd paid them a visit and from being thanked, I could feel that my work had made at least a little difference. I could also feel that, since there were many people growing vegetables and flowers, the disaster victims were starting to feel more positive than before.

The second aspect that impressed the majority of volunteering students I encountered was that of group unity. Students felt, at the end of their volunteer period, that they had become very much 'like a family' and had, at the very least, come to quite enjoy group living (*shūdan seikatsu*). For most students – especially those not actively involved in a student society at university – spending a week in such a socially intense setting with peers was an extraordinary and rare experience, for they generally stay with their parents or in one-room apartments rather than dormitories. Further, the dramatic nature of the experience of working together in disaster areas, and the encouragement of openly sharing or 'spitting out' (*hakidasu*) one's observations, feelings, and worries, seems to have facilitated the formation of close friendships. While some students do experience hardships and stress during their stay in Tohoku, group support appears to mitigate these problems.

The third and possibly most important aspect of students' experience has to do with empowerment through volunteering. One student at the reflection meeting I observed on 23 July exclaimed: 'I realized that I, too, could do something to support reconstruction [in Tohoku]!' (*Jibun de fukkō shien ga dekiru koto ga wakatta!*) Several others also felt that they had made a difference by going to the frontlines of disaster relief, either by 'connecting' (*tsunagaru*) with locals, or by working together as a group, which was more powerful than the sum of its parts (*Minna de yareba ōki-na chikara ni naru!*). This sense of empowerment was also echoed in comments that stressed that there was something about the volunteer experience that could be understood only by those who had experienced it: even just going to the disaster areas (*hisaichi ni tonikaku iku koto*) was in itself of extremely high value. There was, moreover, a sense in which the participating youth seemed to be transcending fundamental mental boundaries as they experienced something that 'could never be felt watching TV' when they confronted the raw 'reality' (*riaru*) of the situation in the tsunami-devastated towns with their 'non-everyday' (*hi-nichijō*) scenes. Each of these themes – including that of empowerment (typically couched in highly modest language where the limits of individual students' contributions are carefully acknowledged) – consistently turn up in the brief but fascinating essays by volunteer participants that are archived on the Youth for 3.11 website.

While some openly stated that volunteering with Youth for 3.11 had been for them a 'life-changing experience' (*jinsei o kaeru keiken*), the students' time in Tohoku was also something that created an even stronger sense of solidarity, at least for the moment, with the people in this region. The triple disaster of 11 March 2011 hence no longer felt like 'other people's business' (*mō taningoto ja nai*). The majority of the 18 students whom I observed in Tokyo made pledges to carry on contributing to volunteering efforts by becoming repeaters or by starting their own initiatives; they felt there was a special opportunity at this particular time for students to act that would not be repeated. Some said they had been inspired by their new experience to strive to contribute after they graduated and got formally employed.

Salient obstacles to student volunteering[19]

Despite the above, it is important to note that eliciting student volunteering in a crisis-hit Japan remains far from easy: the activities of Youth for 3.11 have revealed a formidable battery of barriers that, taken together, go a long way towards explaining the low visibility of student volunteers overall since 3.11. Here I discuss the role of universities, the effects of Japan's graduate system and six other factors, drawing primarily on my interviews with the leaders of Youth for 3.11.

It appears that universities have hindered student volunteering in Tohoku in at least three specific respects: first, by making direct as well as indirect gestures to discourage rather than encourage hands-on volunteer participation in the wake of the triple disaster; second, by declining to award credit in exchange for systematic volunteer activities; and third, by continuing to tacitly accept a graduate recruitment system (*shin-sotsu ikkatsu saiyō seido*) that seriously hampers volunteer involvement in the third year of college.

Regarding the first point, many universities quite explicitly told students, in the weeks that immediately followed 11 March, that they should refrain from volunteering in the disaster zones due to suspected risks. There was a widespread preference for on-campus, local volunteering such as fundraising activities. While commendable, such activities offered universities

---

19   This section draws, with the publisher's permission, on an existing analysis presented in Toivonen 2011.

something of a convenient deflection, for local volunteering implied far fewer risks and liabilities compared to encouraging students to work in the tsunami-hit areas (especially as nuclear fears were still running high). Another important gesture was universities' unwillingness to re-schedule classes and tolerate absences during volunteering. Some individual instructors adopted a pro-volunteering stance, but this has not happened at the institutional level, with even the University of Tokyo feeling the need to point out that volunteering may not cohere with its departments' academic objectives (see Japan Times 2011). The real reasons hardly lie with purely academic factors – Japanese university courses are, with few exceptions, known to be comparatively lax – although there is growing pressure from the Ministry of Education to enforce high rates of class attendance.

As of May 2011, i.e. when the need for volunteer support was the most acute, only six of Japan's roughly 700 universities were offering academic credit for volunteering participation. This is a second major way in which universities limited student volunteering (see Japan Times 2011). In the context of usual humanities and social science curricula at least, it should not have been unfeasible to award credit for volunteer participation considering the numerous 'general education subjects' at Japanese universities, some of which are practically oriented and experiential.

The case of Ryūkoku University in Kyoto, exemplifies the above points.[20] In an official announcement on 14 March, it bluntly told students to refrain from volunteering in Tohoku for the time being, for they might 'cause more trouble than benefit to the victims'. However, over the following month, students and staff collected 17 million yen (approximately $220,000) in donations, equivalent to about $13 per student. While still emphasizing on its website, as of early April, that going to the disaster zones in northern Japan was 'dangerous', in May the university began operating volunteering bus tours to Tohoku, with three tours conducted by August. Revealingly, a key condition of participation was that going on a tour should not in

---

20   This information came from the Ryūkoko University website <http://www.ryukoku.
      ac.jp/npo/news/detail.php?id=2474> accessed 13 December 2011, but the link has
      now been taken down.

any way interfere with class work. With each trip accommodating around 30 students, no more than 100 students could join. This amounted to less than 0.6 per cent of the total student body. In short the university encouraged 'safe' fund-raising activities, followed by a minimal volunteering tour scheme well after the most acute phase of the disaster had passed, and then only for a tiny fraction of its students.

Ryūkoku being a Buddhist university with a stated commitment to humanism, peace and co-existence, a more vigorous reaction might have been expected, but university credos seem in general to have very little positive effect on their volunteering efforts during Japan's present crisis. Meiji Gakuin, an avowedly Presbyterian private university with campuses in Tokyo and Yokohama and 'Do for others' as its motto, found itself grappling with an almost identical contradiction (Tom Gill, personal communication, 13 November 2011). Meiji Gakuin has a Volunteer Centre, which sent no volunteers in the critical first month after the disaster, despite the fact that the university was closed until well into May for fear of aftershocks and power-cuts in the Tokyo region. Indeed, the Volunteer Centre specifically banned students from entering the disaster zone out of safety concerns.[21] Starting from late April just 75 students were sent, for stays of less than a week, in the first year after the disaster, under a project called 'Do for Smile at Eastern Japan'.[22] Most other university administrations were equally ambivalent about hands-on volunteering, and they consistently refused to collaborate with viable 'external' groups such as Youth for 3.11 (even in cases where members of these types of organizations studied at their institutions).

Japan's peculiar graduate recruitment system – a relic that still persists despite most other aspects of its 'life-long' employment system having changed –was a third major university-related barrier to student volunteering. In this highly structured system, virtually all students are expected to dedicate their energies during the third year of college to vigorous

21 Do for Smile @ Higashi Nihon Purojekuto. <http://voluntee.meijigakuin.ac.jp/center/2011pdf/MGVC_2011_2-8-59.pdf> p. 32.
22 *Ibid.*, p. 8.

job-hunting activities (the average student invests approximately eleven months in 'job-seeking activities'; see Kariya and Honda 2010). The hope is that the majority will enter steady jobs in cohort on 1 April after graduating in March. The stakes are high for both institutions (worried about their ranking in league tables) and individuals (concerned, rationally, that they will be excluded from stable jobs should they miss being hired as fresh graduates, or shinsotsusha). Moreover, volunteering experience is not yet something that might benefit one's CV (except in the case of those looking for jobs in Japan's small non-profit and social enterprise sectors). These factors between them effectively remove nearly all job-hunting students from the pool of potential student volunteers. It was no surprise, then, that the three dozen student volunteers I met through Youth for 3.11 were either too young for job-hunting, had already secured jobs, studied at foreign universities, or, in the case of a somewhat radical (or discouraged) minority, had rejected the graduate recruitment system altogether.

The enormous amount of time devoted to job-hunting is a widely recognized problem in Japan. As it happens, 2011 was the first year of a new gentlemen's agreement between universities and enterprises to ban recruitment activities until December of the third year of a four-year undergraduate course, with informal job offers (*naitei*) to be issued only after April of the fourth year. On 19 April 2013, prime minister Abe Shinzō met with leaders of four major employers' organizations and asked them to push the opening of the recruitment season further back three more months, to March of the third year (the very end of that academic year), with informal job offers not to be offered until August of the fourth year. The captains of industry agreed in principle to comply, starting with the 2016 graduating class. Abe's reason for requesting the change was to allow students to concentrate on their studies at least for the first three years at university. If the agreement works, it could also make it easier for third-year students to volunteer. There is, however, widespread scepticism as to whether the agreement will really be effective.[23]

---

23   See for example this article in *Shūkan Tōyō Keizai* from <http://toyokeizai.net/articles/-/13721> accessed 18 August 2013.

Problematic as it is, Japan's graduate recruitment system has one benefit: it leaves the lucky fourth-year students who already have job offers with plenty of free time and a much reduced level of stress. Ironically, one possible outcome of the Abe administration's 2013 deal with the universities could be to reduce the size of this pool of potential volunteers. Meanwhile universities do not appear to be offering any incentives to encourage this year group to engage in full-time volunteering activities.

Groups like Youth for 3.11 offer an interesting challenge to universities by showing how it is possible to work across, and cooperate with, diverse institutions. By promoting student initiative and action more effectively than universities and their bureaucratically burdened volunteering centres do, Youth for 3.11 has been able to activate this key manpower resource, albeit on a very limited scale so far.

Alongside Japan's universities and graduate recruitment system, my fieldwork with Youth for 3.11 also revealed a host of other social institutions and factors obstructing hands-on student volunteer activities:

Limiting beliefs regarding volunteering ('Who can be a volunteer?')

Volunteering, it is observed by the leaders of Youth for 3.11, is still not regarded by most youths as something that 'normal people' do in Japan. Also, others tend to view university students and other youth as too inexperienced to contribute to relief in disaster zones. Housewives and retirees have been the main groups engaging in civil activities in postwar Japan, working-age males being tied to their jobs. Crucially, volunteering is seen to require a high degree of commitment that most young people feel they do not possess. Many thus seriously doubt whether they will be 'good enough' or 'serious enough' to participate. Youth for 3.11 has confronted these limiting beliefs by consistently arguing that 'anyone can volunteer' and that 'you should just give it a try'.

Recently, the organization has stepped up its efforts to counter what it sees as the 'uncool' image of volunteering among youth by arguing that a week of volunteering with Youth for 3.11 is 'more fun than traveling, more educational than studying abroad, more participatory than interning, better for making friends than student club activities and more rewarding than working part-time' (presentation by Tajima Shōhei, Youth for 3.11's Kansai representative, on 21 September 2012 at the Urban Innovation Institute in Umeda, Osaka).

The mainstream media and the state
('Are more young volunteers even needed?')

The mainstream Japanese media has conveyed an inconsistent message as to whether more volunteers are needed or not in the tsunami-hit areas of Tohoku. Self-directed, individual volunteering (*kojin borantia*) has been discouraged as a potential source of trouble (which it admittedly can be, especially from the perspective of established volunteering institutions, if not from that of disaster victims). Student volunteering has certainly not been unanimously encouraged, though specific young volunteers have received a degree of positive coverage. Partly because the Japanese media has conventionally treated youth predominantly as 'problems', helping to construct and spread derogatory labels such as parasite singles, *hikikomori* and NEET (see Goodman, Imoto and Toivonen 2012), it seems overall rather reluctant to consider young adults as self-motivated volunteers and leaders. Youth for 3.11 has countered entrenched negative stereotypes by pointing out that youth organizations can be far more speedy than established ones and that students have not only more positive energy but also flexible minds (*atama ga yawarakai*), allowing them to respond more effectively to diverse relief needs.

Parents ('What if my parents do not allow me to take part?')

Parents exert tremendous influence on their offspring in Japan, far beyond the official legal age of adulthood (20). Most middle-class young adults find it very hard to openly resist their parents' views regarding major life choices, if only for their dependence on the latter for tuition and living expenses. The possible radiation risks posed by the Fukushima nuclear crisis have made parents wary of sending their offspring to Tohoku, although many parts of Tohoku are as far from the reactors as Tokyo. Youth for 3.11 alumni say that the most common stated reason for their peers to give up on volunteering is indeed parental resistance. As for those who do volunteer, their families tend to be either supportive or neutral about volunteer participation.

Friends and peers ('What will my friends say?')

Friends' reactions to their peers' decision to volunteer can be mixed. Most find volunteering respectable but also quite unthinkable at the personal level. However, friends' views often change after their volunteering peer has returned to their home university to share their experiences. Consistent with this, word-of-mouth – peers inspiring peers to sign up – has been a key recruitment channel for Youth for 3.11. Twitter and Facebook have greatly helped to spread the word.

Costs ('Can I afford to go?')

High expenses can be a real barrier to volunteer participation, with a week in Tohoku costing well over 30,000 yen for someone travelling from the Tokyo region and more for those living further afield. To counter this, Youth for 3.11 has striven to make volunteering free or as cheap as possible. Still, especially for struggling students (and there are many in today's Japan), missing a week's worth of part-time work income remains difficult, biasing participation opportunities in favour of those from wealthy families. By 2013 Youth for 3.11 was offering cash incentives such as a 10,000-yen 'rainy season bonus' to subsidize travel and eating expenses (housing already being provided free)[24] and a special offer whereby they would pay all expenses up to 100,000 yen for a three-day stint in Tohoku for 15 students.[25]

---

24   Youth for 3.11 homepage, accessed 30 May 2013. Travel and food expenses from the Tokyo area were stated as 15,000 yen, so this would reduce the cost of participation to 5,000 yen.

25   Youth for 3.11 homepage, accessed 31 May 2013.

The burdens of reciprocity ('Is assistance from a stranger going to make the receiver feel uncomfortable?')

As Slater's chapter in the present volume vividly demonstrates, providing support is not a simple matter but tends to generate a sense of obligation to reciprocate in the receiver of support. This can be predicted to be the case especially where reciprocity is not of general, society-wide nature but concentrates in particular relationships and communities. Accordingly, prospective volunteers may consider it somewhat problematic to engage in relief activities. Such culturally and institutionally rooted hesitations to volunteer have been confronted by Youth for 3.11 by stressing that most tsunami victims do in fact appreciate the presence of students in their areas. Also, great discretion is practiced once in the field: when serving food at evacuation shelters for example, formalities are eschewed and food is distributed in a quiet, non-disruptive fashion, without forcing evacuees to communicate face-to-face with volunteers unless they want to. The aid offered by Youth for 3.11 volunteers has almost never been outright rejected by disaster victims or local officials, owing to the fact that the group relies on collaborating organizations to arrange for volunteering opportunities before dispatching any students.

A socially entrepreneurial approach to civic engagement?

This chapter has charted the activities of Youth for 3.11, a non-profit organization (NPO) that has continuously dispatched student volunteers to disaster-struck areas in north-eastern Japan since April 2011. While growing into the largest organization of its kind,[26] it has found itself confronting

---

26   Other significant student-led volunteer groups include SET (http://set-forjapan. jimdo.com/) and UT AID. The former concentrates on what particular town – Hirota – within Rikuzen-Takata city, where 1,600 people were killed by the tsunami.

a considerable battery of obstacles – from universities' lack of enthusiasm towards supporting student volunteering to parental resistance and the 'uncool' associations of volunteering – that help to explain more broadly why young people have not been among the most visible volunteer groups in Tohoku. Of course, the fact that current university students belong to a shrinking population cohort and are demographically outnumbered by their elders across Japan has been one reason for their lack of presence (it is also worth noting that the 'old' state-guided volunteer institutions of postwar Japan, mentioned earlier, seem to have extremely few young members). But it remains significant and unfortunate that, even at a time of pressing need, promoting student-led youth volunteering has been a formidable challenge, with even the leading organization managing to dispatch, in the 17 months following the Great East Japan Earthquake, 'just' 2,000 students in a country with a student population of nearly 2.9 million (MEXT 2012). So despite Youth for 3.11's relative successes, it has been able to reach less than 0.07 per cent of all students in Japan.

Setting aside the persistent obstacles to volunteering and the ways in which Youth for 3.11 has confronted them, this innovative post-3.11 organization remains interesting for one more general reason: its orientation seems to reflect the emergence of a new socially entrepreneurial style of civic activity that is unlike that of established volunteering groups in Japan. To begin with, though it refrains from employing traditional political terms, the public pronouncements of Youth for 3.11 – including those on its homepage – make it clear that this organization is committed to working towards a society where young people can regularly and substantially participate in the solving of social problems beyond the disaster-hit areas in north-eastern Japan. I mentioned that this is an orientation shared by the related, slightly older NPO Teach for Japan (formerly, Learning for All), but it is in fact the rule rather than the exception, among recent youth-led social enterprises in Japan, to choose mission statements that designate

---

UT AID (<http://utaid.yu-yake.com/>), based at the University of Tokyo, called an end to its operations in March 2013 after making 68 expeditions to coastal districts of Miyagi prefecture.

social transformation as the ultimate goal of practical activity. My earlier long-term fieldwork with youth employment support services such as K2 International,[27] to give another example, indicates that many such institutions do not simply wish to return non-employed 'NEETs' to work – they aspire to make society on the whole more liveable for socially disadvantaged young people (Toivonen 2013). Similarly, while the main objective of what is perhaps Japan's single best-known social venture, NPO Florence, is to 'tackle the lack of daycare services for children who fall ill', its vision is to bring about a society that allows all its members to fully engage in child-rearing, work and self-actualization (Florence 2012). There is no doubt that the triple disaster of 3.11 has served as a further catalyst and an opening of sorts for novel enterprises (many of which are now developing in north-eastern Japan) that aspire not only to provide specific services to a specific clientele, but also to 'scale up' their schemes to spur wider transformations. It is of course far from certain that these enterprising nonprofits – nearly all of which have sprung up since the early 2000s when the related discourses were 'imported' from the US into an increasingly neoliberal Japan following the legal reforms of 1998 – will be able to access the necessary resources to make substantial progress towards realizing their grand visions. What is clear, however, is that, in terms of orientation at least, they represent a sharp departure from the kind of state-guided, obedient civil society entities described in Avenell (2010), and in other well-known studies of civic activity in Japan.

It was indeed partly thanks to its bold vision and emphasis on broad participation that Youth for 3.11 was presented, in July 2012, with a 'Citizen Award' (*shimin-shō*) by the Citizens' Conference for Excellent Non-Profit Organizations (*Ekuserento NPO o Mezasō Shimin Kaigi*). This may suggest that the 'transformational' aspirations of young social enterprises are beginning to resonate more widely within Japan's civil society sector, at a time when various social business competitions and 'social entrepreneurship schools' (*shakai kigyō juku*) are gaining visibility. Along with its inspiring vision, another feature that makes Youth for 3.11 'socially entrepreneurial' is

27   <http://k2-inter.com/>.

its multi-pronged strategy of making volunteering as accessible, as easy and as attractive to its primary target group (i.e. university students from across Japan) as possible. Instead of merely complaining about students' presumed lack of interest or shortage of resources, Youth for 3.11 has attempted to re-frame volunteering as a 'cool' and worthwhile activity, and has made a range of choices available to interested students so that they can volunteer in diverse ways. This emphasis on 'user-friendliness' as well as persuasion instead of high-handed criticism is also shared broadly among emerging Japanese social enterprises from Florence and K2 International to Mother House and Table for Two International. Neither is Youth for 3.11 alone in having bypassed existing power structures and hierarchies (e.g. by swiftly mobilizing via Twitter and by ignoring the chorus of critical voices that insisted 'mere students' could do very little in terms of helping Tohoku) while choosing to collaborate with strategically important, forthcoming partners. It remains to be seen whether or not Youth for 3.11 – interestingly blurring the lines between concepts such as volunteering, social entrepreneurship/innovation and political action – symbolizes the rise of a new type of civil society in Japan that is capable of translating the tragedy and destruction of 3.11 into a positive force for socio-economic renewal in Tohoku and beyond.

References

Avenell, Simon (2010). 'Facilitating spontaneity: The state and independent volunteering in contemporary Japan', *Social Science Japan Journal*, 13(1), 69–93.
Florence (2012). 'Furōrensu bijon' <http://www.florence.or.jp/about/vision> accessed 9 June 2013.
Furuichi Noritoshi (2011). *Zetsubō no kuni no kōfuku-na wakamonotachi* (A country of despair and its happy young folk). Tokyo: Kōdansha.
Goodman, Roger, Imoto Yuki and Tuukka Toivonen (eds) (2012). *A Sociology of Japanese Youth: From Returnees to NEETs*. Abingdon: Routledge.

Japan Times (2011). 'Only six colleges giving credits to students for volunteer activities', *Japan Times*, 8 June.

Kansai Jōhō Netto Ten (2012). 'Kansai kara Tōhoku e: kodomotachi ni tezukuri no yukata' (From Western Japan to North-eastern Japan: Home-made cotton kimonos for children), *Yomiuri TV Kansai*, 20 September.

Kariya, Takehiko, and Honda Yuki (eds) (2010). *Dai-sotsu shūshoku no shakaigaku: Dēta kara miru henka* (The Sociology of Transition from University to Work: Empirical Studies of the Changing Mechanisms of Contemporary Japan). Tokyo: Tokyo University Press.

McJilton, Charles (2013). 'Shien o kobamu hitobito. Hisai shien no shōheki to bunkateki haikei' (People who refuse aid. The cultural background of the barrier against relief aid). In Tom Gill, Brigitte Steger and David Slater (eds): *Higashi-Nihon daishinsai no jinruigaku: Tsunami, genpatsu jiko to hisaishatachi no 'sono go'* (Anthropology of the great earthquake disasters in East Japan: The victims and the 'aftermath' of the tsunami and nuclear accident), pp. 31–62. Kyoto: Jinbun Shoin.

MEXT (Ministry of Education, Culture, Sports, Science and Technology) (2012). *Gakkō kihon chōsa Heisei 24-nen-do (Kōtō kikan, gakkō chōsa, sōkatsu, Table 1)*. <http://www.e-stat.go.jp/SG1/estat/List.do?bid=000001040919&cycode=0> accessed 9 June 2012.

Pekkanen, Robert (2006). *Japan's Dual Civil Society: Members Without Advocates*. Stanford: Stanford University Press.

Schwartz, Frank (2003). 'Introduction: Recognizing Civil Society in Japan'. In Frank J. Schwartz and Susan J. Pharr (eds), *The State of Civil Society in Japan*. Cambridge: Cambridge University Press.

Toivonen, Tuukka (2011). 'Japanese youth after the triple disaster: How entrepreneurial students are overcoming barriers to volunteering and changing Japan', *Harvard Asian Quarterly*, 8(4), 53–62.

——(2013). *Japan's Emerging Youth Policy: Getting Young Adults Back to Work*. Abingdon: Routledge.

Youth for 3.11 (2012). The Youth for 3.11 homepage. <http://www.youthfor311.com/> accessed 9 June 2013.

Zenshakyō (2012). Zenshakyō Hisaichi Shien Saigai Borantia Jōhō (National Social Welfare Alliance Information on Disaster Zone Support and Volunteering). <http://www.saigaivc.com/> accessed 11 October 2012.

DAVID H. SLATER

Moralities of Volunteer Aid:
The Permutations of Gifts and their Reciprocals

> Even the idea of a pure gift is a contradiction. By ignoring the universal custom of compulsory gifts we make our own record incomprehensible to ourselves.
>
> — MARY DOUGLAS, in her preface to Marcel Mauss's *The Gift*

> And what am I supposed to do when some group of strangers spends 8 hours of work digging mud out of my house? Really, what am I supposed to do? How can I repay that?
>
> — ANDO-SAN, widowed housewife in the ruins of Ishinomaki

Introduction

In the weeks and months after 11 March 2011, one of the most necessary jobs was digging out mud left from the tsunami, and clearing dirt and debris from private homes and public spaces. During work with volunteer teams, I found that the first moment of contact with those who needed help was often challenging.[1] Many had lost family members and property; weather

---

[1]   The data for this paper comes from more than 50 volunteer trips I made during the 18 months after the disaster in March, to places ranging from Ōtsuchi in Iwate to Chiba City and even Tokyo. My duties ranged from handing out food and blankets in emergency shelters in March and April to winterizing the temporary housing units when it got cold again. Most of the work was manual labour, with digging mud out of houses being the most common form, but this gradually gave way to beautification

and food could still be concerns. They were often in desperate need of help, an unfamiliar situation to people proud of their self-sufficiency. Accepting assistance from outsiders is not something taken lightly, even in times of clear need. In Tohoku, the difficulty of this situation was compounded by the ambiguity of the groups helping. Often, these were volunteers with no connection to the people or the area, not employed by the state or working in any professional capacity.

This chapter is about the moral choices involved in the giving and receiving of aid, especially when the provider of that aid is a volunteer (rather than a neighbour or the state). When and why does accepting aid from strangers constitute a moral dilemma? How does one accept aid from strangers, and still keep one's self-respect when it is virtually impossible to reciprocate? And how does this dynamic influence the efficacy of aid provision?

The situation in Tohoku is characteristic of a worldwide shift from governmental to non-governmental organizations (NGOs) and non-profit organizations (NPOs) as providers of disaster relief.[2] Some see this shift as part of larger patterns of empowerment of local people, promoting independence from state aid; to others, it is little more than the neoliberal outsourcing of citizen support to non-state providers.[3] We also see a shift

------

of the grounds around the units and then to more complex community care, sometimes referred to as 'care of the heart'. I also led groups of students and business executives, both Japanese and foreign, in an effort to increase CSR (Corporate Social Responsibility) giving among larger companies. We are now engaged in an oral narrative project on the construction of local story repositories, referred to as 'Archives of Hope', at 8 different sites in Tohoku. Besides the very valuable comments I received from fellow contributors, Emiko Ohnuki-Tierney gave me insightful comments on an earlier version of this paper.

2   See Avenell (2012) on the substantial increase of NPO efforts in Tohoku as compared to the 1995 Kobe earthquake. See Nihei (2011) for a more theoretical discussion of volunteerism, as seen through the lens of the gift.

3   Interestingly, the western anthropological literature seems barely aware of this shift to volunteering. In two of the most often cited texts on 'disaster anthropology' there are virtually no references to this now prevalent encounter. See Oliver-Smith and Hoffman 1999, Hoffman and Oliver-Smith 2002. Even sources that criticise

in the status of aid itself, be it development assistance or disaster relief, from a service or even right owed by a state to its citizens, to something more ambiguous. In ways that are reflected in the nomenclature of NGO or NPO, aid is also usually distinguished from both 'charity' and market transactions, but often in ambiguous ways that make the giving and receiving of aid psychologically problematic and morally fraught.

I will argue that at the most intimate level of relief dynamics, survivors in Tohoku find ways to manage the encounter with muddy relief workers traipsing through their living room to work for them, and deliver supplies, by framing the encounter with reference to exchange and reciprocity. This is a common pattern in relief situations, although the gifting traditions of each society will alter the way that exchange and reciprocity are represented and practised. In Tohoku, many survivors treated the goods, services and support provided to them as 'gifts' that ought to be returned in kind, and the impossibility of such a return made the acceptance of such gifts difficult.

An official of Ishinomaki, a city in one of the hardest hit areas of Miyagi prefecture, explained: 'People in this area, they are not used to having things given to them – that is just not how we do it here. If you get something, you give something back'. He continued, 'I would not say that they are very polite – maybe even just the opposite, not even friendly. But (giving back) that is just the way things are done'.[4] On the one hand, the classification of aid as gifts requiring something in return seems paradoxical. The individuals and NPOs providing aid frame it that way, and the aid recipients have almost nothing to give in exchange. And

---

the neoliberal shift in disaster aid do not address this encounter with volunteer aid workers (Gunewardena and Schuller 2008). In the Japanese-language literature Nihei (2011) is a welcome attempt to tackle the topic.

4   Thomas Rohlen (1979) gives an example of this dynamic. As part of a corporate training seminar, a company sent new recruits into the countryside, armed with shovels and brooms, and had them go door to door offering local residents a day's labour for free. Nine out of ten times, they were refused. The incident reminds us of the hesitation of rural Japanese to accept work outside circuits of exchange. Yamaguchi (2012) provides a more systematic treatment, showing how ideas of reciprocity, including this hesitation to enter into relationships of reciprocity, manifested in part through a gift-vehicle, are widespread, particularly in Japanese society.

yet, even under these extreme conditions, for many survivors, the alternatives to the exchange frame are much worse. The classification of aid as gifts to be exchanged transforms the morally suspect and socially problematic dynamic of unrequited receipt, of taking without returning, into a dynamic of reciprocity that at least offers the possibility of ethical and socially valued participation.

And here is a contradiction. The logic and practice of reciprocity works in very different ways to the ethic of 'free gifting' that is behind much volunteer activity, especially as institutionalized through NPOs/NGOs. They generally provide help with no expectation of return – 'with no strings attached'. In fact, even the *expectation* of a return can compromise the moral purity of voluntary assistance. To the recipient, however, to accept without thought of return would violate social and moral circuits of reciprocity. So there are two moral geographies here – two different ways of framing the ethics behind the provision and acceptance of aid, two different ways of doing the right thing, two different ways of creating self-respect and mutual respect – and these differences often lead to miscommunication, at times hostility, and even the failure of aid to flow to those most in need. I hope to explicate the compromises between these moral geographies as seen in encounters between volunteers and Tohoku survivors.

I present here a micro-level case study, similar to the scores of other encounters I have personally had while digging, and similar to the many thousands of encounters between relief groups and tsunami survivors in Tohoku. There are variations, of course, depending on factors such as the extent of the damage, the degree of help from the state, and who is left in the household and community. The following incident occurred in a residential district of Ishinomaki, Miyagi prefecture. Nine of us arrived there in April 2011. Many houses had been washed away, and those that were still standing had been inundated with water and toxic mud throughout the ground floor, making them uninhabitable due to the smell and structural damage. Nevertheless, one local NPO suggested that as many as 10,000 families were living upstairs in severely damaged houses, without water or electricity.[5] Some were sleeping in the evacuation shelters, but returning home by day, working, usually alone, on the impossible task of repairing their homes.

Who was offering aid, with what perceived motive, and with what expectation? The volunteer group I went with this time was in many ways typical of the groups that did much of the work in Tohoku. We were untrained and uncertified, together only for a few days and then disbanded, although we were nominally affiliated with an NPO with no religious or political affiliation. We were given some arm-bands, to look official, but no-one wore them. We came from the Kanto region, around Tokyo, and all were Japanese save for myself (an American), and one other foreigner. Our ages ranged, but each member was fit and strong enough to carry mud and tools from house to house. I was the one to approach the house in the account below because I had the most experience at that point, but I was not the leader of the group in any formal way.

Approaching a house

'No help needed here. We're pretty much OK'. Expressionless, not meeting my eye, the old man, probably about 60 but looking older, stooped and tired, stood in his door frame that had lost its door – instead a piece of plywood was leaning up against the jam. Without thinking, I turned to look over his front yard, strewn with soggy furniture and warped piping, pots and a dresser, a broken globe and a shoe, the back end of a car (axle, wheels and some bodywork). A hundred other things were strewn about. When the tsunami hit, it was as if everything in his house, and those of his neighbours, had been churned in the wild waters and poured out over

5   The term *zaitaku hinansha* (literally, 'residential evacuees') is used for those still living in damaged houses, usually to differentiate them from those who were living in temporary housing because they had no houses at all.

the area. Most of the objects were broken down into smaller parts – bent metal, splintered wood, twisted cloth. Anything flexible – string, hosing, tarps – was blended into the mud. We found a name plate that said 'Chiba'. It might have been dumped there by the tsunami from anywhere, but I will refer to the old man as Chiba-san.

If he noticed me looking at the yard, he gave no indication of it. I suggested, 'Maybe we could just move some of the heavy things. We have many hands here, and ...' I was sure the car would take at least six strong people. I was not sure if he heard me, so I continued. 'And we have come up here to do this ...'.

'Where are you from?' This was the first question many people asked if they were going to talk to you at all – they had to know who you were and why you were there. In Japan, this question is answered by telling what group, town, or company you belong to; your corporate unit, your institutional affiliation. But I was so taken off guard by his denial of any need that I was distracted. Mumbling, I tried to explain that most of us were from Tokyo, but we had members from all over Japan, that I was from the US ... Before I got very far, he apparently lost interest. He gestured vaguely towards the ravaged yard with his arm, and walked back inside. I thought maybe he was coming back out, possibly to give us instructions. That was the protocol – NPO groups had to be invited in by locals, to help as requested. I waited for a few minutes on his front stoop, a few of the other volunteers watching me, wondering what I was doing. I finally decided that the old man's gesture meant that we could work on the yard (but I also knew that it might have been a reiteration of his first words, essentially meaning 'go away'). We began with the car.

The front yard was only about 80 square metres, yet still it took us all morning just to clear it of major debris. There was a lot of glass that had to be treated with great care, but our leather gloves were soon so soaked with mud as to be unusable. We probably worked too hard, making it too clean, at least compared to the rest of the property; the back yard was nearly twice as big, and we never even got to it. When we broke for lunch, one of our members found some water in 2-litre plastic bottles at the edge of our work area, although we never saw who put it there. A peace offering, I thought; a sign saying that even if we were not wanted or welcome, at least it was OK for us to be there on his property. While we worked, someone said they saw him in the window, dark because it had no electricity. 'Is he watching us? That's creepy'.

You cannot talk much while you work, if you want to maintain a good rhythm, but during a break, it became clear that the old man's behaviour had upset some of the more urban Japanese in our group. Some felt unwanted or unappreciated. 'I don't think he really wants any help', said one. 'Actually, he said he did not need our help – I heard him say so'. Someone else suggested: 'That's stupid; of course he needs help. Look at this place. He's just arrogant'. One college student, who had struggled for much of the day, clearly unused to manual labour, said that he thought 'country people' all helped each other out, so they should be used to giving and getting help. 'But he sure doesn't seem very used to it'.

One middle-aged woman in our group was from Tohoku, but from the other side of the mountains, beyond the reach of the tsunami. She explained that 'Tohoku men are like that: they don't talk, and they're not very friendly. Actually', she said with a laugh, 'the men from these parts (this area of Ishinomaki) are supposed to be the most unfriendly, even for Tohoku'. She explained that it is the women who keep neighbourly relations, and after all, 'if you look around, there are not many women around here. No woman in this house, anyway'. She was right – in most of the houses, if there was anyone there at all, it was usually a single older man. Very few women were there.[6] 'So these men, they don't know what to say to others, even their neighbours, let alone a bunch of volunteers from Tokyo'. She obliquely addressed some of the more disgruntled young members: 'We have to understand what they are going through, what they need, but also who we are; we're a bunch of strangers, and it is hard to accept help from strangers'. We all chewed on that for a while, since that was the reason we were up here in the first place. 'It is great that everyone (in the group) is up

6   I was later told that on this little spit of land, more women than men died in the tsunami, because they lacked the strength to climb to safety or hold on against the flows. Also, in cases where a couple survived, the wife sometimes stayed in the evacuation shelter to take care of their little spot on the hard floor while the man returned to their property, to try and clean it up.

here working, but sometimes, the hard part is not giving, not doing work for other people, but receiving, having work done for you ... Besides, I'm not sure how much help we're really giving him, looking at this place'. She did not have much more to say.

We did not see Chiba-san again until the very end of the day. We were leaving at about 4pm, tired and wet, and now slathered with toxic black mud dug out from the sewers, the worst job and one that we had saved until last. There was still work to do, but that would be for another crew on another day.

As I was doing a last check for left tools, I noticed Chiba-san standing just inside the entrance to his shuttered house. From the darkness, he quietly asked, 'Are you coming back tomorrow?' Again I was taken off-guard, and the self-satisfaction of a long day's work disappeared. I said weakly that I was not sure, that we had many other places to clean, and many of the people had to go back to Tokyo. I was trying to think of what else to say when he nodded his understanding and disappeared back through his off-kilter door, leaving me standing stupidly in front of it.

Shortly he re-emerged, holding a small white plastic shopping bag. 'Here are some things from the house ...' he said as he looked down into the bag. 'Not sure if they can be used now, but ...' I nodded as he held the bag out to me. 'Thanks' (*dōmo*), he said in rather flat, not-very-polite Japanese, dipping his head in the barest hint of a bow. By the time I mumbled a thank you in return, he had already gone back inside.

In the bag was a bunch of dirty cups and shot glasses. There were some western-style tea cups, just cheap stuff; some, rougher, Japanese-style tea cups with no handles – I could not tell if they were special or not. Some were chipped but none were broken. The shot glasses all had different place-names on them – souvenirs from his holidays, probably. They'd been wiped down more than rinsed off – he did not have any running water. I counted them – there was one for each of us. I handed them out as we walked back to base.

The reactions from our diggers varied. One woman, an American lady from a US church group, was clearly unsettled. 'But he doesn't have to do that. We're not here to be paid back'. She gave her tea cup back to me, seemingly expecting me to return it to Chiba-san. A young Japanese woman said 'At least he didn't try to pay us. That would have been awkward. I'm sure he has no money anyway'. The young Tokyo-ite, his spirits buoyed by the end of what he experienced as joyless work, took one of the shot glasses and said in a bemused, ironic way, 'Yeah, that is nice of him. I guess for a day of shovelling mud, I get a shot'. The older woman from Tohoku said she thought her shot glass was quite nice. She gave it an extra wipe and put it in her pocket.

The gift and its reciprocals

Just a few weeks earlier, Chiba-san had experienced a monumental disaster. I later learned from a neighbour that his wife had been killed and his workplace destroyed. The damage to his house was too extensive for him alone to do much to improve it. When we came, he let us work, and then evidently felt he had to scrounge around for a return gift. I guess you could say he was returning a kindness, but he was not very kind, not even civil really, certainly not friendly. He showed no signs of appreciation in his words or face. The return was to us, a bunch of people he did not know, whom he did not ask to come, and whom he realized he would never see again. We were outsiders who were just passing through. It was when he realized that this relationship had no future that he decided to reciprocate. That in turn invoked a set of codes that impelled him to dig through the mud in his kitchen to find some set of objects that were set apart, and suitable for us.

I would suggest that the problem was not that Chiba-san was too proud, despite the interpretation of my younger Tokyoite volunteer. I do not think this was an example of one person simply trying to avoid owing something to another. Being indebted to others is a way of life for many. In many agricultural and fishing villages, indeed, in many rural economies (in Japan and elsewhere) where productive activity and labour allocation are structured by seasonal rhythms, debt and its repayment over time is a necessary fact of economic survival. Due to declining economies in

Tohoku, many do other sorts of jobs in the off-season, and thus have even larger networks of labour and obligation, and these networks have to be maintained.[7] Gifts are often circulated among families or other corporate groups, less often between individuals. There are regular and codified circuits of exchange, as seen in the charts published by department stores that guide consumers in their exchanges of consumer goods during the summer and year-end gift-giving seasons, others embedded in patterns of family relationships fixed generations ago (Befu 1968). Other exchanges are more flexible, developing out of the unpredictability and contingency of everyday life; the giving of help when needed or sharing something that is not needed: dropping off extra eggplants or tomatoes when their peak ripeness requires that they be eaten quickly, or fixing a bike for a neighbour's child if it breaks down in your front yard (Rupp 2003: 68). One local official told me: 'you're always exchanging things with everyone up here; from your neighbours to the people you work with or do business with. It's just part of living here'.

As Mauss (1990) reminds us, gifts are not only tokens of exchange; they are the stuff of larger circuits of reciprocity. Being able to reciprocate transforms singular acts of kindness (or, I might add, meanness) into links in larger patterns of exchange that both reflect and constitute sets of social relationships. As Mary Douglas notes, 'A gift that does nothing to enhance solidarity is a contradiction' (1990: x). We need to think of gifts less as objects and more as markers that through their circuits of exchange constitute self and other, community and morality. They are as much about keeping one's place within a community as they are the basis for making moral claims of character. They are thus means for whole communities to keep themselves together as cohesive and productive, and they also provide the collective criteria of personal respectability within the community that create the possibilities for individuals to live up to ethical standards. They

7   See Ishida (1982) for a general discussion of the role of exchange within rural Japanese society in the 1970s, and its connection to social structural dynamics. See Marshall (1985) for the way that gifts mediate relationships among individuals, but also between individuals and the hamlet as a form of strategic practice. Inaba and Takahashi (2012) provide a more psychological/clinical view of social solidarity and gifting.

are, in part, what allows us to be good people, and to be social persons at all. Not to participate in these cycles is not only careless, obtuse or selfish, but also indicates a lack of recognition of these patterns of connection, and indifference to their moral implications. There is quite a bit at stake in gifting.

In Marshall Sahlins' typology of reciprocity (1972), he labels as 'generalised reciprocity' the exchange of objects, goods or services that, without keeping track of their exact value, are still expected to be reciprocated in some way. While these relationships were once commonplace among extended kin or in village society, it is widely assumed that today, in 'modern' society, they function primarily within families, and in particular, between generations. These he contrasted with 'balanced or symmetrical reciprocity', where the gifting of an object is supposed to be returned with an equivalent object, usually in kind, within a more formally recognized period of time. These might not be codified or commodified, but nevertheless, equivalence of value is seen as an objective measure, something akin to market value (rather than say, value deriving from sentimental attachment).

In rural Japan, while both forms of exchange are evident, the patterns of generalized exchange appear to extend far beyond families to numerous durable relationships in which cycles of often dissimilar exchanges become obligations and thus connections that endure for years, sometimes for generations. A classic example is the exchange of labour required to re-thatch roofs on the giant *gasshō-zukuri* farmhouses found in parts of Gifu and Toyama prefectures. This is a major undertaking that takes several days and dozens of workers. It used to be required only once in fifty or sixty years, as smoke from log fires would cure the straw. Each family in the neighbourhood will provide at least one member to help with the work, and will expect the favour to be returned, even one or two generations later – and records are kept. Thus gifts, understood broadly as circulated goods and services, are used to maintain bonds across extended families and within villages.

Chiba-san knew he did not have decades, or even a week or two, to return our gift of labour. He was attempting to balance our exchanges on the day because he correctly saw that there was no future to our relationship (remember, he did ask if we were coming back). There would be no chance to develop generalized exchange between us, and thus he scrambled to do his part in a relationship of balanced exchange. Exchange could not be delayed because our relationship would not be continued. Accounts had to be settled at once. Clearly, Chiba-san was in unfamiliar territory. He may well have been unused to the complexity of gift exchange – women often handle it – but he probably knew he was in a situation where he could not reciprocate properly. This leads us to a dilemma at the heart of relief dynamics in the most stricken areas: how does the recipient of aid maintain the material exchanges required to keep self-respect, if s/he has virtually nothing of material worth to offer in exchange for help received and no period of time to develop such exchanges?

In terms of market value, a few chipped cups bore no resemblance to eight hours of hard labour by nine workers – a point made by one in our group. But at another level, these particular objects were quite appropriate objects of exchange. He chose cups. Cups are symbols of commensality, used for drinking together, a vehicle for sharing – remember that he had already supplied us with water. The fact that he selected exactly nine cups, one for each of us, showed he had taken care to count us, and supply us with objects that were a set, for all of us, but also could be easily divided as we went our separate ways.

He might have said the gifts simply symbolized his 'feeling' – it is not uncommon in Japan to belittle the value of one's own gift by saying, 'this is a worthless thing' (*tsumaranai mono*) a mere token that reflects 'just my feeling' (*kimochi dake*). But he did not say this. Rather, he referred to their possible use, wrapping the morality of exchange in the cloak of utility, a very thin cloak in this case of chipped cups and old shot glasses. Did he imagine that utility was something these urban folk could understand? If so, what sort of utility might these cups have to us? Compromised circumstances force imperfect, if recognizable, attempts to reciprocate.

Different geographies of reciprocity

Theorists of gift exchange, such as Marilyn Strathern (1990) among others, draw a sharp distinction between gifts and commodities, a distinction that does not hold so strongly in Japan. Katherine Rupp follows Dorrine Kondo (1990) Harumi Befu (1968) and even Ruth Benedict (1989 [1946]) in recognizing that in Japan, objects can easily participate in both circuits: their market or use value does not exclude them from being effective vehicles of social and even moral reciprocity. Itō (2011), also based on close ethnographic work, shows that ambiguity is part of the essential nature of the gift itself in Japan. Even cash can be a suitable and unalienated vehicle of exchange (that is, an object that is not reducible to exchange value) in Japan. A colleague mentioned that a fellow digger was offered 10,000 yen by an appreciative house owner in Tohoku. (I do not know if he took it.) This was not unusual, and no one in my digging group thought of such cash offerings as payment in a market transaction. However, many of the larger NPOs have policies against volunteers accepting cash, and sometimes against accepting anything at all. The international NPOs seem to be particularly strict, and one local community organizer explained, 'I have to tell the [local] people here that they should never offer money to a church volunteer. It seems to offend them'. Smaller Japanese NPOs, in contrast, rarely see any harm in accepting gifts or even cash, beyond the depleting of victims' resources (a utilitarian rather than moral concern, to the extent that these are distinguishable).

The issue hinges on the image we discussed above, of humanitarian aid as a 'pure gift'. International agencies tend to view any expectation of a return as a contagion that sullies the purity of the gift. Aid becomes 'interested', as in 'self-interested'. Thus, to give aid properly, a gift must be given selflessly.[8] But to many Tohoku disaster survivors, the problem is exactly

---

8   See Derrida (1994) for the most sophisticated analysis of the problematic of 'purity' in the gift in western cosmology. Hirao (2012) offers a more philosophical analysis of a range of issues associated with Mauss's work. None of these are ethnographic in the normal sense of the term. See Nakazawa (2009) for a treatment of these theoretical issues with some application to Japanese society.

the opposite. As noted by Yamaguchi (2012), receiving a 'pure gift' demands social and moral compromise and forces the recipient into an untenable situation. One older widow in Ishinomaki expressed this predicament when the local volunteer centre suggested that they bring a group over to her house: 'And what am I supposed to do when a bunch of strangers spend hours working at my house? Really, what am I supposed to do? How can I repay that?' The feelings are complex, as she shows in her comment about a previous volunteer group who left suddenly, not saying goodbye, not staying to be thanked. 'I guess they were too busy, maybe too proud of how much work they did', she said with a little resentment. And yet, later in the same conversation, she also expressed her impatience with those volunteers who lingered around, hoping for acknowledgement. The situation of unreciprocated gifts is fraught no matter how one tries to navigate it.

To give without the chance of a return is to shackle the receiver with debt that cannot be discharged. Of course, within the worldview of many aid organizations, an ethic of Douglas aptly associates with 'Christian charity', selfless giving is not only necessary in situations of relief, but also virtuous in itself. But the point is that such giving denies the recipient a possible claim to self-respect, especially in times of abject need. It precludes participation. A 'pure gift' denies any relationship between giver and receiver, because reciprocity is the stuff of the relationship itself. As Douglas points out, 'refusing requital puts the act of giving outside any mutual ties' (1990: xi). In fact, it positions the receiver outside the mutual ties that constitute the moral and social sphere.[9]

9   In a well-known work, Titmuss (1970) argues that a lack of direct reciprocity between giver and receiver (in this case, of blood donations), can be resolved in the generalized and institutionalized circulation of objects or services (for example, giving blood to someone, and getting blood from someone else) in some balanced fashion. While this might be relevant for policy that establishes the moral footing for a blood bank, it does precious little for the immediate, face to face struggle of givers and receivers in many relief situations. Moreover, as Hattori (2001) and Korf (2007) both argue, the invocation of similar ethics of free gifting of aid by NGO relief work agencies can quickly lead to an unbalanced relationship so detrimental that Hattori, following Bourdieu, calls it 'symbolic domination'.

Management by refusal

It is hardly an overstatement to say that for many there are only two choices in the immediate situation: reciprocity or disgrace. To avoid disgrace requires appropriate reciprocity. When this is not possible, the acceptance of aid can be so fraught that people in obvious need may refuse it, as in the cases above and below. In June 2011, near one of the houses we worked on in Minami-Sanriku, I met a young woman, Itō Yūko, still in college, who had come back from Tokyo to check on her mother, with whom she had never got along well. I first asked her if we could work on her mother's house, but she said her mother had not yet decided what to do.[10] Itō-san's mother had been out of the area when the tsunami hit, but her father had been killed. Her mother was staying in a shelter and Itō-san was thinking about taking her to her own small Tokyo apartment. Her mother did not want to leave, in part because her neighbours were still in the area. (Their houses were mostly uninhabitable, but this was one of the luckier communities where most people were given temporary housing in the same place.) Most residents would go back to their houses to clean up when possible. Being away caused worry. But being at the house, like Chiba-san, waiting for the government or an NPO to come and help, was also difficult.

Itō san explained that for her mother, and her neighbours, it was an impossible situation: to reject much-needed help would be both self-defeating and culturally rude. On the other hand, as Itō-san explained, to accept aid, 'from strangers ... who they will never see again, who they cannot even give a cup of tea to ... I guess maybe it is a country thing or a Tohoku thing – Tokyo people probably don't care about this very much – but it makes [local people] feel bad, or weak, or embarrassed. She says that I do not understand, anyway. Maybe she's right'.

---

10 For most people, this decision involved financial considerations, and because the amount of money they would be given by the state was not yet determined, they could not act. Some inundated areas were going to be re-zoned as non-residential, so that houses there would have to be demolished. Many residents are still, more than two years later, in limbo as reconstruction plans are still not decided.

I met Itō-san again in Tokyo and introduced her to an NPO that focused on elder care (which her mother refused to even speak to). On a subsequent trip to Minami-Sanriku, I was introduced by Itō-san to her mother. Her mother had laid out a blue tarp on her floor, and on a barely dry table she had put out a small coffee set. Presenting it as if it were *my* question, Itō-san asked her mother why she did not let NPO workers into her house. 'I have been talking to the neighbourhood leader', explained Itō-san's mother, 'but I cannot just talk to the (NPO) workers, at least not if I don't know them'. Itō-san replied, 'Of course you don't know them – they are volunteers from Tokyo!' Generation and geography separated this mother and daughter in ways that made it difficult to for them appreciate each other's position.

As the weeks went on, Itō-san's mother either did not go back to her house, or else she would sit in the dark house, ignoring those who came to help her. I pointed out that she was talking to me, and I too was working for an NPO. 'Yes', she said, 'but that is different. I know who you are. You are a professor at Sophia University and besides, you helped my daughter'. (In fact, I was never able to help her daughter at all.) She smiled somewhat apologetically and said, 'I had to talk to you'.

Itō-san's mother is not exceptional, especially among older people, in avoiding situations that she could not navigate with respectability. Many local community leaders on their rounds through the temporary housing units regularly have to scold elderly residents for not coming to the door when NPO workers and others came by. As I accompanied one on her rounds, she paused outside one door that the resident would not open, and said in exasperation, 'And I know these people – tomorrow (when I ask why they did not answer the door today) they will say that they did not need anything. That they had nothing to say'. She ominously added, 'You know, they will die in there and no one will know'. In fact, quite a few cases of solitary death (*kodokushi*) have been reported in the disaster zone, usually as the result of older people, removed from networks of family and community, suffering in silence, sometimes unto death. This shows the lengths that some will go to maintain some semblance of respectability, some moral footing on which to navigate, even if it means refusing needed help.

Managing respectability: Framing the receipt of aid

When I say that there are only two choices, reciprocity or disgrace, I refer to responses to gifting. But the giving and receiving of aid can be reframed in ways that go beyond immediate and balanced exchange, thereby displacing the imperative of having to choose between two bad options. Unlike symbolic return gifts like Chiba-san's, or the refusing of help, as with Itō-san's mother, others avoid the challenge of direct reciprocity by reclassifying aid as not a gift but an entitlement or right. Still others maintain the idiom of reciprocity, but define aid transactions in ways that allow reception of aid by embedding it in larger circuits of exchange. Here are some examples of these strategies.

Citizenship frames: Viewing aid as a citizen's entitlement was only possible when the provider was the state or its representatives. An extreme example was televised nationally. On 21 April 2011, then Prime Minister Kan Naoto visited a gymnasium in Tamura City, Fukushima, which was being used as an evacuation shelter.[11] Several elderly evacuees chastised Kan in front of network TV cameras: 'We need to go back home. We cannot stay here – look at this place'. Another one said, 'I am sorry to have to say this, but the government must do more to help us'. Kan replied, 'I am sorry for your situation here'. Another younger man entered the screen, 'But that won't do any good, that you are sorry. We need to go back to our homes'. From the back, off camera, you could hear a voice yelling, 'This situation is unacceptable!' The language may sound relatively genteel when translated, but this was a very intense confrontation. Though Kan's apparent lack of empathy and communication skills probably made things worse, the principle target of the evacuees' anger was not Kan himself but the national government.[12] They rejected his personal apology. Among the other quotes

---

11   See the review of his visit: <http://www.kantei.go.jp/foreign/kan/actions/201104/ 21fukushima_e.html> accessed 20 August 2013.

12   Negative feelings were much stronger toward the national government than the local government, which was often staffed by people from the area, who were thus seen

that day: 'The government, the politicians, need to fix this. They need to help us as a matter of course'. And 'It is their job. It is our right to have some place to live'. This encounter differs from the personal ones I have discussed above, since these evacuees were victims of the man-made disaster at the nuclear power plant as well as the tsunami. Nonetheless, reticence in asking for help, supposedly characteristic of Tohoku people, was striking by its absence.

Note a few things necessary for this frame to be effective as a way to accept help. First, as seen in the rejection of his personal apology, the person of Kan has to be pushed aside for Kan as a representative of the state to be a suitable target of anger. Others whose status relative to the state was ambiguous required conceptual clarification. NPOs are a relatively novel idea in Japan; while after the 1995 earthquake in Kobe (Avenell 2012), there was much talk of 'NPO' this or that, especially in Kansai but in Japan more generally, yet, their status as volunteer non-state actors was not always well understood in rural Tohoku. Some victims saw NPOs as an arm of the Japanese state, so that getting aid from them posed no more moral ambiguity than getting aid from the government, to which they felt entitled in this extreme situation. This framing was harder to maintain if volunteer groups appeared too informal, because then they were less easily mistaken for agents of the state. One volunteer coordinator explained that it was primarily for this reason that NPOs were asked to wear arm bands – 'to make them look official'.

The above case could be seen as an example of reciprocity – a sort of social contract between citizens who pay tax in exchange for rights and entitlements provided by the state. It should be noted, however, that this is a special case because the rights of citizens, in this case to receive help from the state, derive from their status (membership in the state) rather than a prior practice of exchange. One does not become or lose citizenship on the basis of paying tax. In any case, accepting aid to which you are entitled by right poses no moral threat, by definition. This image of a rights-bearing

---

as sharing the same hardship. Interestingly, even TEPCO was often viewed more sympathetically than the national government by many.

citizen, so different from the loyal, obedient and often self-denying subjects of pre-war Japan,[13] has a prominent place in the rhetoric of the anti-nuclear movement. For example, it is often invoked by anti-nuclear activist mothers with children, marching in Tokyo, who argue that they have a 'right' to raise their children free of radiation (Slater 2011; see also Morioka in this volume). Yet, within Tohoku itself, I have only very rarely heard any such invocation – and almost never as a sort of *quid pro quo*, rights to aid earned by paying taxes. People might expect and even feel they deserve help, but not usually as a function of taxes. When it is invoked, it is more often as a function of having an ascribed status as a Japanese, a member of nation, rather than something they do or did (such as paying taxes) to or for a state.

Reciprocity in international relations: Another framing strategy was used to explain the unprecedented visibility of foreign volunteers in the relief effort. A younger man in Minami-Sanriku explained, 'If people like you (author) from foreign countries help, that is great. I guess Japan's Self-Defence Forces helped when the US needed help, so that is good. We're friends, and we can help each other'. The contextualizing of relief work within this distant, impersonal, state-level relationship could define exchange reciprocal relations in ways that would then re-represent individual volunteers as representatives of those nations. This is an example of generalized exchange, where the act of receiving aid is part of a stable relationship of reciprocity assumed to continue over time. The moral terrain was thus managed by reference to the relationships between the Japanese state and whatever country the volunteers were assumed to be from. This, in part, rested on a confidence in the Japanese Self-Defence Forces as an active disaster relief force around the world. As one older man put it, 'Japan helps just about everyone, right? So it is OK'. This framing was especially convenient for explaining the novel presence of volunteer teams from South-East Asian

13   Some have argued that even in the post-war period, this image of a western liberal state, held together by contractual agreements, is more academic projection than reality. See Koschmann (1978), for example. Today, this same confusion is apparent in debates about the nature and function of 'civil society'. See Ogawa (2010).

countries in Tohoku. As one female volunteer from Ishinomaki said, 'It is sort of strange that they should be helping us Japanese – usually, we are the ones helping them'. Others argued that since Japan had helped these countries in the past, it was 'only natural' for them to return the favour. This discursive strategy does require a shift in what constitutes 'balanced' exchange: rather than Japan always giving, secure in the privilege of being an affluent donor country, where a gift of foreign aid is both a sign and performance of its superior geopolitical status, Japan now takes as well as giving. This shift is a diminution of status to be sure, but still a move that allows Japan to avoid being an abject receiver of charity.

When Japan sent aid to victims of the Turkish earthquake in October 2011, we saw a split of opinion. Most people I met in Tohoku expressed empathy for Turkey, but one fisherman in Minami-Sanriku said, 'What is the SDF doing, helping other countries? We need help here, now, in Japan. We need to take care of our own country first'. Here we see competing frames: one of reciprocal relationships (between Japan and other countries), another of citizenship entitlements.

Frames of collective national hardship: 'I welcome (NPOs), the groups who come from Tokyo or Kyoto or some place. College students are good workers, and they can help Tohoku'. Two contrasting reframings are at work in this comment from a man in Tohoku. First, there is a reaffirmation of the nation as a moral community that includes a set of assumed obligations derived simply from being Japanese. Thus, to accept help from other Japanese is unproblematic. 'Of course, people from around here (Tohoku) are all busy trying to dig out their own houses. It is natural for those from different parts of the country to come and help', said one man. Another explained, 'After all, we are all Japanese'. Another older man said, 'Isn't that what is meant by *Ganbarō Nippon* or *Ganbarō Tōhoku*?'[14]

On the other hand, this Japanese help is usually more acceptable when it comes from relatively distant places like Tokyo or Kyoto, rather than close by, such as the same town or city. Some months later, during the late

---

14   'Come on Japan! Come on Tohoku!' These are heavily used post-disaster slogans.

summer, two women in Ishinomaki explained that it was a relief *not* to have volunteers from nearby. 'That idea would upset me. Having someone I sort of knew helping me clean'. She added, 'What if I ran into them later somewhere ... or what if they knew someone I know?' The other women echoed, 'Yes, either your family or strangers, that's best'. One rather disaffected woman, who had not received any help on her house at all, added mischievously, 'Really? I guess so. Your family, you don't have to pay back, and the strangers, you cannot pay back (because they leave)'. This cynical comment clearly embarrassed some of the others (maybe more so in my presence), but everyone knew what she meant and no one objected. The men silently nodded in agreement, seemingly saddened but resigned. In fact, as time went on, these women, and many other men and women in Tohoku, received assistance far in excess of what they could ever pay back. They did not like it or feel comfortable with it, but they could not deny it, either.

Divisive obligations: Who and what should be included in reciprocal exchanges was malleable, especially in novel situations, outside established residence and kinship patterns. In the case of the nuclear disaster, reciprocity was conceptualized differently from the tsunami context. One man who worked near the Fukushima power plant put it thus: 'We had to shoulder the energy burden so that Tokyo could blaze so bright, for the whole world to see. We had the power plants. We took the risks ... although no one told us about these risks, really.'[15] '*Ganbarō Tōhoku*'? Meaningless'. He explained: 'It is pretty strange to hear all this stuff about them helping us, only now that there has been a tragedy, now they don't have their electricity'. Another man, a fisherman from Minami-Sanriku, expressed the same sentiment without referencing the nuclear issue: 'We are forgotten in Tohoku. The big cities have all the rich people, we are poor, and everyone in Tohoku is poor. Now we are even worse off than before'. He continued, 'Maybe the real difference is that now the whole country can see it, with their TV cameras and all ... Maybe they will do something about it now'.

15   See Akasaka (2009) for a discussion of Tohoku as an internal colony.

Again, this is an argument of reciprocity – 'we have given, we have suffered, so we are entitled to receive help'. But here reciprocity is coloured darker: aggressively pointing out fissures and breaks that occurred due to the failure of one side to live up to reciprocal expectations.

These words of anger and resentment are not often heard in Tohoku, at least not as often as they come up in anti-nuclear demonstrations in Tokyo. Demonstrators down in Tokyo often bemoan what they see as a lack of politicization – that the people who are being hurt most are those who are making least noise. The logic of debt and gifts could be a factor here. In this case, it is a function of how reciprocity is temporally bounded – do circuits of reciprocity begin decades ago, with Tohoku sacrificing its safety to accept nuclear power plants to help Tokyo prosper, or do they begin on 11 March 2011, with the disaster and subsequent aid? An example of the latter is a farmer, now living in a flimsy temporary house, unsure if he will ever be able to sell his crop again due to continually dangerous radiation levels. He remarked: 'Of course, people are angry. We were lied to about the danger, and at almost every step of the recovery process, the government didn't care enough to give us full information'. Why then, I asked, is there so little protest and outrage here in Tohoku? Why are there no marches like in Tokyo? He looked at me with a pained expression. 'First, there is no-one to blame for an earthquake or tsunami – after all, that is just nature' – and thus cannot be factored into the calculus of obligation. See pp. 15–21 above on the narrative shifts between narratives of man-made disaster (*jinsai*) and 'natural' disaster (*tensai*). 'My family, like every family, has received so much food, clothes, lots of other things in aid, some things I do not need, but lots of things; from NPOs and regular people, and from the government'. He continued, 'I appreciate them, that someone gave them to me. We needed these things, just to stay alive; otherwise, I would not have taken them. But I needed them and my family needed them'. After another cup of cheap saké he said, 'If we all protest, what does that say? How can I do that? After I have taken all of these goods … I am lucky to be alive. I am not sure I should say anything. I have nothing (negative or critical) to say … Nothing to say out loud, anyway'.

Conclusion

Like any cultural form, 'reciprocity' can be deployed in a range of contexts, with different motives and to different effects. It may function to legitimate feelings, maybe giving voice to anger that is not usually heard, and can even be incorporated into larger strategies of political action and protest. But as the example just above shows, it may also impel us to swallow our anger in silence.

These framings of moral choices occur as individuals and groups navigate new moral terrain, when their old communities and practices are washed away. I have argued that these choices are the foundation to a series of claims about self-respect, considerations that are of particular importance when survivors are stripped of so much else. The complexity of these attempts emerges when we examine the moral implications of these choices. What moral claims and courses of action does each reframing entail? How do these circuits of reciprocity define aid? As gifts? As entitlements? Who are the actors involved and how are they defined within the immediate context (individuals, NPOs, the state)? And maybe of primary importance, what is owed to whom? These are not abstract questions: they are central to the immediate dynamic inherent in the distribution of aid in Tohoku, relevant to aid providers as to the residents themselves, as I hope this article has shown. People do not shed their cultural schema in times of crisis. In fact when everything else has been destroyed, traditional cultural schema are an important support, though they may be applied in ad-hoc sort of ways and to not fully realized ends. We have seen how disaster survivors structure their drastically changed life situations through the invocation of familiar cultural schema, compromising and improvising to adapt them to frame and reframe the circumstances in which they find themselves. But compromise and improvisation only go so far. It should hardly come as a surprise that in Tohoku, as indeed, in many parts of the world, self-respect is such a fundamental necessity that at times, people will choose it even when it compromises survival itself.

References

Akasaka Norio (2009). *Tōhokugaku: Wasurerareta Tōhoku* (Tohoku studies: Forgotten Tohoku). Tokyo: Kōdansha.

Avenell, Simon (2012). 'From Kobe to Tōhoku: The Potential and the Peril of a Volunteer Infrastructure'. In Jeff Kingston (ed.), *Natural Disaster and Nuclear Crisis in Japan: Response and Recovery after Japan's 3.11*, pp. 53–77. London: Routledge.

Befu Harumi (1968). 'Gift-Giving in a Modernizing Japan', *Monumenta Nipponica*, 23(3), 445–456.

Benedict, Ruth (1989 [1946]). *The Chrysanthemum and the Sword: Patterns of Japanese Culture*. Boston: Houghton Mifflin.

Derrida, Jacques (1994). *Given Time: I. Counterfeit Money*. Chicago: University of Chicago Press.

Douglas, Mary (1990). 'No Free Gifts'. In Mauss (1990), ix–xxiii.

Gunewardena, Nandini, and Mark Schuller (2008). *Capitalizing on Catastrophe: Neoliberal Strategies in Disaster Reconstruction*. Lanham, MD: AltaMira Press.

Hattori Tomohisa (2001). 'Reconceptualizing foreign aid', *Review of International Political Economy*, 8 (4), 633–660.

Hirao Masahiro (2012). 'Mōsu to zōyoron no kansei: "zōyo" no rinrigaku tetsugakuteki kōsatsu e no josetsu' (Mauss and the traps of gift theories: Introduction to an ethical-philosophical consideration on the gift), *Ritsumeikan Bungaku*, 625, 1051–1063.

Hoffman, Susanna, and Anthony Oliver-Smith (eds) (2002). *Catastrophe and Culture: The Anthropology of Disaster*. Santa Fe, NM: School for Advanced Research Press.

Inaba Misato (2012). 'Shakaiteki kōkan no keitai ga shakaiteki rentai ni oyobosu eikyō no hikaku' (Comparison of the effects of exchange forms on social solidarity), *Shinrigaku Kenkyū*, 83(1), 27–34.

Ishida Takeshi (1982). *Japanese Society*. New York: Rowman & Littlefield.

Itō Mikiharu (2011). *Zōtō no Nihon bunka* (The Japanese culture of gift giving). Tokyo: Chikuma Shobō.

Kondo, Dorrine (1990). *Crafting Selves: Power, Gender, and Discourses of Identity in a Japanese Workplace*. Chicago: University of Chicago Press.

Korf, Benedikt (2007). 'Antinomies of generosity: Moral geographies and post-tsunami aid in Southeast Asia', *Geoforum*, 38 (2), 366–378.

Koschmann, Victor J. (1978). *Authority and the Individual in Japan: Citizen Protest in Historical Perspective*. Tokyo: University of Tokyo Press.

Marshall, Robert C. (1985). 'Giving a Gift to the Hamlet: Rank, Solidarity, and Productive Exchange in Rural Japan', *Ethnology*, 24(3), 167–182.

Mauss, Marcel (1990 [1925]). *The Gift: The Form and Research for Exchange in Archaic
Societies*. London: Routledge.

Nakazawa Shin'ichi (2009). *Junsui na shizen no zōyo* (Purely Natural Gift). Tokyo:
Kōdansha.

Nihei Norihiro. (2011). *'Borantia' no tanjō to shūen: 'Zōyo no paradox' no chishiki
shakaigaku* (The birth and death of 'volunteering': Sociology of knowledge of
the 'gift paradox'). Nagoya: Nagoya University Press.

Ogawa Akihiro (2010). *The Failure of Civil Society?: The Third Sector and the State in
Contemporary Japan*. Albany: State University of New York Press.

Oliver-Smith, Anthony, and Susanna Hoffman (eds) (1999). *The Angry Earth: Disaster
in Anthropological Perspective*. New York: Routledge.

Rohlen, Thomas (1979). *For Harmony and Strength: Japanese White-Collar Organization in Anthropological Perspective*. Berkeley: University of California Press.

Rupp, Katherine (2003). *Gift-Giving in Japan: Cash, Connections, Cosmologies*. Stanford: Stanford University Press.

Sahlins, Marshall (1972). *Stone Age Economics*. Chicago: Aldine.

Slater, David (2011). 'Fukushima women against nuclear power: finding a voice from
Tohoku', *Japan Focus*, 9 November. <http://japanfocus.org/events/view/117>
accessed 23 June 2013.

Strathern, Marilyn (1990). *The Gender of the Gift: Problems with Women and Problems
with Society in Melanesia*. Berkeley: University of California Press.

Takishita Yoshihiro (2002). *Minka ichiku: gasshō-zukuri ni kurasu* (Reconstructing
traditional houses: Living in a thatched cottage). Tokyo, Kōdansha International.

Titmuss, Richard Morris (1970). *The Gift Relationship: From Human Blood to Social
Policy*. London: Allen and Unwin.

Yamaguchi Makoto (2012). *Zōtō no kindai: Jinruigaku kara mita zōyo kōkan to Nihon
shakai*. (Modern gift-giving: Japanese society as seen from the anthropology of
gift exchange). Tokyo: University of Tokyo Press.

EPILOGUE

BRIGITTE STEGER

Still Missing …

5 June 2011: Yamada bay is beautiful, but you cannot see it from the town because of the tsunami protection wall. So I walk around the harbour; it is almost empty. Two men are measuring how much the harbour has sunk. At one of the fishing buildings, a worn-out middle-aged man with a tight and hypertensive red face is looking under the debris. I ask whether he is a fisherman. He says 'Yes', adding '*kā-chan dete konai*' (literally, 'mummy hasn't come out'; meaning 'my wife is still missing'). He speaks as if he does not actually notice me, but neither does he seem surprised that a stranger is talking to him; he appears completely detached from his feelings.

He tells me that his house was destroyed and he now lives with his sister. During the tsunami, he stayed out in the open sea to keep the boat safe. I comment that it is a relief that he still has his boat, but, 'No', he says, 'it belongs to a relative'. He explains that in a week from now, people who are missing will be declared dead. He keeps looking around and explains that he is searching for something that might be of use. I wonder whether there is still anything to be found. He answers that there is still useful stuff under the debris, though he wouldn't know where to store it. He repeats '*kā-chan dete konai*', and it is clear that it is really his wife he seeks under the debris. It feels as if he has only one week left to find her.

16 July 2011: Today is the second mass funeral ceremony at Ryūshōji, the temple where I am staying. About 300 people attend, and some of them are unable to find a place inside the temple hall. The priest's wife tells me that today's ceremony is for those who are still missing, but have now been provisionally declared dead. In Yamada, there are 477 people dead and 257 missing. A few people have urns with the ashes of body parts that have been identified through DNA testing. Some do not even have pictures of the deceased, as their house and all its contents have been completely destroyed. Others rely on pictures their relatives might have, and make copies for the funeral.

Confirming the death of a close person is important financially, for life insurance and compensation claims; but also emotionally. It is always difficult when a loved one dies, but particularly upsetting when you cannot find closure. How important this is, I learn from Haruko,* a kindergarten teacher who has just retired. Hurrying over the debris, she had been injured badly enough to require an operation on 31 March. On her way to the hospital in Miyako, she received a phone call informing her that the body of her 'obaya' (literally, grandmother; meaning her mother or mother-in-law) had been found in the ruins of her house, sitting at her usual place. 'When I heard this, it was a great relief. Now I could undergo the operation without any worries. Until then, I'd suffered quite a bit of anxiety, but now I thought, thank goodness they've found her!'

The eighty-minute ceremony is held by the temple priest and two younger monks. It begins with a minute's silence, followed by prayers and chants. A group of potters from Mie prefecture have sent *jizō* in different shapes and colours for the mourners. These are small statues of the Ksitigarbha bodhisattva, who works to ease the suffering and shorten the sentence of those serving time in hell, as well as delivering the faithful into Amida's western paradise and answering the prayers of the living. The *jizō* are for people to take home. Everyone is composed; I do not see anyone crying.

After the ceremony, outside in the temple courtyard, there are tears. One girl from Sachiko's* elementary school class had been 'swallowed by the tsunami', and was missing from the graduation ceremony at the end of March. Many class-mates and teachers are here at the temple today. They gather around her crying mother and try to comfort her. I have to fight back the tears, even though I do not know the girl, nor can I hear what people are saying.

There is no consolation when someone close dies, especially one so young. But observing and documenting these moments inexorably connects us more closely to our interviewees, providing the human element for our research.

I would like to thank all of those who shared their time, thoughts and feelings with us in the aftermath of the disasters of 11 March 2011.

---

*   Asterisks indicate pseudonyms.

Notes on Contributors

ALYNE DELANEY, born in 1970, is from the United States and received her doctorate in cultural anthropology from the University of Pittsburgh in 2003. Since 2007 she has worked as an associate professor at Aalborg University (Denmark) in the Research Centre for Innovative Fisheries Management (IFM). Her research interests include social organization, coastal cultures, gender and social sustainability. Her publications on Japan include 'Transition in *nori* cultivation: Evolution of household contribution and gendered division of labor' in *Cahiers de Biologie Marine* (Vol. 52, 2011), and she has also published articles on European fisheries, particularly community studies and social impact assessments. < http://personprofil.aau.dk/116078>

TOM GILL (Thomas P. Gill) was born in the United Kingdom in 1960, and received his doctorate in social anthropology from the London School of Economics in 1996. He is a professor in the Faculty of International Studies of Meiji Gakuin University, Yokohama, Japan. His research interests include marginal labour, homelessness and masculinity. Since 2011 he has been studying the victims of the Fukushima nuclear disaster. His numerous publications include *Men of Uncertainty: The Social Organization of Day Laborers in Contemporary Japan* (2001) and 'Failed Manhood on the Streets of Urban Japan: The Meanings of Self-Reliance for Homeless Men' in the collection *Recreating Japanese Men*, ed. Sabine Frühstück and Anne Walthall 2011). <http://www.meijigakuin.ac.jp/~gill/>

IKEDA YOKO earned her PhD in Cultural Anthropology from City University of New York in 2009, with a dissertation titled 'Digging up the Earth in New York City: A Community-based Environmental Movement'. A Japanese-language article on the same topic appears in Waseda University's *Journal of Cultural Anthropology / Bunka Jinruigaku Kenkyū* (Vol. 13, 2012). She experienced the earthquake of 11 March 2011 in her hometown of

Kōriyama city, Fukushima. She is an interdisciplinary independent scholar and her wide-ranging research interests include environmental issues, Japan's 'lost generation' and theatrical representations of American cultures.

DAVID MCNEILL was born in Northern Ireland in 1965 and received his doctorate in Sociology from Napier University, Edinburgh in 1998. He has taught at universities in Ireland, the UK, China and Japan and currently teaches media and politics part-time at Sophia University. He first came to Japan on a two-year government scholarship in 1993. Since returning to Japan in 2000, he has worked as a journalist for *The Irish Times*, *The Independent*, *The Chronicle of Higher Education*, *The Economist* and others. His co-authored book (with Lucy Birmingham) on the 3.11 disaster, *Strong in the Rain: Surviving Japan's Earthquake, Tsunami and Fukushima Nuclear Disaster*, was published in 2012. Much of his work is available online at *Japan Focus*. < http://www.japanfocus.org/-David-McNeill>

RIKA MORIOKA was born in Osaka, Japan, and has lived mainly in the United States. She received her PhD from the University of California, San Diego, in Medical and Cultural Sociology in 2008. Her research interests include social determinants of health and illness, social change in dominant and counterculture groups, and the gendered division of labour. Her publications address death from overworking and activism against it; gender effects on risk perception in post nuclear-disaster Japan; and the meaning of rehabilitation to patients in US drug addiction treatment programs. In addition to academic research, she is also active in international development, having worked for organizations including the United Nations. She currently heads a development agency in Burma.

NATHAN J. PETERSON, born in 1981, is a doctoral candidate earning his degree from the University of Iowa in Art History specializing in East Asia. Since receiving his MA in 2007, he has spent several years studying, researching and teaching in both China and Japan. He spent ten months living in Miyako, Iwate prefecture, after the 3.11 disaster. Since 2012, he has been teaching at Tianjin University in China. The US Embassy in Beijing published his bilingual photo essay *Learning Is as Limitless as the Roads We*

Travel (*New Communication*, autumn 2012). His research interests include contemporary art, Buddhist grottoes in China and Shinto rituals in Japan.

DAVID H. SLATER was born in the United States in 1960. He holds a doctorate in Anthropology from the University of Chicago and is an associate professor in the Faculty of Liberal Arts at Sophia University, where he also serves as director of the Institute of Comparative Culture. His research interests range across capitalism, social class, labour, youth culture, urban ethnography and social media. His many publications include *Social Class in Contemporary Japan: Structures, Sorting and Strategies* (co-edited with Ishida Hiroshi; 2011) and *Alternative Politics: Demonstration and Youth Activism* (co-edited with Patricia Steinhoff; forthcoming). <http://www.fla.sophia.ac.jp/professors/2012/slaterdavid>

BRIGITTE STEGER is Senior Lecturer in Modern Japanese Studies at the University of Cambridge, specializing in the anthropology of daily life. Her PhD was on the social history and cultural anthropology of sleep in Japan and she has published award-winning books and many articles on this topic. In 2011 she stayed at a tsunami evacuation shelter in north-eastern Japan, where she interviewed people about their lives at the shelter. Her most recent books are *Manga Girl Seeks Herbivore Boys: Studying Japanese Gender at Cambridge* (co-edited with Angelika Koch; 2013) and *Sekai ga mitometa Nippon no inemuri* (2013). <http://www.ames.cam.ac.uk/general_info/biographies/japanese/Steger.htm>

TUUKKA TOIVONEN was born in Helsinki, Finland in 1979. He holds a PhD in Social Policy from the University of Oxford (2009) and is Lecturer in Social Entrepreneurship at Goldsmiths, University of London, and Research Fellow in the Study of Contemporary Japan at the Nissan Institute, University of Oxford. He has recently served as a visiting scholar at the universities of Tokyo, Kyoto, Keio and Kobe, as well as at GLOCOM. Toivonen is the author of *Japan's Emerging Youth Policy: Getting Young Adults Back to Work* (Routledge, 2013) and the co-editor, with Roger Goodman and Yuki Imoto, of *A Sociology of Japanese Youth: From Returnees to NEETs* (Routledge, 2012). <http://www.tuukkatoivonen.org>

JOHANNES WILHELM was born in Japan in 1970 and received his doctorate in Japanese Studies from the Rheinische Friedrich-Wilhelms-Universität Bonn in 2009. Since 2010 he has been lecturing at Vienna University, where he was appointed an assistant professor in 2013. His research interests include coastal fisheries in northern Japan, rural socioeconomics and history. Since 2011 he has been studying the victims of the tsunami disaster in an area which he has known since childhood and has studied professionally since 1998. His publications, mainly in German and Japanese, include studies on coastal culture in Sanriku, the history of European-Japanese relations and Okinawa. <http://www.wilhelm.jp/site/>

Index

Note: Page numbers followed by *f*, *t,* and *n* indicate figures, tables, and notes.